# DOWN TO THE SEA
## A BISHOP'S LIFE AND MINISTRY

# Down To The Sea
## A Bishop's Life and Ministry

*by*

BISHOP BILL DOWN

The Memoir Club

© Bishop Bill Down 2004

First published in 2004 by
The Memoir Club
Stanhope Old Hall
Stanhope
Weardale
County Durham

British Library Cataloguing in
Publication Data.
A catalogue record for this book
is available from the
British Library.

ISBN: 1 84104 050 9

Typeset by George Wishart & Associates, Whitley Bay.
Printed by CPI Bath.

*For Sally and our family, with love.*

# Contents

# Illustrations

# Acknowledgments

I WAS PRIVILEGED to serve with The Missions to Seamen (now The Mission to Seafarers) for 27 years, during which time we lived and worked in South Shields, Hull, Fremantle and London. In 14 years as General Secretary I travelled some two million miles by air, visiting and linking up the staff at the 118 seafarers' centres operated by the Society, often in partnership with Christians of other denominations. I experienced at first hand the wonderful hospitality and welcome Christians everywhere extend to fellow Christians they have never met before, and I want to express my thanks and appreciation to the worldwide family of The Missions to Seamen, and to all who made my journeys so fulfilling, rewarding and easy to bear.

As retirement drew near I was approached by The Memoir Club with an enquiry as to whether I had considered writing the story of my life and ministry. I had had this in mind for several years and I agreed to do it. I want to thank them for spurring me into action and for their unfailing support and encouragement. Particular thanks are due to David Bourke, who has edited *Down To The Sea* chapter by chapter as I have written it. He has been marvellous: encouraging, constructively critical, and positive. I have enormous respect for his opinions and judgment, and we have become good friends through correspondence.

My skills on the computer are strictly limited, and I am most grateful to Susan Adams, a parishioner in Leicester, for so willingly and competently typing this book and putting it on floppy disks. Nothing has been too much trouble for her, and she has made my task much easier.

Thank you to the host of friends I have made in many parts of the world for your love, your support, your loyalty and your company. I remember you often in my prayers.

Our family means everything to me, and I want to thank my wife Sally, our children and their spouses and our grandchildren for their love and support. They are an integral part of the story.

# Foreword by H.R.H., The Princess Royal

BUCKINGHAM PALACE

Here is the story of a remarkable priest, pastor, and, in the course of time, bishop. Bishop Bill served first in the parish of St. Paul's Salisbury, then joined The Missions to Seamen in South Shields, before moving to Australia and rising eventually to be General Secretary, having overall charge of that world-wide organisation. Which is where I met him when I became President of the Missions to Seamen in 1984. One of the very few truly ecumenical organisations, his example of welcoming and engaging with everybody and anybody, and wherever, and his humour and commitment were an inspiration to everyone with The Missions. Service by example is not always easy; Christ's example has never been easy to follow, but Bill Down is very close to getting it right, which may explain why he was then consecrated and appointed Bishop of Bermuda in 1990; later still he became Parish Priest and Assistant Bishop in the Diocese of Leicester, before retiring to Witney in the Oxfordshire Cotswolds, where he now lives and works as Honorary Assistant Bishop of Oxford.

When he was Assistant Bishop of Leicester, Bishop Bill persuaded me to become Patron of the Leicester Cathedral Appeal in 1998, and his drive, gentle persuasion and deeply rooted Christian approach were instrumental in the success of this Appeal. Bishop Bill is also renowned for composing amusing and highly appropriate Graces for any occasion, and I suspect many of you will have been unknowingly entertained by them. And finally, and by no means least, his thought provoking humour makes him an inspirational preacher. This book allows us to enjoy the man and his mission.

*Anne*

# CHAPTER ONE

# A Momentous Day

May 24th 1959 was a landmark in my life. On that day I was ordained deacon in Salisbury Cathedral, to serve as Assistant Curate of St Paul's parish in the city of Salisbury.

I was approaching my twenty-fifth birthday. I had just completed five years at Cambridge University – the first three at St John's College reading French and Latin for my Bachelor of Arts degree, and the last two at Ridley Hall preparing for ordination. I was engaged to be married. I was still experiencing the lingering effects of having spent more than a year in bed suffering from tuberculosis of the lungs at the end of my school career. I was just getting back into full active participation in football and cricket, two of my keenest interests. And I was more than a little apprehensive as to how I would cope with the life of a priest in the Church of God: on the one hand I believed that this was what I was being called to do, but on the other I felt both unworthy of the call and inadequate for the task. The prospect both excited and scared me. On May 24th 1959 I committed myself irrevocably to my calling, for better or worse. I could only leave the outcome to God. It was truly a momentous day.

## How It All Began

Reaching the decision to go ahead with ordination, and making that commitment, was the culmination of a long build-up of influences and events stretching back to the beginning of my life. I was born on July 15th 1934 in the village of Ash in Surrey, just below the Hog's Back. Our home, a new semi-detached house, was situated between the parish church and the railway station, both of which played an important part in my early years, though for very different reasons. I was the younger of two children, my sister Paddy having been born sixteen months before me. I was baptized in the parish church, and christened William John Denbigh – William, because the first male child in every generation of our branch of the Down family had been named William for as long as anyone could remember; John, my paternal grandfather's second name; and Denbigh, after my mother's youngest brother, who was just nine years older than me.

Paddy and I were much-loved children. We had a fairly strict upbringing from parents with strong Christian moral principles, and who were hard pressed financially at the beginning of their married life. Mum came from a devout Baptist family background, and Dad spent six months at Wells Theological College before deciding that ordination was not his calling. Both sets of grandparents and all our aunts and uncles were unfailingly kind and generous to us. But even if our upbringing was strict, we also had a lot of fun. As we grew up, there were other young families in the road where we lived, and we enjoyed many happy hours playing together in a large, neglected and overgrown field behind the houses. There was little or no bullying, and we all got on well together most of the time; there was plenty of space for all of us to express ourselves boisterously and uninhibitedly. We boys played football and cricket for hours on end, sometimes joined by Dad, who was an outstanding games player. As a student he had played football for Exeter City in the old Third Division of the Football League, and we loved it when he joined in. He demonstrated a wide variety of footballing skills, showed us how to hold a cricket bat and how to bowl, and was always willing to teach us.

**Church**

I did not take kindly at first either to Sunday School or Church. Sunday School was held in the church hall on Sunday afternoons. The hall itself always had a dusty, musty smell, which I can still recall very clearly, and we were split up into small classes taught by some very worthy (and as I thought, very ancient) ladies. At the end of each class we were given a stamp to stick in our attendance book. It was usually a reproduction of a classic Christian painting, and I was frequently mystified by them; I could not work out their relevance to me. I was often bored at Sunday School, though I am sure that that was my fault. It did, however, have its memorable moments. One Sunday afternoon I was firmly and unceremoniously ejected for fighting with another boy and making him cry. I had the commonsense not to go home until everybody else did, but I didn't get away with it. When we got home Paddy took great delight in recounting my escapade, and I was duly marched round to the teacher to apologise for my behaviour. I did apologise, and with as much grace as I could muster, but to this day I firmly believe the other boy deserved exactly what he got!

We were also taken to church, sometimes on a Sunday evening when Mum was free to take us, but I had very little idea of what was going on. There were occasional visits to the Rectory too. Paddy and I played with the Rector's daughter, while Mum and the Rector's wife enjoyed tea together. My participation in these outings came to an abrupt end after I was discovered attempting to sweep the chimney with the Rector's shaving brush.

My attitude towards Church changed when I was getting near my eighth birthday. The choirmaster at the parish church asked Mum if I could join the choir. She was understandably reluctant at first – she was well used to my singing, which was not particularly melodious – and she made it very plain to me that if I did join I would have to attend choir practices and the services; no excuses would be tolerated. I joined the choir, and remained a member until my voice broke when I was fourteen. I was not a great asset, but I heard the Bible read Sunday by Sunday, I learned to sing the Psalms, and I sat through any number of sermons. I joined in in the usual choirboys' games – noughts and crosses, flicking rolled-up pieces of paper at the other boys, whispering little items of gossip – and I learned to dodge the choirmaster's disciplinary strikes. But I absorbed the words of Scripture, and the worship of God became part of my life. Later on I came to appreciate the value of this background.

At the age of fourteen I was confirmed by the Bishop of Guildford in our parish church. It was 1948, and our preparation classes were held in the church one evening a week throughout the winter. It was a long cold winter, and the heating was never operational in midweek. The boys and girls had separate classes. I can picture the Rector now as if it were yesterday. He would sit in his overcoat perched on the back of one of the pews facing us, and we would wait expectantly for him to topple off one day. He never did! I cannot remember much about the classes, but two moments do stand out. The first was when he told us that the world is round, and you can deduce this from the fact that the first view you have of a ship coming over the horizon is of the top of the mast. It was a moment of real enlightenment; I had never understood it properly before. The second was when he was giving us our instructions for the Confirmation service. On no account, he said, were we to put hair cream on our hair that day; the Bishop didn't like getting his hands greasy. It was a mistake to tell us that. Normally I never put hair cream on my hair, but perversely I couldn't stop thinking about it. On the big day I went to Dad's jar of Brylcreem and smothered my hair with it. I can still see the look of distaste on the Bishop's face as he prepared to lay his hands on me, and I felt bad about it afterwards.

After I was confirmed, and my voice had broken, I left the choir and attended church once a Sunday for several years. I was seriously questioning how much I believed of what I had heard and been taught, and I became very sceptical. I knew that I needed to be convinced of the truth of Christianity, and several years passed before I came to a real deep-seated belief and trust in Jesus Christ.

**The Second World War**
I was five years old when the Second World War started. We had been staying with our grandparents in Exeter, and I can recall vividly standing with Mum and Dad on St David's railway station on the morning of September 3rd, 1939, waiting for a train to take us back to Ash. The platform was crowded. Several special trains filled with troops came through. We waited a long time

for our train. Then an announcement was made over the loudspeaker system: war had been declared upon Germany. There was a sense of shock and apprehension everywhere. To a five year-old it was confusing and frightening.

My memories of the War are very clear. We lived just three miles from Aldershot, the home of the British Army. Our house was situated a hundred yards from Ash railway station, where there were extensive and important sidings. A lot of trains, including ammunition trains, passed through the station every day. The close proximity of the church and the station made the station and its sidings an easily recognisable target from the air, and I remember the noisy and terrifying night when enemy aircraft bombed an ammunition train parked for the night in the sidings behind our house.

I remember being issued with a gas mask early in the War and carrying it to school every day. I can still hear the sound of the air raid warning siren and recall our rapid descent into the air raid shelters at school. I can still remember the cold and crowded conditions of nights spent in the air raid shelter we shared with our next-door neighbours. I can recall the blackout curtains, the hooded headlights of the few cars still on the roads, the rationing of food (especially sweets!), and such slogans as 'Careless talk costs lives' and 'Dig for Victory'. I can remember the hostility which greeted some Italian prisoners-of-war who were set to work in the fields near us, and how by their graciousness they overcame much of the hostility. I recall the unaccustomed accents of troops from Canada, Australia, the United States of America and New Zealand. I can recall the gloom which greeted bad news in the early years of the War, and also the visible lifting of the spirits of grown-ups when Winston Churchill spoke on the radio. One of the most vivid of all my memories is of a German aircraft spiralling down in flames during the Battle of Britain in 1940.

In the long summer holidays during the War we went to harvest camps with Mum and Dad. Dad was a schoolmaster, and also a Flying Officer in the Royal Air Force Volunteer Reserve. He had a degree in Geography, and both taught in school and trained navigators. He helped to run the harvest camps, at which the older boys helped with the gathering in of the harvest. In the summer of 1944 the German V1 and V2 rockets ('doodlebugs' as they were widely known) caused consternation everywhere. At the camp seventy of us watched, horrified and spellbound, when the engine of one cut out just short of our field. We threw ourselves to the ground, and waited in suspense. In the event it glided over us, a few hundred feet above the ground, and plunged into a farmhouse three miles away, killing the occupants, whom we knew.

For me personally harvest camp that year came to an abrupt end when I was rushed away to hospital. On a Thursday night fifteen of us were taken ill with stomach pains, vomiting and diarrhoea, and a local doctor came to see us on the Friday. He diagnosed colic, and everybody except me recovered quickly. My pain persisted, however, and despite urgent phone calls from Mum and Dad, the doctor did not come again until the Tuesday. When he did eventually come he examined me thoroughly, and immediately sent for an ambulance. I was taken to St Thomas's Hospital, which had been evacuated from London to Hydestile, near Godalming, where the senior surgeon was preparing to return to London at the end of his weekly visit. My appendix had burst, so he changed his plans and operated on me straight away.

For ten days or so my life hung in the balance, and then, with more than a little assistance from the ward Sister, the noxious fluids which were poisoning me suddenly poured out in a torrent – to the Sister's unrestrained delight. I spent a further six weeks in hospital, my progress being slow and uneven. My spirits also were at a low ebb in the early weeks, since I was being treated with the then new drug M & B, which became noted for its depressing, as well as its life-saving, qualities. Visitors were allowed just twice a week, and I eagerly looked forward to Mum and Dad coming; after they had gone I often shed a few tears.

As my recovery progressed, I began to take a lively interest in my surroundings. Our ward was a long wooden hut with thirty-six beds; it had been built quickly when part of the main hospital in London was bombed. Most of the other patients were men from the London area, and I was the only one under eighteen. There was a lot of quick-witted banter, and there was a good atmosphere which was helped enormously by the cheerfulness of the nurses. When I had been there about three weeks, the hospital Chaplain (who was also the parish priest) stopped by my bed one day. He said he was glad to see me looking better, and asked how I was spending my time. I proudly showed him my brand new stamp album, into which I was transferring my very limited collection. He came again a few days later bearing a large Kraft margarine box, which he deposited on my bed. 'There you are', he said, 'these are from one of my parishioners. They'll keep you going for a while!' He then went on to the next patient, and when I opened the box I saw that it was crammed full of stamps. It was a wonderful gift, one which I have never forgotten. He took my thanks in his stride, and he was the first clergyman who made a real impression on me. It took me months to sort out the thousands of stamps in the box, and I treasured the box itself for many years.

There was at least one other major benefit of my stay in St. Thomas's. Every week the senior surgeon who had operated on me conducted a formal ward round. It was a formidable occasion, because he always came with a large team of doctors and students. On his second or third visit I plucked up the courage to ask him a question which had been bothering me. I said, 'Two days before this started I smoked three cigarettes up a tree. Do you think it had anything to do with it?' With a deadpan expression he replied, 'I should think so.' With those four words he put me off smoking completely, and I have smoked only an occasional cigar or pipe ever since.

After I came out of hospital I went to stay with Mum's parents in Weston-Super-Mare to recuperate. For three months I was confined to bed for half the day, and I read prodigious numbers of books. After six months I was fully recovered, and returned to school for the summer term, where I took a late sitting of the eleven plus examination, and passed. Harvest camp in 1945 was a joyful and memorable occasion: the War in Europe had already ended, and the Japanese surrendered while we were there.

When the War ended more than half of my life so far had been lived in wartime. It had made a great impression on me. Mum's three brothers all served in the Royal Navy, two of them in a succession of dangerous postings. Dad was in the Royal Air Force Volunteer Reserve and was often away, and his sister's fiancé was also in the R.A.F. I loved them all, and we were constantly anxious about them. At a young age I realised the fragility and vulnerability of human life, and I have been very aware of it ever since. With the uncomplicated thinking of a child I hated the Germans and Japanese for the bombs they had dropped on us, the torture they had inflicted, the fear and anxiety they had caused, the suffering of the troops, the grief of those whose loved ones were killed or injured, and the cutting off of our food supplies. It was the influence of our headmaster at the grammar school I attended which led me to see things differently later on.

**Education**
At the age of four and a half I started school at Ash Walsh Memorial School. We had first-rate teachers with large classes. I got on well in class and the other children were very friendly in the main. We were sometimes bullied on the way home by some bigger children, and it was both unpleasant and frightening, but we learned how to avoid the worst of it.

Looking back over those early days at school, I realise the debt of gratitude I owe to the teachers. It was wartime, and they were more than fully stretched. We were given a good basic grounding in all subjects, and the discipline was firm but fair. We learned poetry, our tables, and passages from the Bible by heart, and we were encouraged to take the approach to the grammar school selection examinations in our stride. I cannot recall any great sense of anxiety as we sat them. I learned not to tell tales, and also not to say I had been punished at school when I got home!

In 1945, despite having missed most of the school year because of my burst appendix, I was awarded a place at Farnham Grammar School, an all-boys school with three hundred pupils and a long and honourable history. We were well taught, and we were also encouraged to participate in a variety of sports and extra-curricular activities. It was a very happy school with a good academic record. The masters took a keen interest in our progress and discipline was firm but light. I recall an occasion, however, when my irreverent sense of humour got me into hot water. It was in a Latin lesson, and in the previous lesson the master had been talking about 'ambrosia', the food of the gods. At the beginning of the next lesson he checked up on us by asking what was the food of the gods. Quick as a flash I answered, 'Fish and chips!'. It got a good laugh, but it also got me a salutary caning. I deserved it but I thought it was worth it, and there were no hard feelings on either side afterwards.

We had a wonderful Headmaster, F.A. Morgan. He had won the Military Cross during the First World War, and was nearing retirement. He taught Latin and Religious Knowledge to the Sixth Form. He was a brilliant and inspiring teacher who really held our interest. He could also be fiery and impatient. But he was never afraid to apologise handsomely and publicly if he misjudged a boy or a situation, and he was respected and loved. Early in 1947, just eighteen months after the end of the Second World War, he visited every form in the school to tell us that he had agreed to bring two German boys into the school on a permanent basis. He told us that he expected us to make them as welcome as any other newcomers, and warned us to expect no sympathy if we made their lives a misery. The two boys duly arrived, and were soon an integral part of the school. For me it was a great lesson in understanding, forgiveness and acceptance.

In 1950 I sat the last of the old School Certificate examinations. I passed satisfactorily and went on into the Sixth Form to take the new General Certificate of Education Advanced Level examination in English, French and Latin. I also took up German, with a view to taking the Ordinary Level examination. I really enjoyed the Sixth Form. I enjoyed the academic work, and I played football and cricket for the school teams. In 1951 I won the cup awarded for the highest batting average in the cricket team. I was looking forward to going on to University and then, I hoped, into the Royal Navy as a career. I was a reasonably good linguist, and I hoped that I would be able to learn Russian in the Navy.

Early in 1952 the bottom dropped out of my world. Following a visit to the mass X-ray unit with the whole school, I was diagnosed as having tuberculosis of the lungs. I was the only boy in the school with anything wrong. It was then still the early days of the new drug treatment which revolutionised the treatment of the illness, and I was afraid that I was going to die. I was ordered to bed immediately, and I stayed there for fifty-three long weeks. It was seven weeks before a hospital bed became available, and then I spent nearly ten months in the King George V Chest Hospital at Hydestile near Godalming. It was a traumatic, life-changing experience. Up to that time my life had proceeded fairly smoothly, even living through a world war; now all of a sudden I realised clearly that I was indeed very mortal. My Christian faith was not strong, and I felt frightened, vulnerable and sorry for myself.

I was put in a ward with twenty-three other men. Four were in single rooms, twelve in two-bed rooms, and eight in a large room. For the first three months I was in the 'eight-bedder', as it was known. The other patients came from a wide variety of backgrounds, and at seventeen I was the youngest by seven years. All but one of them came from the London area. There were two who had fled from East European countries, one of whom was not at all grateful to the National Health Service for his free treatment and was a thoroughly unpleasant person. There were two who had each spent three years in hospital and who were now steadily and encouragingly making good progress after treatment with an experimental wonderdrug. The other three were mature men, two of them from semi-professional backgrounds. I was allocated one of the corner beds, and I observed carefully the things that caused friction in our very intense little world. I made a few clumsy mistakes, but in general I got on well with everybody. I co-operated fully with the medical and ancillary staff and hoped and prayed that I would get better. I was very anxious about whether I was in fact getting better, and progress seemed agonisingly slow – if indeed there was any at all. I was at odds with myself and I was having to learn to be patient the hard way.

After three months I was transferred to a two-bed room, and this proved to be a happy move. My room-mate was a young Pole, and he was good company. Over the next six months I had various room-mates, all of whom went home before me, which was very frustrating. When I had been in hospital for six months the Medical Superintendent made a ward round with a visiting specialist from the United States of America. As they stood at the end of my bed discussing my case, the Medical Superintendent said casually, 'We're going to keep him in bed for another six months to make sure there is no recurrence.' The prospect of another six months in bed thoroughly depressed me, and my morale was low for a while.

It was one of the nurses, Sheila Evans, who brought me to my senses. I had been particularly ungracious to her one day when she turned on me and said: 'You know what your problem is, don't you?' 'No,' I replied. 'You've always been a big fish in a little sea,' she said. 'Well, now you're a little fish in a big sea!' It hit me hard. It hurt to be told that, but as I thought about it I realised that it was true. I also realised that if I was going to get better, my whole attitude had to change. If I were to die, the world would not stop. I had to start helping myself. I needed to be more positive. The next day Sheila apologised for what she had said. I told her not to apologise: what she had said was true, and I was grateful. That incident did change my whole attitude, and not long afterwards I began to experience definite signs of recovery.

Towards the end of my time in hospital I was greatly encouraged to hear that I had been awarded a place at St. John's College, Cambridge, to read Modern and Medieval Languages, starting in the following year. And on April 1st 1953, almost ten months after being admitted, I was finally discharged from hospital. It was a great day. During the next five months I gradually got used to being up and about again and to resuming a normal life.

In September 1953, at the age of 19, I returned to school to complete my Advanced Level examinations. In many ways it was a difficult year. I was now much older than my fellow pupils, and had lived for a year with older men in harrowing circumstances. I had put on a lot of weight because of the enforced inactivity, and I was embarrassed by it. For many months I lived with the dread of a relapse at the back of my mind. At the end of it I passed my examinations, and in October 1954 went up to St. John's College, Cambridge, to begin my three-year course. In my first week events occurred which shaped the whole of my future life from that point onwards.

**Conversion and Commitment**

Because of my recent illness, a kindly tutor allocated me very comfortable rooms in Chapel Court for my first year at St John's and I felt very privileged. A few days after my arrival a fellow student, John Bausor, knocked at my door. He came in and, after introducing himself, asked me point blank if I was a Christian. I replied that I thought so. What did I mean, I thought so? he asked. I repeated my answer, namely that I thought so. 'What do you think a Christian is?' came the next question. I replied that it was someone who tried hard not to harm anyone and also tried to do some good. 'What do you think about Jesus Christ?' he asked. 'Who was He? Who is He?' I could not give a coherent answer. He then invited me to go to church with him on Sunday evening. I accepted, and we arranged a time to meet. Something went wrong on the day and we failed to meet up with each other. But I went along to the church anyway, and listened to a sermon from The Revd. Bertie Rainsbury which changed the pattern and course of my life.

He began his sermon to a packed congregation of students in Holy Trinity church by talking about the many and various ways people follow seeking satisfaction in life. Some think it can be found by accumulating a lot of money. Others seek it through acquiring valuable possessions. Many seek it through self-indulgence of one kind or another. None of these, he told us, brings real deep lasting satisfaction. True real deep lasting satisfaction in life comes when you acknowledge your sins and failures, and commit yourself willingly and wholeheartedly to love and serve the crucified and risen Jesus. The living Jesus stands at the door of your life, knocking, seeking to come in. For Him to come into your life you need to invite Him yourself. It is up to you. When the living Jesus comes into your life a change takes place in you. The Bible comes to life for you. You have a sense of purpose in your life. You have the inner peace that comes from knowing that your sins are forgiven and that you are loved and valued by God.

Deep within me I knew that this was what I wanted and needed. During my illness I had come to realise how fragile and inadequate my faith was. I had watched a number of men die slowly, some of them very bitter in their outlook. I listened as one man told me that he no longer believed in God, because if there was a God He would not have allowed him to suffer as he had. I had come to realise how self-centred I was, and had also come to the conclusion that if I got better, I wanted to spend the rest of my life serving other people. I realised how ungrateful I had been for the many blessings I had received. I had prayed fervently, but without any conviction that my prayers rose higher than the ceiling. I had been afraid that I was going to die, and I desperately wanted to live. I had been angry and resentful that it was I, and not somebody else, who was ill. I was ashamed that I had been thoughtless and inconsiderate at times in my relations with other patients. I had sometimes been full of self-pity. At the same time as I was seriously ill, I was also going through the painful process of growing up. It had been a really tough time for me.

An incident from that period of my life had made a great impact on me. It was in the early days of my illness. I woke suddenly in the middle of the night, hot and sweating. I had been dreaming, and as I woke I found myself saying, 'If I get better, I'll be a priest'. Later, in the cold hard light of day, I told myself that this was no more than a subconscious attempt to bargain with God, something like, 'You get me better and I'll serve you'. I did my best to put it out of my mind, treating it lightly because of how I viewed it. But the memory would not be erased. It came back again and again.

As I sat in Holy Trinity Church listening to the sermon on that first Sunday evening of my life in Cambridge, I knew that I wanted a sense of purpose in my life. I knew that I wanted the inner peace which springs from knowing that God loved me and valued me. I knew that I wanted to move on in my life. When the preacher asked those who wanted to know more about committing themselves to love and serve Jesus to come forward and tell him so, I did just that. I was introduced to a theological student from Ridley Hall, John Wheatley Price, who gently and wisely talked to me about being a Christian. That night, in the quiet of my room, I offered myself to Jesus and asked Him to lead me through life. John and I became good friends, and he was a tower of strength to me in those early days of my new-found faith.

When I committed myself to Jesus, some undramatic but noticeable changes occurred at the deepest level of my being. I discovered a new sense of purpose: to serve Jesus, and to serve Him in a practical way. The Bible became important: now it was a book with a relevance for me, showing me myself as I really was, pointing to the way I should follow and bringing me into contact with God. I found that I needed to re-think many things: there were some bad habits to cut out and some new ones to nurture. I learned that following Jesus involved my mind and my will as well as my emotions. I found that I wanted to talk to God about many things and to listen to what He was saying, though I was not sure how or where to start. I wanted to talk to other people about my new-found faith, though I was hesitant to take the plunge. I became aware of a new source of strength within myself which enabled me to tackle fresh challenges. And almost imperceptibly I began to experience a deepening sense of security and peace. I made many false steps, but I knew I was on the right track.

My day-to-day life at once took on a new direction and impetus. I began to attend church regularly and I drew a lot of inspiration and encouragement from a succession of brilliant, powerful and thought-provoking preachers from a wide range of backgrounds. For more than a year I attended Bible Studies and meetings organised by the University Christian Union, but I didn't become a member; I knew beyond doubt that I had committed myself to follow Jesus, but I could not bring myself to accept some of what I thought were its rigid attitudes. But I am deeply grateful for the clear and passionate way its members witnessed to their faith and proclaimed the eternal truths of the Gospel. Quite simply, they brought me into the presence of the living Jesus.

## Cambridge

The five years I spent in Cambridge were exciting, challenging, formative, and immensely satisfying.

When I arrived at St John's College in October 1954, the only person I knew in Cambridge was my sister Paddy, who was doing a teacher-training year at Hughes Hall. She had just graduated from Girton with First Class Honours and a university prize for French. She was formidably able at her subjects, and I had always known that academically she was brighter than I was. I had much to live up to in the Modern Languages department!

During my first year I was still tiring easily after my illness, but as the year progressed, I shed the excess weight I had gained through inactivity and felt distinctly better physically. I was unable to play football and cricket during my first two years because of continuing medical treatment, but I could play golf, and this became a great love even though I have never succeeded in getting my handicap into single figures. I worked hard at Latin, because there was a lot of reading to catch up on. I put in less time at French, because it had always come easily to me. At the end of our second year a college friend, Maurice Tyler, and I spent the best part of a month travelling around France and walking in the Pyrenees in preparation for our French oral examination. When the time for the examination arrived, the conversation section was conducted by Paddy's former Director of Studies, Alison Fairlie. There was little wrong with my spoken French, but she tied me up in knots with some of her questions. Eventually she admitted defeat and with a broad smile asked me how my sister was getting on. It was the only uncomplicated question she asked! I passed the examination with Second Class Honours, as I did all my examinations at Cambridge.

In my second and third years at St John's I was preparing for the final examinations. My particular subjects included medieval French and medieval Latin. We were superbly taught in both subjects, and I became fascinated by the medieval Latin literature and history; it was all bound up with the life and work of the Church, and our tutors, Professors Raby and Brittain, brought it all to life for us. They succeeded in making examinations seem secondary to our enjoyment of the subject, and they took a personal interest in all of us.

Becoming a committed Christian in my first week in Cambridge had a major influence on the way I spent my time. I did my best to get my academic work done as early in the day as possible and to enjoy the life of the College and the University as fully as possible thereafter. I attended debates at the Union, was an avid spectator at the University rugby matches, played golf at the Gog Magog course just outside the city, umpired for the College cricket team until I was able to play again in my third year, got involved in the life of the College, talked well into the night with fellow students, and worshipped in the College chapel on Sunday evenings.

On Sunday mornings I worshipped at Holy Trinity Church, and through worshipping there became involved with the Cambridge Pastorate, a loosely structured association of students keen to know more about the Christian faith. It was a lovely group of people – open-minded, joyful, questioning, committed Christians. The Vicar of Holy Trinity, Stanley Betts, attracted well-known Christian leaders to preach in the church on Sunday morning, and submit to a barrage of questions at tea at the Vicarage in the afternoon. There were no holds barred in the questions we asked and the comments we made; if we hadn't been able to follow what a preacher had been saying, we told him so! Those Sunday afternoon teas were splendid occasions: crowded, lively, thoughtful, good-tempered, humorous, and purposeful. The Chaplain of the Pastorate, Bill Skelton, who was also Chaplain of Clare College, was a remarkable and much loved man. He had won a D.S.O. and Bar and a D.F.C. and Bar in Bomber Command during the War, and he was a true friend and wise counsellor. He was also a bachelor, and many of the female students eyed him longingly!

Towards the end of the Long Vacation in the summer the clergy of Holy Trinity Church led a team of fifty or so students on a pastoral and evangelistic mission to a particular parish or group of churches. The students were split into teams, each with a student leader nominated by the clergy. We prepared for the Mission during the Easter term with group instruction and individual team meetings, and then met up in the parish in the second half of September for the Mission. We were accommodated by parishioners, and had our lunch and evening meal together in the church hall or, on one Mission, in a works canteen. The task of the students was to visit the homes of the parish to give information about the Mission and to promote interest in it; to conduct meetings in pairs in peoples' houses; to mix with church members in parish groups and at church services; and to be prepared to witness to what our faith meant to us whenever an opportunity presented itself. It was very demanding and challenging as well as being hugely satisfying.

I went on my first Cambridge Pastorate mission in 1956 to Hornchurch in Essex. As the time for the Mission drew closer, I became more and more scared. I began to think that I could not face it. The more I thought about it, the more daunting it appeared. Eventually I wrote to Bill Skelton telling him that I was too busy to go. Twenty-four hours later, thoroughly ashamed of my cowardice, I wrote to him again saying that I would be there after all! It proved to be an unforgettable experience. The sense of fellowship among us grew day by day. We enjoyed visiting in pairs and conducting home meetings. We found it very satisfying to share our Christian experience and we learned a lot. We made lasting friendships. New people came to church and heard the Good News of Jesus. Our vision of the Church expanded and blossomed, and we had the joy of seeing people committing themselves to Jesus Christ. For me personally it was the moment when I realised that God had taken me just as I was, with all my weaknesses and failings, and was using me in His service. It was much-needed encouragement and reassurance as I contemplated life in the ordained ministry.

Earlier in 1956 I had attended a selection conference for those seeking training for the ordained ministry of the Church of England. I had never forgotten the experience of waking in the middle of the night when I was ill and hearing myself saying that I would be a priest if I recovered. After I had committed myself to love and serve Jesus in October 1954, I gradually became aware of a disturbing and compelling conviction that I was actually being called to be a priest. I truly did not like the prospect. As a teenager I had known that I wanted to serve in the Royal Navy, and although that was no longer possible, I very definitely did not want to be ordained. I had not been impressed by some of the clergy I had known, and although I had little conception of what was involved in a priest's life, I was adamant that it was not for me. But the nagging conviction that this was what I was being called to do just would not go away, and eventually it dawned on me that nobody was going to force me to do it; rather, it had to be my own conscious decision to offer myself willingly. With many misgivings I told Mum and Dad what I was thinking. They were very supportive and I was deeply grateful; it was the first hurdle crossed. Then I told our Rector, who was also very encouraging. There were, however, people who were not supportive, including a very respected family friend whose immediate reaction was: 'You're surely not going to waste your life like that!' In a strange way that served only to strengthen my resolve.

So in January 1956 I attended a Selection Conference in Farnham Castle, then the home of the Bishop of Guildford. I was very nervous. I was acutely conscious of my ignorance of the Church, of my faults and failings, and of my own reluctance to hear God's call. It all spilled out in an interview I had with one of the selectors. 'I suppose you've always wanted to be a priest, haven't you?' was one of his first questions. 'No, I haven't', I replied, 'and I don't know that I want to be one now!' 'Well, why are you here, then?' he very reasonably asked. 'Because God won't leave me alone', I said. We discussed this and the reasons for it, and I left the interview convinced that I had put paid to any possibility of being recommended for training. I was surprised, therefore, and excited, to receive a letter from the Bishop telling me that I had been recommended. So later that year, when I went on my first Cambridge Pastorate Mission, and saw for myself that God takes us just as we are and uses us in His service and for His purposes, I began to think that maybe I really might be a round peg in a round hole in the ministry of the Church. But I still had concerns about it, and these persisted right up to the day of my ordination.

It was in October 1956, at the beginning of my third year as an under-graduate, that I first met Sally, who later became my wife. It was at one of the Pastorate 'Meet the Preacher' teas at the Vicarage at the beginning of the academic year. There were a lot of people there, and I noticed Sally at the far side of the room. I thought she looked lovely, so I set about finding out as much as I could about her. She had just come up to Newnham to read Classics. For both of us it was a busy year, but we often came across each other and exchanged a few words at Pastorate meetings. I was attracted by her vivacity, her outgoing personality, her balanced commonsense outlook and her sense of humour. She sang with the Cambridge University Musical Society and mixed easily with everybody. She was a committed Christian and worshipped regularly at Holy Trinity church.

When the time came to prepare for the next Pastorate Mission – to Darlaston, in the Black Country – and I was appointed as one of the team leaders, I chose her as a member of my team. As the Easter term progressed, we got to know each other better through the meetings of the Mission team, and after our examinations were over I asked her out a number of times. In July 1957 I started my ordination training at Ridley Hall, and as she lived at Great Shelford, just outside Cambridge, we continued to meet. I believed I had found 'Miss Right'; but the question was, would she have me? It was on a free day spent at Lichfield during the Mission that we discovered we were in love. As I told her mother later, 'There we were, and off we went!' A year later, on her twenty-first birthday, we became engaged to be married. Two years after that, on July 29th 1960, we were married at Trumpington church, where she had worshipped all her life.

I started my ordination training at Ridley Hall a few weeks after graduating from St John's. It was lovely to stay on in Cambridge as a graduate. I had known a number of Ridley men when I was an undergraduate, and I felt very comfortable with its thoughtful and purposeful Evangelical emphasis. I applied for a place there after I was recommended for training by the Selection Conference, and was interviewed by the Principal, Cyril Bowles. He suggested that I should switch from modern languages to theology at the end of my second year as an undergraduate, and said that he would offer me a place immediately if I agreed. After much thought and much good advice from Dad, I came to the conclusion that it would be best to complete my Modern Languages course first. Cyril accepted this, and told me that he would write to me again when the meeting to allocate places was held at the end of the academic year. The end of the year came and went without my receiving any notification, and I was getting anxious and frustrated. Eventually I wrote a letter to Cyril withdrawing my application, and another to the Principal of Wycliffe Hall in Oxford applying for a place there, and I walked down the lane from our house to post them. It was August, and a fine day, and it was South Devon (my parents had moved to Newton Abbot in 1956) in the height of the holiday season. To post the letters I had to cross a busy main road. The traffic seemed endless and I waited and waited for a gap. As I waited I had second thoughts about what I had written: I wondered if I was writing more out of pique than real conviction. I turned round and went back up the lane and re-wrote the letter to Cyril. By return of post I received a letter from him explaining the delay and offering me a place. Afterwards I realised that if I had gone to Oxford for my theological training, I might never have got to know Sally; I shall always be grateful for that heavy traffic which caused me to have second thoughts.

The two years I spent at Ridley were unfailingly interesting, often very enjoyable, always challenging, occasionally frustrating, and sometimes daunting. At the end of the course ordination loomed large, the prospect still exciting and scaring me. Never far away was the desire and longing to be a good and faithful priest, coupled with a concern that I might not be up to it. I had to tell myself frequently that if I truly trusted God, then I had to trust Him in everything – and stop worrying! His strength would be made perfect in my weakness.

The staff at Ridley, ordained and lay, were outstanding and there was a great sense of fellowship and common purpose. I think that everybody loved Cyril

*Mum, Dad, Paddy and myself at home, Newton Abbot, 1956.*

Bowles, the Principal. He was always ready to listen, and he had a wonderful gift of helping you to make up your mind for yourself. He was kind, considerate, compassionate, open-minded, clear-thinking, generous, encouraging – and human! He gave a firm unambiguous lead to the life and work of the college. He was a genuinely good and holy man, and his Christian witness had a profound influence on us all. It did not come as a surprise when his abilities were recognised with his appointments first as Archdeacon of Swindon and then as Bishop of Derby. It was a great joy for me when he agreed to preach at my own consecration as a Bishop in 1990. At Ridley he gathered a fine staff team around him – priests of proven ability and high calibre – and I believe we all felt well cared for and well prepared for our life in the ordained ministry of the Church.

The daily routine of life in Hall was a good discipline. Morning Prayer was at 7:10, followed by a time of silence before breakfast at 8:15. Group Bible studies, lectures, sermon preparation classes, group tutorials and private study filled the mornings. The University very generously allowed us to attend some courses of lectures given by the Faculty of Divinity, and I shall never forget the sheer brilliance of Professor Owen Chadwick's Church History lectures. Nor shall I forget Professor John Burnaby's on Christian Doctrine. He lectured at 12 noon in an upstairs lecture room situated above an Indian restaurant. At about 12:15 tantalising aromas of curry wafted up from below, and good resolutions about eating Ridley's rather spartan lunch too often went by the board! On three days a week we had intercessions in chapel at 1:05 p.m. and Evening Prayer preceded dinner in the main hall. We had a lot of freedom, but it was expected that we would not miss chapel services. And nobody seemed to mind that a number of us occasionally slipped out to the Granta pub during the course of the evening!

There were a lot of very able men among the students at Ridley in my time there. Some later became archdeacons, deans or bishops; others filled a variety of important ministries in a wide range of places; some served overseas; and a number discovered that their calling was to serve God in a lay capacity. The much loved and highly respected evangelist David Watson was in my year both at St John's and Ridley. All of us learned a great deal together and from each other in a very positive and mutually supportive atmosphere. One of the happiest features of Ridley life was the active encouragement we received to involve our wives, fiancées or girl friends in the life, work, worship and practical preparation for ministry for which the Hall exists. Sally's college, Newnham, is situated next door to Ridley, and we found it deeply helpful to be able to worship together in the chapel and to be involved together in some of the practical courses. I also walked to lectures with her some mornings.

At the beginning of my second year at Ridley it was time to be thinking about where I would begin my ministry. I had no firm ideas about where I wanted to serve, except that I knew I did not want to be in the Guildford diocese where I had grown up. At the time I did not know why this was, but I believe now that it was because the memories of my long illness and the possibility of a relapse were still very much with me, and I could not easily forget the trauma. I was not consciously worried about it, but tuberculosis was never far from my thoughts. I felt I wanted a completely fresh start. When the Rector of St Paul's, Salisbury, Theo Dobson, made a visit to Ridley to seek an Assistant Curate, Cyril Bowles suggested that I should talk to him with a view to going there. Theo and I got on well together, and in due course I was advised that I would be ordained in Salisbury Cathedral on May 24th 1959. As I was still unmarried, I would live in lodgings in the parish for a year; there was no Curate's house in the parish.

Another happy feature of my time at Ridley was the close proximity of Sally's home at Great Shelford, five miles away. Whenever possible we went there for Sunday lunch in term time, and I thoroughly appreciated the change from college meals. Sally's mother and father and three younger brothers – John, Michael and Nicholas – all made me very welcome, and it was good to be able to escape for a while from the demands and challenges of ordination training and to be part of a happy well-balanced family. I treasured those visits, and also the times we spent together there and at my home in Newton Abbot during vacations.

The last few weeks before ordination were a delight. I had completed all my examinations, and there was a lot of free time to prepare myself for what lay ahead. It was Spring, the weather was beautiful, and Cambridge looked at its best. I was still concerned about how I would cope with life in the ministry, but I was determined to go ahead; my mind was made up. As I walked into the grounds of South Canonry, the home of the Bishop of Salisbury, for the ordination retreat, I was as ready for it as I would ever be – which still didn't feel very ready!

CHAPTER TWO

# Salisbury 1959-1963

## Ordination

T HE DAY OF MY ordination as a deacon in Salisbury Cathedral on May 24th 1959 stands out in my memory as freshly and vividly as if it had happened yesterday.

Three peaceful days in retreat at the Bishop's lovely South Canonry residence in The Close were ideal preparation. There were just two of us to be ordained: Max Williams as priest and myself as deacon. The Archdeacon of Wiltshire conducted the retreat in a relaxed way, and the glorious early summer weather made reflection by the river at the end of the Bishop's garden very pleasant indeed. There was a lot to think and pray about as I contemplated the future: I was excited by the prospect of at last getting on with the task ahead of me in the parish; I was apprehensive as to how I would get on in the ordained ministry; and I was looking forward to marrying Sally a year later. When May 24th dawned, the time of waiting and agonising was over.

The service was unforgettable. In the graceful historic Cathedral the atmosphere of centuries of worship was almost palpable, and I got caught up in it. The organ thundered out the hymns. The choir's singing lifted my spirit and my thoughts. The Bishop's charge rang out with solemnity and power. I read the Gospel, conscious of the momentousness of the occasion. I was aware of family, friends and new parishioners around me. It was awe-inspiring, a glimpse of eternity in the here and now.

## St Paul's

After the ordination service there was a large and happy family lunch party at the historic Red Lion Hotel, and it was good to be able to relax for a few hours, albeit in an unfamiliar and uncomfortable dog collar. Then after a brisk walk across the water meadows with Sally, it was time to make my way to St Paul's, the church where I was to serve as curate, for Evening Prayer. I duly read out my licence to officiate as required by law and was introduced formally to the congregation, who made me feel very welcome. My ministry had begun.

As I made my way to my lodgings at the end of a full day, I suddenly felt very lonely. I did not know anybody in Salisbury very well. I had one room of my own in a house where there were two other lodgers, and that room had to

*Curate at St. Paul's, Salisbury, 1960.*

serve as bedroom, study and office. I had very little money, and was greatly relieved when the parish treasurer very considerately paid me half a month's salary in advance. It was all a bit overwhelming. But I need not have worried. My landlady, Mrs Shephard, was wonderful. She made me very welcome and treated me like a son. In the year that I lived with her I came to appreciate that I had a real home there. She was very kind to Sally, too. Sally had got a job teaching Latin at South Wilts Grammar School for Girls and was living in self-catering lodgings; Mrs Shephard regularly made her an apple pie to keep her going through the week.

As soon as I got settled in, I threw myself wholeheartedly into the life of the parish. At that time St Paul's had a population of around seven thousand people. Within its boundaries lay the railway station, part of the city's shopping area, a psychiatric hospital, Church and State Infant and Junior schools, a large compact area of Victorian terraced and semi-detached houses around an unsightly gasometer, part of a large modern council estate, a number of pleasant roads with larger houses, two complexes of almshouses, the cattle market and a marvellous recreation ground by the side of the River Avon. The church itself was a spacious Victorian building set in large grounds encompassing the Rectory and its garden, the church hall, car parking space and a complex of almshouses.

It was on the recreation ground that I established real contact with some of the young people of the parish. I had arrived in Salisbury in early summer, and many of the parish's evening activities were about to close for the holidays. On fine evenings informal games of cricket and football took place on the large recreation ground and I often went there to watch what was going on. It was not long before I was invited to join in one of the games of cricket, and after I clouted the ball into the river a couple of times with lusty hits I was readily accepted. I became part of the scenery there, and when our parish youth group resumed its activities in the autumn we got a number of new members.

Throughout my time at St Paul's I played cricket for the Old Manor (psychiatric) Hospital, a team which included both staff and patients. My Rector was Theo Dobson: he was chaplain to the hospital and he wanted me to be involved there too. Some of the patients attended services at St Paul's on Sundays, and I became good friends with one of them, Frank, who acted as fixture secretary for the cricket team and Chapel Warden at the hospital. He had been a patient there for nearly thirty years, a shell shock casualty of the First World War in which he had served with distinction as a commissioned officer. We played golf together on my day off most weeks provided he was well enough. He insisted on everything being done properly, and he reduced me to tears of helpless laughter on one of his more volatile days. Bemoaning the lack of discipline of his fellow patients in the chapel he bellowed, 'I keep forgetting that I'm not in charge of soldiers now – just a bunch of bloody lunatics!' The cricket matches we played against other psychiatric hospitals were often unusual – and always unpredictable. I vividly recall a match in which as I was facing the incoming bowler one of the slip fielders suddenly yelled out at the top of his voice, 'Sodom and Gomorrah!' If the ball had been straight I would not have had a hope of playing it.

During my early weeks in the parish I was busy finding my way about and getting to know people. In the new and unaccustomed experience of my pastoral work I made a whole host of mistakes. But people were kind and I made many friends. I did a lot of visiting, and learned to listen attentively. There was always a group of sick or housebound people whom I visited regularly and frequently, and I was humbled when some of them told me how much my visits meant to them. One afternoon when I visited a lovely old woman in her nineties, who was a devout Christian, I could see that she was

*Salisbury, Old Manor Hospital Football Team, 1963. (Myself 2nd from right, front row.)*

close to death. She was fully alert, however, and as she lay back on her pillows she smiled contentedly and said: 'I'm going to a wonderful home'. Her straightforward sincere witness to her faith made a great impression on me. I visited many elderly people, and I came to treasure their wisdom and their willingness to share their knowledge and experience of life. And I drank endless cups of tea!

In September the full programme of Church activities resumed and I found my days crammed with work. I was responsible for a weekly children's evening programme with a missionary emphasis and also for the youth club. The youth club was small in numbers when I arrived, and the Rector gave me clear instructions before the winter programme got under way. He told me to be firm about the fact that it was a church youth club and that young people belonging to it would be expected to attend church at least once a month. I should also have a regular 'God slot' at some time during the club evenings. From the start the club grew and grew. Club evenings were informal and provided young people with a great opportunity just to chat and listen to records. At 8:30 everything stopped so that announcements could be made and a brief but pertinent prayer said. I insisted on silence for this, and it took a while to achieve it, so I was very thrilled one evening when a newcomer who kept interrupting was firmly told by a lad who had himself been fairly rebellious at one time: 'We shut up when he's talking!' We had a full programme of sporting and social activities, arranged interesting and enjoyable outings, and put on musical plays to raise funds. The club continued to grow. It was very much a team effort, with the co-leader, Rene Haines, playing a vital role. She was the mother of two young children, a tireless worker for the Church, and a second mother to many of the young people; they loved her because they knew she was sympathetic, that they could speak frankly to her without shocking her, and that she would respect a confidence. After a year the club had outgrown the hall and so the Parochial Church Council took the decision to build a second, smaller, wooden hall.

The Youth Club was only one of a wide range of activities into which I was plunged. In a typical week I took part in all the Sunday worship; conducted the daily assembly at our Church Infant and Junior schools on one morning; taught one lesson to a class of nine year-olds on another day; participated in a midweek celebration of Holy Communion; prepared talks, lessons and sermons; organised and ran a children's early evening club called 'Discoverers of the Way'; attended meetings of parish groups; took part in the Bible Study meeting; called on families about baptisms or funerals; visited the sick and the elderly; made house-to-house calls as time permitted; played football or cricket on Saturday afternoon; and cycled sixty miles a week in the course of my duties. I loved what I was doing and I felt that I was a round peg in a round hole. I was learning fast.

I could not have had a more encouraging and helpful Rector than Theo Dobson. He combined a willingness to let me do things my own way with clear guidance when it was needed. He was concerned that I had a full day off each week and he ensured that I did not preach more than once a fortnight in my first year. He encouraged me to play football and cricket, while insisting that church engagements took precedence if there was a clash. This policy had a highly amusing consequence on one occasion. In my first game for the Hospital Staff football team in the local league, I scored five goals and made headlines on the back page of our local paper. Everybody was asking me if I was going to repeat the feat in the next game. Unfortunately I was already committed to conduct a wedding at the time the match was due to be played, so I had to withdraw from the team. My replacement failed to make it clear that he was not me, however, and so he received the rough treatment which had been lined up for me!

Theo was wonderfully well organised in his daily work; I learned a lot from him about efficient administration. He was very thorough in introducing me to the many and varied aspects of life in the ordained ministry. He had a fine intellect, and he was very human. He was a devoted husband and father, and I felt greatly privileged when he and his wife Anne invited me to baptise their baby daughter Sheila a few weeks after I arrived in the parish. And thirty years later I was very thrilled when, despite severe physical disabilities, he came to the service in St Albans Abbey when I was consecrated Bishop.

*Salisbury, Sally and myself at Youth Club party.*

I was ordained priest in Salisbury Cathedral on June 12th 1960 after a year as a deacon. As I approached ordination, I found myself in a calmer and more settled frame of mind than the previous year. During that year I had experienced for myself the truth that God takes His servants just as we are and uses our efforts for His purposes. I had learned that people are usually willing to forgive a young minister if he shows that he is willing to learn from his mistakes; that 'a soft answer turneth away wrath'; and that 'more things are wrought by prayer than this world dreams of'. I knew that I had much to learn, but I also knew from experience that God could be trusted. I was looking forward to the new responsibilities and opportunities that ordination to the priesthood would bring.

**Marriage**
Six weeks later, on July 29th 1960, Sally and I were married at Trumpington

Church, just outside Cambridge. It was the church in which she had grown up and where she and her parents sang in the choir. Her father was churchwarden and treasurer of the Parochial Church Council at the time. It was a wonderful occasion. We were married by the Vicar, David Maddox. The preacher was Philip Goodrich, chaplain of my old college, St John's, and later to be Bishop of Worcester. Theo Dobson celebrated Holy Communion. We were surrounded by friends and family, and it was lovely to see a good representation of junior clergy, friends from College days. The reception was held in the splendid setting of the Garden House Hotel in Cambridge, and we spent the two and a half weeks of our honeymoon first in the Lake District and then in South Devon.

We set up home in a comfortable upstairs flat in Swaynes Close, just outside St. Paul's parish. Since there was no parish house for a curate, and there was also an acute housing shortage in Salisbury, we had had to scour the city to find somewhere to live, and it had proved very difficult. Eventually our organist put us in touch with a relation, Trixie Gummer by name, who had accommodation available. We were delighted to move in there, and we had a kitchen, a large lounge-dining room, a bedroom and a bathroom. We loved the small apartment.

Our dining table looked out over the pavement, and as we ate our meals we had a marvellous view of the passers by. Some of them became a familiar sight, and we attributed names to them as we speculated about their appearance and possible occupations: there was a man in a brown overcoat and flat brown cap who was always hurrying along exercising a dog on a leash and whom we christened 'The Sleuth'; there was a tall middle-aged man with a shock of curly hair whom we named 'The Author'; there was a lady of eccentric appearance who always wore knitted dresses and whom, for some reason, we christened 'Freda'; and there were several nuns who called regularly at the house next door and whom we dubbed 'The Anglican Sisters of Mercy.'

After we were married, Sally continued to teach Latin at South Wilts Grammar School for Girls, and she also played an important role in the life of St. Paul's parish. She was elected to the Parochial Church Council, was a regular participant in the weekly Bible Study group, played the piano for one of the Youth Club's musical productions, and in 1961 came to Switzerland with a party of twenty-five Youth Club members whom I took there for a holiday. We were very happy, and very busy, and I enjoyed getting to know some of her teaching colleagues.

A welcome feature of a curate's life in the diocese of Salisbury at that time was the receipt of a special cheque from the diocese a few days before Christmas, a gift arising from a benefactor's generosity. My salary as a deacon was £350 a year, so a cheque for £20 coming out of the blue at Christmas was riches indeed. Financially it was a real struggle to make ends meet; with a monthly cheque of £27 after a small deduction for Income Tax, I never had much left over.

The first call on my income was my weekly offering to God. Before I was ordained I had made up my mind that my financial commitment to God's work ought to be the first ten percent of my income, and Sally and I agreed that this would be our policy when we married. We have adhered to it throughout our married life and have never been in debt. There were a number of times when there was almost nothing in our bank account, and Sally worked wonders in running our household with the most modest resources, but we have always managed to cope – just! Our policy was very simple: if we could not pay for something we did without it. It was tough at times for our children, and we had been married for eleven years before we had a bank balance of £100 at the end of a month.

The question of our giving to God arose a few months before I was ordained. A wonderful old retired priest came to Ridley Hall to talk to us about his ministry, and he told us how he had arrived at his own policy and practice of giving. He reminded us of the Old and New Testament teaching on the subject, and stressed that giving is a matter for individuals to decide for themselves according to their circumstances and consciences. I was very struck by a passage he quoted from St Paul's second letter to the Christians at Corinth:-

> Remember this: Whosoever sows sparingly will also reap sparingly; and whosoever sows generously will also reap generously. Each man should give what he has decided in his heart to give, not reluctantly or under compulsion, for God loves a cheerful giver. And God is able to make all grace abound to you, so that in all things and at all times, having all that you need, you will abound in every good work.
>
> *2 Corinthians 9 Verses 6-8*

Until the time of that talk I had not given much attention to the question of personal giving, partly because I had never earned my living until then and partly because I had nothing to give financially anyway. So Sally and I decided that the first portion of our income to be allocated each month would be our giving to God.

## The Diocese of Salisbury

Alongside my life and work at St Paul's, I had to learn at the outset of my ministry to take my place in the wider life of the diocese. In my year as a deacon the diocese loomed large on my horizon. I was required to sit two three-hour examinations about books I had had to buy and read, and I had to report to the Rectory to take the papers under examination conditions; later one of the Bishop's examining chaplains would invite me to discuss my papers with him. It was not very demanding but I felt quite strongly that I had already done sufficient to demonstrate my academic capabilities, and I could think of other more profitable ways of training a deacon. Then there were the Rural Deanery Clergy Chapter meetings to attend; it was good to get to know the other clergy in the deanery and to know what was going on, but I confess that I often found the meetings very tedious.

Every year there was an excellent residential course for junior clergy. They were organised by Canon Eric Heaton, a noted Old Testament scholar, Chancellor of the Cathedral and a delightful person. He brought interesting and lively speakers to lead these courses and I came to really value them.

From time to time there were major diocesan festivals, services and important occasions, and I attended most of these. In my first month all the clergy were officially cited to attend a specially convened Synod to discuss Christian Stewardship. We had to wear cassock, surplice, scarf and hood; we were checked in on arrival and we sat in some discomfort in the Chapter House of the Cathedral. It was very impressive, and I remember it very clearly – especially some of the wonderful characters who spoke. One of the most inspiring services was a Young People's Evensong. It was organised by Ernest Teale, the Deputy Director of Education for the diocese, and it was very innovative and bold. A jazz band played before the service and accompanied some of the hymns; the hymns and canticles were set to new or modern tunes; the sermon was preached by a guitar-playing visiting Canon; and it all took place in the hallowed surroundings of the Cathedral! It was too much for a middle-aged man who stood up to protest as the procession of clergy, mainly 'of riper years', made its way up the aisle at the beginning of the service to the strains of 'Moon River'. He roundly denounced 'These modernistic clergy with no fire in their bellies.' The enormous impact of the service put his protest into perspective; it was a truly magnificent act of worship. It was imaginative, dignified, lively and purposeful; it lifted our spirits immeasurably.

**Becoming Parents**
Sally taught at South Wilts. Grammar School for Girls until Christmas 1961, when she resigned because she was expecting our first child. She kept wonderfully well throughout her pregnancy and we looked forward eagerly to the baby's arrival. She went into labour just before midnight on Thursday May 17th 1962, and I drove her at once to the Maternity Wing at Odstock Hospital. When she had been examined and admitted, I was advised to return home and get some sleep, as the birth was not imminent. It was a warm bright moonlit night, and I was much too wide awake and excited to sleep, so for two hours I drove slowly along deserted country lanes by the side of several of the rivers which converge in Salisbury, marvelling at the beauty of creation. Throughout the whole of Friday and all of Saturday morning I waited

anxiously for news of the birth. The waiting seemed interminable, and I even had to withdraw from our Saturday afternoon cricket match! Eventually in mid-afternoon a nurse came out of the delivery room and told me we had a fine healthy baby son weighing just under nine pounds. She said that I could go in and see them both, and it was a wonderful moment. We named him Andrew William, and we were very proud and doting parents. He brought an exciting new dimension into our lives, and he was thoroughly spoiled by the people of St Paul's!

**Life in the Parish**
Throughout my years at St Paul's I saw a pattern of ministry gradually emerge. I established relationships with people of all ages and backgrounds. I could see that if I was to be of any use to the people with whom I came into contact every day, I needed to be in touch both with God and with the real world. Any advice I might give had to be thought through carefully, expressed simply and be realistic. I saw that the young people looked to me for a lead and that I must combine enthusiasm, high spirits and energy with sensible policy and consistent uprightness of life. I learned to preach without reference to the script I always wrote out in full. I became known and trusted in the community, and I was very conscious of the need to be responsible. Parishioners would tell me about the problems of their neighbours and ask if I could help. Some of the situations were heartbreaking, difficult and time-consuming, others had a lighter side to them. All were important. Here are just some of the things that happened.

A young woman with four children under the age of five was suddenly and tragically widowed. Without her husband's income she found it very hard to make ends meet. I visited her regularly and gave her advice about where and how to apply for assistance. She was receiving support from the National Assistance Board (as it was then called), but in my view this was woefully inadequate. I advised her to appeal against their judgment, and a date was set for a hearing. As she could not afford to pay a solicitor to represent her, I offered to go with her myself to speak on her behalf. So in due course I found myself facing a formal tribunal with very little knowledge as to how to proceed. The Chairman carefully and patiently explained the set-up to me, and as I listened I realised that he was doing his best to help me. I caught on quickly and made my case to a largely sympathetic audience. I was absolutely thrilled when the tribunal significantly increased the widow's weekly benefit.

A close relative of two members of our congregation was employed by one of the large State-owned industries, and one day I got a message to say that he had been admitted as a patient to the psychiatric hospital. I went to see him and found him greatly distressed – so distressed in fact that he could not bring himself to tell me why he was there, though he did ask the psychiatrist to tell me in private. He had been arrested and charged with an indecency offence. He had pleaded guilty in Court and his case had been adjourned on condition that he underwent psychiatric assessment and treatment as an in-patient. His employers had suspended him on full pay. I visited him frequently, and the psychiatrist advised me that his patient was suffering from a physical ailment which was largely responsible for his acting out of character. When the Court reconvened to consider the reports he was given a conditional discharge, and the magistrate expressed the hope that his employers would now reinstate him. In fact they declined to do so, and sacked him.

I was incensed, partly because the offence involved had not been committed at work, and partly because it had been made clear by the hospital that the patient's condition had been treated and cured; there was little fear of a relapse. I made a strong plea to his employers to reconsider their decision, and I included letters of support from the psychiatrist, the hospital authorities, the magistrate who had heard the case, and others. I also sought to enlist the support of his trade union representative, but was sharply rebuffed. His employers rejected my plea, and I was shattered. I was determined not to give up easily, but I did not know what to do. Then out of the blue I received a telephone call from a well-spoken man who told me that he was not going to give me his name but would give me some information which might help me with the appeal. He proceeded to tell me the names of three people employed by the same nationalised industry who had been found guilty of similar offences and who had retained their employment. It was just what I needed. A tactful call to his employers indicating that I would request our Member of Parliament to raise the matter in the House of Commons produced the promise of a review. In due course our parishioner was reinstated. I was greatly relieved, and I had learned the value of determination and perseverance.

One day when I was visiting round the parish a member of our congregation came running out of a house and stopped me. She told me that she had just gone in to check on one of our congregation, a lovely old man who had recently been widowed, and had found him in a state of collapse; he appeared to have taken an overdose. We rushed back in and found him barely alive. We rang for an ambulance and got him off to hospital. Then together we cleaned up the house: the poor man had been so devastated by the loss of his wife that he had not had the will to pick himself up and try to get on with his life, and the house was a mess. Thankfully he recovered in hospital, and we were able to arrange for him to be properly looked after in the future.

There were some young people in the parish whom I knew and who got into trouble of one sort or another. Some just did not want any assistance, but with others I was able to provide support and help. I was delighted when one of them, with the considerable assistance of the Vicar of a rural parish, obtained a job on a farm. The young man had committed a serious and reckless offence, but was determined to make a fresh start when he came out of the detention centre. He settled well in his new environment and as far as I know he never slipped back.

And there were many happy, satisfying and amusing events.

In the summer of 1961, when I had been ordained for two years, Sally and I took 25 members of the Youth Club to Switzerland for a ten-day holiday. It was a wonderful trip. Most of the organisation, including the collection of all the money, was undertaken by the young people themselves, and at the end of the trip the accounts balanced exactly. By that time the Youth Club had a membership of about sixty, all of whom attended church at least once a month. It had been a real struggle to achieve this and a few battles had had to be fought on the way. Every year several of them came forward for Confirmation, and some found their marriage partners within the group; forty years on we are still in touch with a significant number of them. We took two parties to Lee Abbey for training weekends. We entered teams in inter-church Bible Knowledge competitions. We put on plays and musical productions to raise funds. We organised a second overseas holiday, this time to Austria. Our aim was to meet the social and spiritual needs of our young people within the family of the Church.

Early in 1962 Sally and I bought our first car. I had passed the driving test in 1961, much to the amazement of some of my friends, and I came in for a lot of teasing at the Youth Club. One lad asked me if I had worn my clerical collar when I took the test. When I said I had, he scornfully expressed the opinion that the examiner had had no option but to pass me! And a Bank Manager friend dismissed it by saying to a mutual friend, 'Well, if he can pass, anybody can!' I wondered whether I should feel insulted! The car we bought was a 1940 Austin 8 four-door saloon. It was black, had a large dent in the boot, had had only one owner and had travelled 135,000 miles. It was my pride and joy. Its registration letters were CHR, so we christened it 'Charity'. Flat out, down hill and with the wind behind, I could get it up to 50 m.p.h. We had endless pleasure from it, and after it got a puncture one Saturday I discovered that the New Testament reading for the next morning contained the words, 'Charity is not puffed up.' There was suppressed laughter in church next morning! 'Charity' continued as our car for two years. Then, with a change of job, I was given a vehicle to go with my work, so 'Charity' had to go.

One of my earliest weddings brought a tricky moment. The bridegroom was a highly accomplished craftsman with little formal education. He was also a very nervous man. At the wedding he dried up completely, unable to say a word when I asked him to repeat the promises after me. Three times I asked him, and three times he failed to respond. In desperation I glanced at the best man, who was looking equally worried. He drew back his foot, gave the bridegroom a sharp kick on the ankle, and hissed: 'Speak, you bugger!' It worked like a dream.

## Time to Move On

When we had been in Salisbury for a little over three years it was clear that the time had come for us to consider seriously my next appointment. Our time at St Paul's had been very satisfying and enjoyable, but now that we were a family of three, our living accommodation was inadequate, I was feeling that I was beginning to dot the i's and cross the t's, and I was ready for a fresh challenge.

I took stock of what I had learned at St Paul's.

I had come to see how vital it was for me to spend an unhurried time of quiet alone with God at the beginning of the day, when I could read Morning Prayer, meditate on the Bible readings, think about the day ahead of me, pray, and commit myself afresh to God's service. I had learned the need to respect absolutely things said to me in confidence. I had learned to keep silent when necessary; to be loyal to my superiors when people wanted to grumble about them; to listen carefully to all sides of a contentious issue before venturing a firm opinion; to apologise without reserve when I got things wrong; and to learn from my mistakes. I was developing the confidence to trust my own judgement and to take steps of faith when I believed them to be necessary, and also to stand firm when I believed I was right and people were grumbling at me. I was aware that I needed to be better organised in my work. I was discovering different ways of communicating the Gospel. I knew too that I was making a lot of mistakes, that I had only just launched out into the deep, and that I had a huge amount to learn. But I had made a start and now it was time to move on.

Invitations to consider new appointments began to arrive – offers of second curacies, priest-in-charge positions, even one or two incumbent's posts – but somehow none of them seemed quite right. I had a gut feeling that I wanted to do something different from parochial ministry for a while, and also that I wanted to demonstrate to myself that the Gospel could be communicated effectively in an all-male community. Sally and I thought seriously about offering to serve with the Church Missionary Society, but I had anxieties about serving in a tropical climate in the light of my history of tuberculosis.

Then one day I played golf with a good friend, Don Lewin, the Area Secretary of The Missions to Seamen. Don had been Port Chaplain in Dublin and was a great enthusiast about his work. He asked me what I was going to do after St Paul's, and when I told him that I did not know, he asked me if I had ever considered serving with The Missions to Seamen. I said that I had not and he then proceeded to describe its ministry. He painted a fascinating picture and after our game I went home and thought about what he had said. At the back of my mind was my love of the sea and my thwarted ambition to serve in the Royal Navy. Sally and I discussed it at length and I wrote to The Missions to Seamen for information. I liked what I read, and applied to serve as a chaplain. I was interviewed by the Candidates Committee in January 1963. The interview was notable for some abrasive questions from one of the laymen present, to which I replied courteously but firmly. However, the atmosphere was lightened as I left the room by a whispered aside from the Deputy General Secretary, Tom Kerfoot. 'Don't worry about that crusty old bugger – he's always like that!' A few minutes later I was told that I had been accepted.

In due course we were advised that we would be going to South Shields to learn the job, and our time in Salisbury drew to a close.

CHAPTER THREE

# South Shields 1963-1965

## A First Glimpse

BEFORE WE MOVED to South Shields in June 1963 for me to join the chaplaincy staff of The Missions to Seamen, Sally and I had made a brief visit to see where we would be living and working.

We travelled by train, and the journey from Newcastle to South Shields along the south bank of the Tyne was fascinating and revealing. We crossed the river by the famous bridge and wound our way towards South Shields through places which had previously been unknown or just names to us: Gateshead, Low Fell, Felling, Hebburn, Jarrow and Tyne Dock. We passed factories, industrial complexes, shipbuilding yards, dry docks, collieries and rows and rows of densely packed terraced houses. At the time the shipbuilding industry was in recession and everything looked run down. It was very different from rural Wiltshire in the Spring!

At the station in South Shields we were met by Richard Hughes, Senior Chaplain of the Tyne and Blyth station of The Missions to Seamen. He drove us straight to the seafarers' centre, the Flying Angel Club, on the Mill Dam, right in the heart of the port and close to the Market Square. It was a large, old, rambling three-storey building on to which a new entrance and offices had been built. It had thirty-eight bedrooms of varying size and standard, a large concert hall, cinema, a restaurant which doubled in the evening as a dance hall, a canteen, recreation areas and a chapel. The chaplain's and the administrative offices were located in the new entrance area, together with the reception desk and a magnificent memorial to seafarers from the area who had died in the Second World War. There were more than twenty full-time or part-time staff and a good number of voluntary helpers. The bedrooms were fully booked throughout much of the year, and some two thousand seafarers from the ships in port visited the centre each month. All this we picked up as we were taken round the centre, where we stayed overnight and had our meals. It was a valuable opportunity to experience the atmosphere for ourselves.

Next morning we were taken on a tour of the area. We saw the smoke-blackened buildings, the rows of terraced houses, the piles of coal outside the miners' homes, the corner shops, the dingy pubs and the many fish-and-chip shops. We saw the impressive Marine and Technical College, where deck and engineering apprentices and officers prepared for their certificates of competence. We drove through Laygate, an area of the town where the families of many Middle Eastern seafarers lived. We went on to the mouth of the River Tyne, with its magnificent entrance and impressive view of the coastline to the north, and we passed a long, wide, well maintained stretch of grass on top of the cliffs. It was soon all to become very familiar to us.

Then we were taken to see the house where we would be living, our first home of our own. 13 St Michael's Avenue was a three-bedroomed house in the middle of a long terrace, opposite one of the hospitals. There was no front garden, and only an enclosed concrete yard at the back. The kitchen was minute, and the bathroom and upstairs landing were enormous. Hot water was produced by the breakfast room fire. We were very excited by the prospect of moving in and were accumulating furniture during our last months in Salisbury. We were thrilled to receive the gift of a quantity of good solid old furniture from a generous priest friend of my family. On our way back to Salisbury Sally and I thought about what we had seen and heard, and we realised how great the change in our lives was going to be. I resolved that I would give my best efforts to the task for two years. If at the end of that time I felt that I was not suited to this ministry, I would then seek to return to parish life or move to some other type of ministry.

**The Missions to Seamen**
When I became a chaplain of The Missions to Seamen, my knowledge of the Society and its work was very limited. My mother was parish secretary for the Society in Newton Abbot and we had heard a little about it from her. As a theological student I had visited the seafarers' centre in Manchester and heard the chaplain talk about his work. I had listened to enthusiastic reports from Don Lewin, Area Secretary in Salisbury and formerly chaplain in Dublin; and I had read the publicity material sent to me by the Society's Head Office. I had very little first-hand knowledge of ships and how they operated. My knowledge of a seafarer's way of life was limited to what I had read and to the wartime experiences of my uncles. I knew that the Society was the third largest missionary society of the Church of England, and that it worked in every continent.

The Missions to Seamen was formally constituted in 1856, bringing together under one flag a number of separate port chaplaincies. Its aim was to promote the spiritual welfare of seafarers at home and abroad, ashore and afloat. Its ministry was to be practical, pastoral and evangelistic, and by the end of the nineteenth century it had spread to every continent. It did magnificent work in the two world wars, and it was a basic principle that the Society was there for all seafarers irrespective of any considerations of race, rank, religion, or absence of it. It operated under the auspices of the Church of England and of the Anglican Church worldwide. That was all I needed to know when I started. Answers to the further questions of how it carried on its ministry, what was expected of a chaplain, how a seafarers' centre operated, and how my own abilities and personality could be used best, would hopefully emerge as time passed.

I was eager to learn, and on the very first ship I visited I became aware of the wonderful reputation the 'Flying Angel' (as the Society is affectionately known to seafarers all over the world because of its logo) enjoys in the maritime world. On the British India cruise ship *Dunera* I found myself in an open area in the middle of dozens of boisterous and excited teenage school children embarking on an educational cruise. I looked around and saw a door marked 'Officers – Private'. I went through it, and heard voices in a cabin with its door open. I knocked, and a pleasant voice invited me to come in. The Chief Officer greeted me. 'Good morning, Padre,' he said, 'from The Missions to Seamen, I see. Sit down and have a beer.' In the course of conversation it emerged that I was a very new chaplain visiting his first ship, and the officers spontaneously told me how much the 'Flying Angel' had meant to them in their careers, particularly in ports overseas and when they had been cadets. My education began on day one.

### The Shipping Scene on the Tyne

For a chaplain beginning his ministry among seafarers, Tyneside, and South Shields in particular, was a wonderful place to start.

The Flying Angel Club of The Missions to Seamen was situated on the south bank of the River and about a mile upstream from its mouth. It was close to the town centre, and near the offices of the National Union of Seamen, the Shipping Federation and the River Police. On either side were the drydocking firms of Brigham and Cowan and The Middle Docks, with the smaller firm of Tyne Dock Engineering alongside Brigham and Cowan. The terminal for the North Shields/South Shields ferry was a few hundred yards away downstream. In North Shields there were the large and important fish quay, the terminal for the passenger ferry to Bergen in Norway, and Smith's Dock, a large ship repair yard. Up river on the south side were John Redhead's shipbuilding and ship repair yard, mineral ore and general cargo berths, a tanker berth, coal staithes, and Palmers and Hawthorne Leslie's shipbuilding and ship repair yards. Beyond the Tyne bridge in Newcastle lay the Dunston coal staithes. Up river on the north bank was a tanker berth, Clelands shipbuilding yard, Swan Hunter's and Vickers shipbuilding and ship repair yards and, in the centre of Newcastle, the Newcastle Quay.

The Missions to Seamen operated a small launch, *Hope The Good*, named after a distinguished former chaplain, and it was invaluable for our ship-visiting. Many ships moored in midstream, and it was a great advantage to be able to visit them and to cross the river at points between the South

Shields/North Shields ferry and the road bridges in Newcastle ten miles upstream. I loved the launch work and became adept at scaling rope ladders, making fast alongside ships in midstream, climbing gangways and quayside ladders, leaping on to ships' gangways, and hauling supplies of books and magazines on board.

Our launchman, Bill Egan, was a great character. He had served for many years on deep-sea ships, and he looked after the launch like a baby. He maintained the engine, kept the boat immaculate, and was very protective of the paintwork. He also had a fine flow of invective, acquired over the years at sea. It appeared on a notable occasion when, in order to assist a family travelling from a distance, I arranged to scatter the ashes of a deceased former seaman from the launch outside the harbour entrance on a Saturday afternoon. Bill was not best pleased at having to give up his Saturday afternoon, and he was even less happy when the day turned out to be cold, wet and windy. He didn't want to go out, but the family had come from a long distance, and as we thought it was safe to go, we went. The sea was rough, and when we hove to to conduct the simple service the launch was rolling wildly. At the exact moment when my colleague was pouring the ashes into the sea a sudden gust of wind from an unexpected quarter whipped some of the ashes inboard. Bill received them full in the face, and his expression of displeasure was so awesome that even the family had to laugh.

I soon became familiar with the main features of the River, and slowly came to understand the roles of many of the officials who are an integral part of any port: Customs, Port Health, Immigration, Port Authority, ships agents, ship chandlers, union officials and so on. I became acquainted with individuals in many of these jobs. I came into contact every day with seafarers from many countries and different backgrounds, and learned about their culture. I began to be able to recognise different types of vessels and I watched with keen interest the building of new ships and the repairing and refitting of older ones. I came to know the representatives of other Christian and secular organisations concerned with the welfare of seafarers. I met the River Policemen and the tug crewmen who visited the Flying Angel Club, and learned more about their jobs. I found the whole shipping scene endlessly fascinating, and my own work deeply satisfying.

## Being a Chaplain Among Seafarers

Chaplaincy in the maritime world was very different from parochial life. As a curate in a parish I spent most of my weekday mornings combining a time of quiet alone with God, reading, preparing talks, sermons and meetings, visiting the church school, conducting services, and administration. The afternoons and evenings were given over to visiting and parish activities. I lived and worked in the same place and among the same people every day. As a chaplain in the shipping world, my daily programme was much less predictable and much more flexible. After a short morning service in the chapel, the chaplains, lay reader and student assistant sat down with the Senior Chaplain's secretary to review the previous day's activities, take necessary decisions, and plan and allocate the day's duties. We then went our several ways.

Most of the rest of the morning was spent visiting the ships. I saw this as being at the very heart of our ministry. In going to the ships, we were representing our Lord Jesus Christ and His Church. We were ambassadors for Him among seafarers from all over the world. By just being there we were showing His care and concern for them. We were there as the servants of the servants of the Lord. I always wore a clerical collar and a Flying Angel lapel badge so as to be instantly recognisable – and a navy blue battledress and trousers to keep my shoreside clothes clean! It was important to visit all the ships, if possible, because if we did not, the seafarers might well be unaware that the Church was there and available to them in the port.

Throughout my time in South Shields I visited at least a hundred ships every month. The first thing I did was to take a good long look at the ship, noting what type of vessel it was, its condition, and its port of registration. Once on board, I made it my practice to go first to the Captain or Chief Officer to ask permission to visit the ship: they were responsible for the ship and for the crew, and it was also their home; I was a visitor, and observing proper procedures was important. I would speak to them about the seafarers' centre and its daily programme, and then tell them (if they were at a remote berth) that we would provide transport from the ship to the centre and, at the end of the evening, from the centre to the ship. The provision of transport was important: taxi fares could be prohibitively expensive, and in every port there are unscrupulous characters on the lookout for the unsuspecting seafarer with money in his pocket, a few drinks inside him and walking back to his ship on his own. It was a real bonus that English is the international language of the sea, because it meant that I could always communicate with at least some of the people on board.

Once permission to visit the ship had been granted, I was free to go around and meet everybody. It was important not to intrude on or disturb the working life of the ship, but it soon became clear what were the best times to visit the various departments. In the middle of the morning the engineers took a coffee break, which they spent in their duty mess clad in their overalls, and that was a good moment to talk to them. The cook and the catering staff could always be found in the galley, and they usually welcomed a chat as they worked. Half an hour or so before lunch many of the officers gathered in their lounge for drinks, and this was a suitable moment for meeting them. And there were always some seafarers working or relaxing in their cabins; they were usually glad to talk. I found most seafarers very welcoming; they were pleased to see a visitor – especially one who was not trying to sell them anything! I learned how important it was to introduce myself clearly by name, and to say that I was a chaplain of The Missions to Seamen. Conversation usually flowed freely from that point, and I seldom introduced the subject of religion: it cropped up quite naturally, and if the seafarer asked questions about it I did my best to answer simply. One of the questions most frequently asked was, 'Why do you do what you do?' It made a good place to start.

Every day I met fine people of different faiths and traditions, and it made me work out as best I could where I stood as a Christian in relation to them. I came to the conclusion that my calling was to be faithful to our Lord Jesus Christ, to be loyal to that part of the Church of which I was a member, to work on the principle that all of us are made in the image of God, to witness to my faith by word of mouth and by quality of life and service, and to leave the sorting out to God. I was aware, too, that in the maritime world it is the Christian Churches who have given a lead in providing a comprehensive service to all seafarers without distinction.

During the course of ship-visiting we were occasionally faced with unusual requests. One morning I was visiting a Scandinavian ship and called on the Captain. He asked if I could do anything to help one of his officers who was suffering from severe toothache. Time was short, because the ship was due to sail later that day. I telephoned our own dentist and explained the situation to him. He told me to bring the officer to the surgery straightaway, so I went to his cabin to give him the good news. He got up and picked up two large bottles of whisky. He took the top off one and had a long drink. In the minibus on the way to the surgery he again fortified himself generously. I took him into the dentist, where he politely told the dentist, 'No anaesthetic!' The tooth was quickly removed, whereupon the grateful patient presented the dentist with the second bottle! On the way back to the ship he celebrated his freedom from pain with a further substantial intake, and I was very happy and relieved when I returned him, safe if not entirely sound, to the Captain! On another occasion a captain asked me if I would take his non-English-speaking wife to a good hairdresser. All went well until the hairdresser asked me how the lady wanted her hair styled!

In the chaplains' offices at The Flying Angel Club we dealt with a wide variety of situations and problems. Chaplains of The Missions to Seamen act as honorary agents for two wonderful charities caring for sick and retired seafarers and for the dependent relatives of deceased seafarers, the Royal Alfred Merchant Seamen's Society and the Shipwrecked Fishermen and Mariners Royal Benevolent Society. With Tyneside being home to a very large number of merchant seafarers, and with every application for financial assistance being scrutinised and recommended by a chaplain, we regularly spent time with people in real need. It was time-consuming, but very worthwhile – and the Church was seen to care.

Sometimes it was an emergency which brought a person to our office, as on December 23rd 1963 (my first Christmas as a seafarers' chaplain), when a middle-aged lady came in late in the afternoon in great distress. She had just received a letter from one of her husband's shipmates in which he expressed the hope that her husband was recovering well – he had been taken ashore into hospital in Hong Kong, seriously ill. The letter had been posted several weeks earlier, but she had had no indication at all that her husband was ill. She was beside herself with worry. By the time she had told me the whole story it was 5:30 p.m., or 5:30 a.m. on Christmas Eve in Hong Kong. I said that I would get in touch with our chaplain there as quickly as possible and ask him to investigate. I sent him a telegram setting out the problem and requesting information urgently. At 11:00 a.m. the next day, Christmas Eve, I received a reply. The chaplain had traced the seafarer and had visited him in hospital. He was making a good recovery, having been desperately ill, and was hoping to fly home for the New Year. His wife's happiness and relief were a joy to behold, and I realised what a wonderful thing it is to belong to the worldwide family of the Church and to be able to ask a fellow Christian on the other side of the world to act so swiftly.

At other times it might be a shipping company contacting us by phone to ask us to break news of the death of a seafarer at sea or overseas to his family. It was a heartbreaking, demanding task which we took very seriously. It was always difficult. Early in my time in South Shields I was asked to tell the parents of a young seaman that he had died whilst swimming on his birthday. With the ship at anchor outside a port in the Black Sea, he had dived into the water and on to a concrete post below the surface. He had died instantly. When his father came to the door I told him what had happened as gently and straightforwardly as I could. He was absolutely shattered, and we went through to the kitchen to tell his wife. Their grief was heartrending; it emerged that they had had three children, and all had died in tragic circumstances. My heart went out to them and I did not know how to begin to comfort them. I wanted simply to put my arms round them in love and sympathy, but I hesitated because I knew that I was not much older than their son. Instead I said some well intentioned but totally inadequate words, and I knew I had failed them. I helped with the arrangements for a memorial service in their local church and I kept in touch with them. And I took to heart the lesson that just being there with people in their grief, and not talking too much at that stage, is very important. Talking comes later.

Not long after that I was asked by a shipping company based in Newcastle to go to a young wife and tell her that her husband, an outstanding young engineer officer, had died at sea from a gastric complaint. When I got to the house, she was out. A neighbour told me that she had gone shopping with her two year-old daughter, and also where her parents lived. As they lived nearby, I went to them and gave them the news; I asked them to stand by to help. When I got back to the house, the young woman was just returning, wheeling her daughter in a pushchair. When they had gone in I went to the door and rang the bell. She invited me in and as gently as I could I broke the news. I spent much of the day with her and with both sets of parents, and in the days that followed I dealt with many of the arrangements that had to be made. The shipping company was wonderful and I was very moved by the trust they placed in us.

A challenge constantly facing us was how to communicate effectively with seafarers having little or no command of English. I compiled a list of the languages we encountered most frequently on the waterfront, and enlisted the help of my sister and brother-in-law, both excellent linguists, in translating our leaflet advertising The Flying Angel Club into various languages. Eventually I carried leaflets in eighteen languages in a large box in our minibus, and they proved very useful. Then it dawned on me that we did not need words at all: pictures were what was required. So a new leaflet was prepared, with small cartoon pictures portraying what was available at The Flying Angel Club, a simple map showing our whereabouts, and the telephone number in bold print. It was immediately successful and it set me thinking about ways in which the Gospel could be communicated visually.

At the heart of our lives and work was the chapel, a simple quiet place with seating for about seventy people. Its main feature was a magnificent carved oak reredos: the central panel, behind the altar, portrayed Jesus making Himself known to His disciples after His resurrection as they returned from a fishing trip; one side panel depicted a contemporary dockland scene, and the other a modern passenger ship. The reredos was a daily source of inspiration: the Crucified and Risen Jesus at the heart of our daily work. Every morning the chaplaincy team gathered for a time of worship, reflection, prayer and spiritual refreshment. A short service was held every dance evening, and there were morning and evening services on Sundays. The walls of the staircase leading down to the chapel were covered with plaques commemorating seafarers who had died at sea in peace or war. It was a place with an atmosphere, a holy place.

### Life at the Seafarers' Centre

It soon became clear that the ministry of visiting seafarers on board ship and the ministry of welcoming them in The Flying Angel Club were equally important. Seafaring is a unique way of life. Seafarers are away from home, family and friends, for weeks, months and sometimes even years at a time. They are normal people and they miss shore life. At sea they live in close proximity to the same group of people for long periods of time and they cannot get away from them. Boredom can be a major problem; after all, out of sight of land one stretch of water looks much like another. It can also be dangerous; even today an average of two ships a week of 500 deadweight tonnes or more are lost at sea through storms, fog, collisions, fire, fraud and other causes. It can also be very lonely. When they go ashore in a foreign port, they may well not speak the language or be aware of local customs; they may experience problems exchanging currency or paying for a telephone call home; and if they do not speak the local language, they are at real disadvantage since there are always people on the lookout to exploit a stranger. It was against the background of loneliness and danger at sea and temptation and danger ashore in the nineteenth century that the Churches realised that the provision of shore-side centres open to all seafarers was an urgent necessity, and took appropriate action. Seafarers' centres today are very different from the early ones, but the need for them is just as great.

Our Flying Angel Club in South Shields was well used. It was old and scruffy through constant use. Most of the thirty-one bedrooms on the top floors were sparsely furnished, but were adequate for a seafarer needing a bed just for a night or an inexpensive base whilst studying at the Marine College for Certificates of Competency. The other seven bedrooms were larger, better equipped and more comfortably furnished; they were usually occupied by seafarers standing by a ship, or waiting to join one, and whose companies were paying the bill.

In addition to our residents a large number of seafarers from ships loading or discharging cargo came into The Flying Angel Club. We visited these ships as soon as possible after arrival, and this was always both exciting and challenging. We never knew quite what to expect, who we might meet, or whether many would speak English. The prospect of going on board an unfamiliar vessel could be quite daunting, and I always said a brief prayer as I went up the gangway. Almost always we were well received, and I came to love ship-visiting. Arranging transport to and from the centre often required imagination and improvisation when crew members did not speak any English; it could involve making noises and appropriate actions as if driving a motor vehicle, writing a time on a piece of paper, and then waiting for enlightenment to appear on a seafarer's face!

There was always at least one member of the chaplaincy team on duty in The Flying Angel Club in the evenings. On three evenings a week we ran a dance, with music provided by a pianist and drummer and partners coming from the Harbour Lights Guild, a group of ladies of varying ages who came specially to provide a welcome to men cut off from female company for long periods of time. The Guild had a simple but strict code of conduct designed to promote good fellowship and safeguard reputations. On evenings when there was no organised social programme we sat and chatted with the seafarers or joined with them in games of table tennis, darts or snooker, or talked to the voluntary workers in the canteen.

A regular feature of our winter programme for seafarers was the Saturday afternoon trip in the minibus to the Football League matches at Roker Park, Sunderland, and St. James' Park, Newcastle. These trips were greatly appreciated by the seamen and I myself became a dyed-in-the-wool Sunderland supporter. On the return journey after the match, and on the other trips we organised, serious questions about the Christian faith and the Church often emerged, and it was a real challenge to answer simply and directly.

Throughout my time in South Shields I was constantly being faced with new and unfamiliar situations, and I was very glad that during my first eighteen months I could always seek the advice and guidance of Richard Hughes, the Senior Chaplain. However, I had no chance to consult him (he was away on emergency duties in Brazil) when I received a visit one summer evening from a group of senior police officers, trade union officials and the Deputy High Commissioner of India. They told me that the Indian crew members of a bulk carrier, the *Finnamore Meadow*, had walked off the ship that morning in protest against some of their working conditions and were refusing to return until their grievances had been dealt with. Negotiations had gone on all day, but no solution had been reached. It was deadlock. The police officers and the Deputy High Commissioner asked if we would accommodate the 44 seamen for the night so that negotiations could begin afresh in the morning.

I thought very hard for a few moments, and then consulted our very experienced Lay Reader, Sid Wilson. He pointed out that we should be careful not to give the impression that we were taking sides and I was grateful for his advice. I told the assembled group that we would accommodate the seamen if the ship's Captain agreed, and we went off together to talk to him; he said that it would be very helpful if we would take them in. So we set out mattresses and blankets in our concert hall, and in the morning gave them all breakfast. Negotiations dragged on and eventually the seafarers were transferred to an Asian hotel. As I drove them there, I was asked several times what would happen to them if the dispute were not resolved amicably. I spelled out the implications for them and was greatly relieved when the dispute was settled the next day and they returned to the ship. In the course of those few days I learned a lot about the shipping industry.

There were some great characters among the domestic staff and the voluntary helpers at The Flying Angel Club. Many of them had family links with seafarers and others had spent years working with us. Mary Allan, our chief receptionist, was married to a seaman. She was responsible for booking seafarers into the residential accommodation, dealing with the pensioners of The Royal Alfred and Shipwrecked Mariners Societies and actually paying their pensions, and answering the telephone. She called a spade a spade, treated everybody alike, and had a wonderful sense of humour. She was popular and highly respected. Edith Penman, the Chaplain's Secretary, ran the office very efficiently and kept us all up to the mark administratively; she had a vast knowledge of the shipping world, and particularly of Tyneside shipping personnel. Bill Egan, our launchman and general handyman, was an absolute gem. Grace, Kitty and Elsie in the kitchen were a law unto themselves. Joe, one of the stewards, had a fine command of English when roused; he had a short fuse, and when a seaman made an improper suggestion to his wife, who was one of the bedroom cleaners, Joe decided to speak to the man himself. After the incident he told me that he had said to the seaman that if he repeated his suggestion, he 'would put his hands down (the seaman's) throat and pull his balls up past his tonsils.' He couldn't understand why the picture he had conjured up was making me shake with laughter! Inspector Cram of the River Police was a regular visitor and kept us in touch with the goings-on on the River. Harry Malcolm, secretary of the Tugworkers Union, was a wonderful friend; he was a regular at the Sunday morning celebration of Holy Communion, and did all sorts of jobs about the place. There was a great feeling of fellowship and dedication among the staff and voluntary helpers, and it certainly was the real world we were dealing with.

## Memorable Moments

In a busy seafarers' centre, where hundreds of people passed through the doors every day, where seafarers of all ages and a wide variety of countries and backgrounds were constantly coming and going, and while many languages, including Geordie, were spoken, it was hardly surprising that there should be occasional unforgettable moments, some amusing and others deadly serious.

One occurred soon after my arrival. A very large cook came into The Flying Angel Club. He was six feet four inches tall, and must have weighed at least 250 pounds. He told me that his name was John —— ; he had just missed his ship; he had nowhere to spend the night; and he had no money to pay for a room. I asked him the name of his ship, and he replied, '*The Sir Alexander Kennedy*', a collier sailing between the Tyne and the Thames. I exclaimed that it was two days since she had sailed, but he assured me that I was wrong. Unconvinced, I rang the Lloyds Hailing Station to check. 'She sailed two days ago, Padre', came the reply. When I put this to him, all the cook would say was that it seemed that it had only just gone! However, we still had the problem of where he was going to spend the night, and against my better judgment I let him have a room for the night. In the morning he slipped away early, leaving a wet bed behind him. I then discovered that he was on a blacklist of persistent offenders, and that I should not have allowed him to stay. I was in trouble with the staff, so I asked them all to tell me immediately if he came in again.

Two days later, in mid-afternoon after the pubs had closed, one of our stewards came rushing up. 'Padre, Padre,' he said, 'John —— is here again!' I asked where he was, and on being told I went down to the canteen area to confront him. He was standing talking to several of his mates and they had all obviously been drinking. My heart was in my mouth as I went up to them.

'Mr ——', I said.

'Yes,' he replied.

'I must ask you to leave.'

'Why?'

'Well, last time you were here,' I said, 'you didn't pay for your room, you left a wet bed, and you told me a pack of lies. And now you've had too much to drink. So please leave!'

'Get down on your knees in that chapel!' came his reply.

'Why?' I asked.

'For daring to ask me to leave!' he shouted.

I told him that I did not want him in the building, and that if he did not leave voluntarily I would call the police. We argued for a while, and I had succeeded in manoeuvring him to the side door when he suddenly turned to face me and shouted, 'I'll call your bluff. Get the police!' I went back upstairs and rang the police. A few minutes later a mini arrived driven by one of the biggest policemen I have ever seen; he was wearing a peaked cap, with a black and white checked band round it. I took him downstairs to the cook, who by now was sprawling on a bench near the side door.

'Come on, son,' said the policeman. 'Up and out!'

'Why?' asked the cook.

'Because the Padre doesn't want you here, and if he doesn't want you he doesn't have to have you.'

The cook looked up at the policeman's peaked cap. Then he looked at me.

'Would you mind sending for the regular police?' he asked. The policeman had had enough. Bending forward, he hauled the cook to his feet, and stood face to face with him, their noses just inches apart.

'Look, son; what the hell do you think I am? The bloody postman?'

Together they went out of the side door, and I could hear some well-chosen words of advice coming from the policeman. Some time later the cook came back to apologise, and we made our peace with each other. We became good friends, and I never had any more problems with him.

While I was still fairly new to serving among seafarers, I sometimes had difficulty understanding the English spoken by some of the overseas seamen – and also by some of our British seamen! An Asian seafarer came up to me in the Flying Angel Club one day and asked me where the Peace Room was. I took him to the chapel, where he looked in and then shook his head vigorously. With an unmistakable gesture he indicated that it was the men's toilet that he was looking for!

During my time in South Shields The Missions to Seamen opened a new Home Mission in Sunderland. Far-reaching changes in the pattern of shipping using the port had meant that the large old seafarers' centre had become obsolete and had been sold. A comfortable modern house had been purchased and adapted for use as the chaplain's home and a place to which seafarers could be invited. It had good recreational facilities and a lovely small chapel. Richard Hughes and I were invited to the official opening, which was to be conducted by the Bishop of Durham. Just as the Bishop was about to begin the formal part of the proceedings, a small but very well-endowed lady came up to us bearing a plate of assorted cakes and jam tarts. Standing very close to Richard, she looked up at him and said, 'Oh, Father Hughes, may I press you to a tart?' The Bishop chose that very moment to start the service, and silence descended. Unfortunately Richard and I were helpless with laughter, and it took us ages to calm down.

**Emergency Duty in Belfast**
In the middle of 1964, a year after our arrival in South Shields, the General Secretary of The Missions to Seamen asked me to take charge of the station in Belfast for a few weeks in an emergency situation. The previous Senior Chaplain there had moved a few months earlier to the chaplaincy in Wellington, New Zealand; the incoming Senior Chaplain would not be arriving for another three months, and the Lay Reader in temporary charge was unwell and finding the situation very stressful. It was felt that he needed a complete break for a few weeks. I was happy to accept; it would be good to have an opportunity to see for myself the work of another seafarers' centre.

The Flying Angel Club in Belfast was very impressive. The building was eight years old and had been brilliantly planned to meet current and future needs. It had a magnificent chapel: simple, dignified, beautifully furnished, and already with a hallowed atmosphere. Entry to the chapel was from the multi-purpose hall, which had a well equipped stage and a first class canteen. The reception area, offices and recreational amenities were of a similar high standard, and the excellence of the whole set-up made me appreciate the value of careful and imaginative planning.

When I arrived in Belfast, morale at The Flying Angel Club was low. The previous Senior Chaplain, Ted Matchett, had been there for eleven years and had been greatly loved. The new Senior Chaplain, Joe Parker, was an unknown quantity. The Lay Reader, Allan Jones, was very unwell and unable to operate fully. The staff were doing their best to keep everything going but

*South Shields, leaving presentation, 1965.*

were struggling, and the voluntary helpers were losing heart. The ship was drifting without a rudder. I saw my task as being to prepare the way for the new Senior Chaplain and to rekindle failing enthusiasm. I visited the ships, and spent time with committee members and voluntary helpers. The dance nights in the club were popular, but even these were deteriorating: the girls were becoming discouraged, drifting in late and leaving early, and the band had got slack about time-keeping. On the first dance evening I observed what was happening: there were plenty of seafarers but not many girls, and the band arrived half an hour late. Towards the end of the evening I talked to the girls individually about how I hoped to liven up to the dances, and when the leader of the band told me they were ready to play the last dance I told him that as they had arrived late they could either play on for an extra half hour or I would reduce their payment proportionately. It was a defining moment. I did not know what the band leader would do. In the end we compromised – but it was the last time that the band was late!

I enjoyed visiting the ships in the port and I watched the building of a variety of new ships in the Harland and Wolf shipyard with interest and admiration. It was good to experience the atmosphere of Belfast as I stood shaking a flagday tin on one of the street corners. It was a joy to travel round the Antrim coast on a day off and to visit The Missions to Seamen in Dublin on another. I was uplifted by the worship in the chapel. I crammed a lot of activity into three weeks and made many new friends. I was sad to leave when the time came, and it began to dawn on me that I had a gift of being able to motivate people. When I moved to Hull sixteen months later, the experience in Belfast proved invaluable.

## In Charge

When I had been in South Shields for about fifteen months, Richard Hughes was asked to take charge of The Missions to Seamen centre in Santos, Brazil, during an emergency. He would spend about a year there and return to South Shields afterwards. While he was away, I would be acting Senior Chaplain at South Shields. I was ready for the extra responsibility, though I was very aware of my inexperience.

My time in charge got off to a bad start when I broke two bones in my right foot. I was stepping off a low stage, but failed to notice a thin wire stretched a few inches above the stage. I tripped and landed awkwardly. My foot was in plaster to just below the knee, and for three and a half weeks I had to be driven everywhere, which was very frustrating. But as I look back I can see that this period of enforced inactivity was very useful: it gave me an opportunity to analyse carefully how our Flying Angel Club ran, to note exactly who did what, and to organise my own office as I wanted it. The building was old, and badly in need of upgrading, refurbishing and redecoration. I brought all this to the attention of the Committee of Management (a splendid group of high-powered shipping, business and professional people), and they encouraged me to get on with the most urgent jobs and draw up plans for the future. I was very aware that I was in temporary charge and that I should therefore not start anything that Richard would not wish to continue on his return, so I got on with a programme of extensive redecoration and planning for a new lounge to replace an unsightly and under-used open area in the main part of the building.

I was desperately keen to make a success of my tenure of office as Senior Chaplain, and as a consequence I made a number of elementary mistakes. If I saw a job in the centre that needed doing, I often did it myself to save time. I found myself getting bogged down by administration simply because I was not ensuring that those who should be doing particular jobs were actually doing them. And as I gave my attention to the running of the centre, the number of ships I was visiting was declining. After a few months it became clear to me where I was going wrong. I sat down to work out how to do my job more efficiently, and came to the conclusion that I must do first the jobs that only I could do, I must ensure that our paid staff actually did the work that they were employed to do, and that I should praise and encourage good work in public and rebuke as necessary in private. In that way I sorted out my own priorities, and ship visiting and daily contact with seafarers were soon back at the top of the list.

The temporary nature of my appointment brought many frustrations, not least the need to preserve the status quo as far as possible, but it was very beneficial to me in preparing for the next stage in my ministry. Towards the end of my year in charge I was appointed Port Chaplain of Hull, the third largest port in England at that time. I began to look forward to putting into practice what I had learned in South Shields.

**Partners in Service**

As I visited ships and made my way round shipyards, dry docks, coal staithes and cargo berths, I saw for myself that The Missions to Seamen was one among a number of Christian and secular charitable organisations serving seafarers. The Roman Catholic Apostleship of the Sea operated a fine well-equipped seafarers' centre, Westoe Towers, near the Marine College in South Shields, and had its own very active chaplain. The inter-denominational British Sailors Society ran a hotel for seafarers in Jesmond, a mile or so from the centre of Newcastle. Next door to us on the Mill Dam in South Shields was the Lutheran German Seamen's Mission, and across the water in North Shields there was the Norwegian Seamen's Mission. In South Shields the Merchant Navy Welfare Board, a government-aided body, operated a beautifully furnished and equipped Merchant Navy Hotel. And up-river in Hebburn, Simpson's Hotel catered mainly for Asian seamen.

From the outset I visited ships of all nationalities and all types: merchant ships, naval vessels, international fishing vessels, and supply boats. Soon after arriving I met the Roman Catholic chaplain, Father David Head, on board a ship. He greeted me very cheerily and said that he was glad to meet me as he had heard about me from seafarers. Then he asked me how we could work together. I was stunned; to my shame, I had never even thought about this, and he took me by surprise. It was at the time when Pope John XXIII's great vision of the unity of the Church was beginning to make an impact on the Churches, though it had not really impinged on me. We agreed to meet and discuss collaboration, and it was he who began my ecumenical education. Not long after this I was visiting a German coaster when I came face to face with one of the German pastors. An awkward moment occurred when he asked me very courteously why I was visiting a German ship. I explained that it was my understanding that all the seafarers in port were our parishioners, but that did not seem to impress him. He was very friendly, though, so Sally and I invited him and his colleague to have dinner with us and discuss a mutually acceptable way of working. We came to an amicable agreement whereby German seafarers would always be welcome at The Flying Angel Club if they chose to come, but the chaplain of The Missions to Seamen would not normally visit German ships. Forty years on Pastor Heinz Neumann, the pastor in question, and I enjoy the best of friendships.

All the organisations serving seafarers on Tyneside were kept very busy, and we enjoyed friendly relations whenever we met. As I look back from a distance of forty years, I can see why the International Christian Maritime Association, which came into being in 1969 to promote and enable ecumenical collaboration, was able to make such a dramatic impact on the maritime scene; the seeds had already been sown.

### Family

Our house in South Shields was our first home of our own and we were very happy there; it was lovely to be on our own together as a family. Within a year of our arrival our daughter Helen was born. It had been agreed and arranged that the birth would take place at home, and in the middle of a cold March night the two midwives arrived. They were very pleasant, and highly efficient. They very firmly told me to go downstairs and leave them to it. I was to keep the fire going (in order to burn the afterbirth), to have plenty of hot water available, to make tea at regular intervals, and keep out of the way! At about 3 o'clock in the morning I heard the cries of a new-born baby, and soon one of the midwives called out that we had a fine healthy baby daughter weighing eight and a half pounds. In due course I was allowed into the bedroom to see mother and daughter, and it was a very joyful moment. We named her Helen Mary: Mary, which was Sally's second name, and Helen, a name we both loved. A few weeks previously I had been going upstream on the launch on a crisp bright frosty morning when I saw a beautiful silver ship just ahead of us. I was struck by her beauty as the sunlight shone on her. The ship's name was *Helen*. When I got home I told Sally what I had seen, and we agreed that if the baby was a girl we would call her Helen.

On the morning after her birth my domestic duties began with a vengeance. There was twenty-two months-old Andrew to look after and all the other jobs to do. The local Council had agreed that we could have a home help for two weeks, and Doris, who came, was wonderful. I enjoyed having some time away from work and being with the family, and it was lovely having Helen at home with us right from the time of her birth. Andrew was fascinated by her and he pottered about helping me very happily. The worst part of it all was my cooking!

### Leisure

I worked long hours at The Flying Angel Club, arriving at home at midnight two nights a week, and Sally and I treasured my day off each week. We made trips round Northumberland and Durham and fell in love with the rugged beauty of the hills and coastline. In the summer I played cricket for the Durham diocesan cricket team, and there was great jubilation when we won the *Church Times* cup in 1965. Most dioceses entered teams in this competition, and it was keenly contested. First of all we won our regional group, and then progressed to the quarter-finals and the knockout stage. Excitement mounted as we won our two matches and got into the Final, which was to be played at Southgate in London.

I drove the team to London in the Mission minibus on the day before the Final and we spent a very enjoyable evening there. The day of the Final dawned bright and sunny and we dismissed our opponents, Bath and Wells, reasonably cheaply. We knocked off the runs for the loss of four wickets, and we were ecstatic. One of my treasured memories of an unforgettable day is of seeing our captain, Frank Chase, stripped to the waist and with a bottle of sherry in his hand, declaring to all and sundry in the pavilion that he had been 'trying for this for twenty years, and if anyone begrudges me it, I hope they drop dead!' Nobody dared to disagree! After a splendid celebratory dinner I drove the team back to County Durham, eventually arriving home at 5:30 a.m. The last people to be dropped off were Frank Chase and his wife Hilda. As we approached the Vicarage, they discovered that neither of them had brought the house key. Marital harmony evaporated for a while! My day was made, though, when Frank had to go to his curate's house to ask for the spare key, and the curate came to the front door in his nightshirt and nightcap.

### Moving On

As the time approached for Richard Hughes to return from Brazil and resume his role as Senior Chaplain, Sally and I were invited to the Headquarters of The Missions to Seamen in London to discuss my next appointment. The first posting considered was Lourenço Marques in Mozambique, but it was eventually ruled out because of the unsuitability of the climate for anybody prone to asthma and/or eczema, both of which have afflicted Sally from time to time since early childhood. We were then asked to consider Hull, which had had a turbulent history for the past ten years. We went to have a look at the port, the city, the seafarers' centre and the house. It was an exciting challenge, and after we had discussed it fully, we agreed to accept.

I looked back over the two and a half years I had served in South Shields, and I could see that it was a great place for a new and inexperienced chaplain to begin his ministry amongst seafarers under the guidance of an experienced Senior Chaplain. I had learned a lot about ships and shipping generally; about shipbuilding and ship repairing; about how a port works; about seafaring and seafarers; about the physical dangers involved in life at sea and moving around dockyards; and about the great brotherhood of the sea, an intangible but very real bond linking all who go to sea and reflected in immediate action to assist any fellow seafarer in danger. I had learned a lot about ministry among seafarers, although I was also aware that I had only begun to scratch the surface of the complex and fascinating maritime world of which I was

*Durham Diocese, Winners of Church Times Cricket Cup, holding our captain aloft, 1965.*

becoming a part. I had made many friends from a wide variety of backgrounds, and I knew deep down that this was what God was calling me to do. I could not have been happier in what I was doing. I was now looking forward to being responsible for The Missions to Seafarers in Hull and to making my own decisions.

# CHAPTER FOUR

# Hull 1965-1971

## The Prospect

I WAS LOOKING FORWARD eagerly to our move to Hull. I was thirty-one, and had been ordained for six and a half years. This would be my first appointment in charge, and I felt that I was ready for it. The port was busy, with ninety ships a week coming and going. The Flying Angel Club, our seafarers' centre, was old, shabby and poorly equipped. However, there had been official notification that a compulsory purchase order for it might be served by the City Council, in which case a new centre would have to be planned and built. The Committee of Management of The Missions to Seamen had a reputation for being tough with its chaplains, but I had worked harmoniously with a strong committee in South Shields and I was cautiously confident that I would be able to cope; I certainly would not be looking for confrontation. There had been an unfortunate succession of problems with the chaplaincy staff over the previous ten years, and my predecessor had left in acrimonious circumstances. I was sufficiently experienced to have worked out the broad principles on which I would base my ministry, and I intended to start as I meant to go on; I particularly wanted to involve the staff in our daily prayers – ours was a Christian mission, and I wanted everybody to see it in that light. For the rest, I would take a long look at everything before making changes, and I would consult fully when making important policy decisions.

## Early Days

We moved into our new home during a spell of bitter wintry weather in November 1965 and were soon happily settled there. It was a pleasant, mature, semi-detached house in Anlaby, one of the western suburbs of the city; it had four bedrooms, an inefficient and expensive-to-run central heating system, a big garden, and, as we later found, wonderful neighbours. I was soon at work at the Flying Angel Club, where my first task was to get to know my colleagues and familiarise myself with the building.

On the first morning I arrived early, and had a thorough look round. I was not impressed or encouraged by what I saw. The building itself was an old Georgian house set back in an open courtyard. The front door was situated at the top of three steps and there was a glassed-in reception desk in the entrance hall. It was a dark, drab and unprepossessing place. The ground floor was the public area, and consisted of a nicely carpeted but poorly furnished television lounge; a large L-shaped room which served as a dining area, games hall and function room, and had a splendid parquet floor, pleasant wallpaper and attractive curtains; and a small chapel, which was approached by a dark corridor. This had been converted from a bathroom when the Committee of Management sold the main centre in Posterngate and had never quite lost the atmosphere of its previous usage. The administrative offices were inconveniently located on the first floor, which made supervision of the ground floor activities very difficult. On the second floor there were fourteen simply-furnished but adequate bedrooms. I had known what I was coming to, and close examination of the building confirmed my view that in the long term it was inadequate and unsuitable.

At ten o'clock that morning (the time appointed by my predecessor) I rang the chapel bell to announce morning prayers. Nobody came, and I said the service by myself. It was a bad moment, and as I knelt there I said to God: 'Lord, I know what I've got to do, but please show me where to start.' Afterwards I went into the kitchen, where the steward and his wife, Sid and Ada Lawtey, the bedroom cleaner, Annie Johnson, and my secretary, Doreen Smith, were having a coffee break. I sat down with them, and spoke with them of my hopes for our work. I also told them that as we were a Christian mission, I would like to start every day with prayers in the chapel with them. The service would last about ten minutes, and afterwards we would all have coffee together and talk about the day's programme. Everybody was happy with this and we arranged that Sid would cover reception duties while we were in chapel. We agreed also that we would start the service at 9:15, so as not to curtail prime ship-visiting time. The next morning everybody was in chapel and the pattern was set. I was thrilled and thankful that it had happened so swiftly and easily; it seemed very important to me to establish some priorities right at the outset.

As the days and weeks passed, a number of positive factors emerged. Our staff members were hard-working, pleasant and efficient, although Sid, who was seriously handicapped by a severe leg injury sustained at sea in the Second World War, could be curmudgeonly at times. My secretary, Doreen, was a gem; she had been secretary to one of the directors of a large shipping agency before leaving to have a family and had recently returned to part-time employment. She was extremely competent, interested in, and supportive of, what The Missions to Seamen stood for, and not afraid to express her opinion. Her husband, Len, was a highly qualified District Nurse and he became a key voluntary worker. I thanked God for them both; we became firm friends as well as colleagues.

The Committee of Management included influential people in the shipping, business and professional fields and who showed themselves to be very interested in what I set out to do. The chairman, 'Skidder' Watson, had a

*Hull, setting up Christmas Crib, 1965.*

reputation in The Missions to Seamen for being awkward and overbearing towards chaplains, but he and I established an excellent relationship after a small but significant contretemps at the outset. It happened like this. Late one afternoon I rang him up to ask him if he would reconsider a minor decision he had made before my arrival. He brusquely repeated what he had previously decided, and put the phone down. I was incensed, because he had not given me an opportunity to say why I thought we should think again; and I was sorely tempted to ring back straight away and have it out with him. Common sense prevailed, and I waited till the next morning, when I rang him early and asked if I could come and see him. He agreed at once and asked what it was about. I replied that I would rather wait to tell him face to face, and about an hour later I went to his office. I told him why I had come and why I would like him to reconsider his decision, giving full reasons. He recognised the validity of the argument immediately, and agreed that we should change the decision. Then he asked me what was really bothering me. I replied that it was his putting the phone down on me without listening to what I had to say that had incensed me, and that I could not work like that. He apologised at once and his gracious response set the tone for what became a wonderful friendship. He gave me strong support in committee meetings and the whole atmosphere was open and friendly.

A long-established feature of the programme of the Flying Angel Club was the twice-weekly dances. When I arrived there was a total of seven ladies who came to act as dance partners and hostesses to the seafarers. A major problem was that they were never all there together, and to have three or four hostesses and fifty or sixty men was never going make for a successful evening. After several weeks of driving up to fifty seafarers from their ships to the club, only to find that there were almost no hostesses there, I knew that I had to do something about it. When repeated requests to the hostesses failed to bring any new recruits, and requests to the churches met a similar fate, I went into action myself. I contacted the Matrons of the city's two main hospitals, and asked if I could call on them. The first visit was unforgettable. Matron Bruce belonged to the old school. She was Scottish, near to retirement and a martinet. She listened attentively, and then said very simply: 'Young man, I will support you. I'll ask six of my nurses to come to your centre next week. But there is one condition: a senior member of my staff will come to look after them!' I agreed willingly, and went off to call on the other Matron. By the time I got there they had obviously been on the phone to each other already. I was promised another six nurses and my cup of joy was full. On the following Monday twelve nurses duly came to our dance evening, and I had brought more than forty seafarers in the mini-bus. We had a wonderful lively evening, and both seafarers and hostesses thoroughly enjoyed themselves. After several more similar evenings I knew that that particular hurdle had been crossed, though I experienced a fairly rough passage for a while from some of our original hostesses, who were not keen on my having brought in the nurses.

As the weeks passed, more young and not-so-young women asked to become hostesses and were welcomed and absorbed into the fellowship. We had a simple but strict code of conduct designed to safeguard everybody, and the dances went from strength to strength. An important feature of them was the prayers at the end of the evening; these were deliberately kept brief, because of language problems, but I insisted that all the hostesses stayed for them – it was an integral part of our Christian witness. We ensured, too, that every hostess had transport home every dance evening. And there was also a delightful postscript to my visit to Matron Bruce: the senior member of staff who accompanied the nurses from the beginning joined the permanent staff of The Missions to Seamen as a Lady Warden six months later, and was posted to Walvis Bay in South West Africa.

Another problem at our dance evenings early on was that we did not serve any alcoholic drinks. During the course of the evening a number of the seamen would come up and ask where they could get a beer, and when I told them that there was a public house a few doors away along the street, they would slip out and not return until closing time, when they would come back to get a lift back to the ship. After a lot of thought I came to the conclusion that it would be right for us to serve beer at the Flying Angel Club: most seafarers were accustomed to having a drink when they went ashore to relax; we could ensure that nobody drank too much; and we would be driving them back to their ships at the end of the evening in any case. What settled the matter for me was the experience I had already had of seeing at first hand some of the unpleasant, unsavoury and dangerous situations involving seafarers which regularly occurred in some dockside bars. I felt that we could and should provide a better, safer service. I therefore proposed to the Committee of Management that we should apply for a licence to sell beer, and they agreed unanimously. The Archbishop of York, Donald Coggan, signified his cautious agreement, urging strict supervision and promising to visit the club to see how it was all working out if the licence were to be granted. The police supported our application and one of the magistrates argued strongly on our behalf. We were duly granted a Licensed Seamen's Canteen permit to serve beer. The impact was immediate; the seafarers stayed at the club for the whole evening and we had no trouble. I found, too, that in the relaxed atmosphere of an enjoyable evening seafarers often asked to speak to me privately about matters which concerned them.

At the very beginning of my ministry in Hull it was clear to me that if The Missions to Seamen in Hull was to fulfil its calling, our aim must be to visit every ship in port as soon as possible after its arrival. No more than about fifty seafarers a week were visiting the club when I arrived, and it was imperative that we took the message to the ships that we were there and very much in business. In the first full month I visited 168 ships, and throughout my time in Hull I visited around 100 ships a month. I was assisted on three mornings a week by a wonderful Lay Reader, Charles Shores, who was nearly eighty. He faithfully visited the coastal vessels in the Albert and William Wright docks, and proved to be a wise and sympathetic counsellor. I had his help for two and a half years before he became ill and eventually died, and I treasured his friendship and presence. The ship-visiting produced good results, the numbers of seafarers using the club increasing steadily, even though we had little to offer in the way of recreation and entertainment on non-dance evenings.

A very important early visit was to Bishopthorpe Palace, where I went to be licensed by The Archbishop of York for my ministry in Hull. There were a number of priests to be licensed, and after the formalities the Archbishop spoke at length to each of us. When he reached me, I mentioned to him in passing that the next day I would be visiting the lightships at the mouth of the Humber for a Christmas service and to deliver specially prepared hampers. He immediately expressed a wish to visit them himself, and asked me to try to arrange this for a day six months or so ahead. The following day, during the

*Hull, taking Christmas Fare to Lightship crews, 1965.*

course of the voyage, I raised the question of a possible visit by him with the officials of the Humber Conservancy Board. They agreed to the suggestion with enthusiasm and we fixed a mutually convenient date with the Archbishop. I was greatly encouraged by the Archbishop's interest and he was a tower of strength to us all at 'the Mission' – as indeed was the Bishop of Hull, Hubert Higgs, also.

Six weeks after my arrival in Hull, on Boxing Day 1965, a major marine disaster occurred in the North Sea. In mid-afternoon, in moderate weather conditions, the oil rig *Sea Gem* suddenly broke up and sank. A coastal cargo vessel, the *Baltrover*, was passing close to the rig at the time, and one of the stewards happened to look out of a porthole. As he looked, he saw two of the rig's ten legs suddenly buckle, and the whole structure begin to tilt and slide slowly down into the sea. He raised the alarm and the ship put about and went to the rescue. They picked up nineteen of the thirty-one crew on board and radioed that they were making for Hull. They asked that appropriate arrangements should be made for the reception of the survivors, who had gone into the water just as they were and had lost all their belongings. The ship's agents rang me to ask if I would stand by to meet the ship when it arrived two or three hours later and make all the necessary arrangements to accommodate the survivors. I had just returned from taking a party of seamen to Hull City's Football League match, and I had to re-focus my thinking quickly. There were many arrangements to make in a short time: beds had to be prepared, meals provided, clothes found for nineteen men who had lost everything and staff made available to deal with the rush of enquiries which would surely pour in. And it was December 26th, Boxing Day, which meant that most organisations were shut down and many people were on holiday! I knew that we could provide the beds, the meals and the staff at The Flying Angel Club, but clothes were a problem. I made a phone call to the Women's Royal Voluntary Service, and explained what had happened and what was being arranged. They turned to with a will and when the ship berthed at 10:00 p.m. they were there with a wonderful array of clothes for all the survivors.

As we went on board the ship, I was taken to two cabins where the bodies of two men who had not survived their ordeal had been laid out. Alone and silently, I committed their souls to our Heavenly Father, gave thanks for their lives, and prayed for the families they had left behind. I gave thanks, too, for the rescue of the others. Then it was time to work again among the living: to get them to The Flying Angel Club, arrange telephone calls for them to their homes, provide meals as necessary, and listen as they talked about what they had been through. Gradually everything settled down and about 3 a.m. I went home for a few hours sleep. I was back at the Flying Angel Club not long after 8 a.m., by which time transport had been laid on by British Petroleum, the rig's owners, to take the men to their homes. It had been a hectic evening and night, and our Flying Angel Club featured prominently on the television and radio news bulletins. We had played our part quietly and efficiently, and the resultant publicity enhanced the reputation of The Missions to Seamen in Hull.

New Year 1966 saw me looking forward with cautious optimism. The headquarters of The Missions to Seamen sent me a student assistant, Stephen Doe, who had a lovely outgoing personality, was prepared to work hard, and made a great contribution to the life of the Flying Angel Club in the six months he spent with us. Between us we visited most of the ships in the port and spent a lot of time on board with the seafarers. We steadily recruited more hostesses for the dance evenings, and their enthusiasm and reliability were most impressive. I saw them as being a vital and integral part of the Church's outreach to the seafarers who visited us. We laid great emphasis on Christian standards, and it was heartening to see how they responded and became a Christian fellowship. The Committee of Management took a keen interest in what was happening, and it was good to be able to report increased and increasing numbers of seafarers visiting the club and steady progress being made on a number of fronts. Six months after my arrival, the licence to serve beer in the club was granted; it met a social need and was not abused. There was a new atmosphere in the Flying Angel Club, a feeling that a fresh start had been made, great things could be achieved, Christian service was exciting and satisfying, and we were moving forward together.

Around Easter 1966 we received a letter from the City Council informing us that they intended to purchase compulsorily the Flying Angel Club as part of the scheme to redevelop that area of the city centre. I was absolutely delighted. It meant that we could plan and design a new seafarers' centre to cater for the needs of the seafarers of the future. A suitable site would have to be found, negotiations for appropriate compensation for the loss of our current building would have to be undertaken, and money would have to be raised to bridge the gap between the proceeds from the sale of our present building and the cost of a new and better one. The news gave added impetus to our work; we all now had something very special to look forward to.

Our Committee of Management reacted with enthusiasm and wise counsel to the news. They were people who, by their ability, determination and hard work, had reached positions of authority and influence in the city and beyond. 'Skidder' Watson, the Chairman, was an executive with Northern Dairies; Edward Good, the Honorary Secretary, was a partner in his family's shipping agency; Ted Bickersteth, the Honorary Treasurer, was an executive director of Reckitt and Colman, as also was Paddy Field; Stanley Craggs was a ship owner; Dick Cockin was a solicitor; Robin Fenton was a director of a shipping agency; Muriel Bird was a wealthy and generous lady who was also the Chairman of our very active Women's Auxiliary Group; Bob Fewlass was an executive with the Ellerman Wilson shipping company; Captain Alfred Newlove was a retired master mariner and an Elder Brother of Hull Trinity House; Judy Waites represented the Ladies Harbour Lights Guild, our hostesses; and Mrs Metcalf was the charming President of our Women's Auxiliary. They were unanimous in supporting the project. They formally requested our architect, Harold Hollingsworth, who had designed and was currently overseeing the building of our new Asian Seafarers' club, to work with themselves and me over the compulsory purchase negotiations, the selection of a suitable site, and the planning, design and building of a new centre. It proved to be a long road; it was two whole years before the foundation stone of the new building was laid.

The first major public event of 1966 was the opening of our new Indian and Pakistani Seafarers' centre, built on the same site as a previous one. For many years a number of large British shipping companies had employed crews from the Indian sub-continent, and in ports around the United Kingdom special provision was made for their needs. One of the main relaxations of these crews was watching films made in their own countries. The Government-supported Merchant Navy Welfare Board obtained regular supplies of these films (which often lasted between three and four hours) and circulated them to seafarers' centres around the coast. Whenever there were ships in port with Indian or Pakistani crews, the seafarers' centres would be packed night after night if a film was being shown, even if it was the same film on successive evenings. It was nothing unusual for there to be up to 150 seamen crammed into whatever premises were available to see the film. In Hull, where there were many ships with Indian crews (all seafarers from the sub-continent were recognised as Indian before partition in 1947), a very generous benefactor had donated a building near the docks specifically for the use of Indian seamen, and it was this building that was being replaced.

The building of this new centre was well underway before my arrival and a date in April 1966 had been set for its official opening by the Archbishop of York. It was a delightful single-storey building, with a well-equipped cinema, a large recreation room generously stocked with Asian games and musical instruments, a quiet room/library, and residential accommodation for the Warden, Bill Taylor, and his wife. Bill, an ex-soldier, had spent many years in India and loved his work amongst the seamen. He was held in high regard and affection by them. From the day it opened an average of 1000 seamen a month made use of its amenities. Most had very little money to spend (they sent the bulk of their wages home to support their extended families in India and Pakistan), and almost the only things they bought were aerograms and soft drinks. It was a very specialised ministry, one in which listening and practical caring were vital, and I thanked God for Bill and his wife. There were Bibles and Christian books available in the Quiet Room, but very few were taken. It was good to have the Archbishop with us for the opening, and he obviously enjoyed the occasion.

The next major event of 1966 was the Archbishop's promised visit to the lightships. He allocated a full 24 hours to the visit, and we had arranged for him to make an early morning visit to the Fish Quay, a tour of the main docks, a six-hour visit to the lightships out in the North Sea at the mouth of the Humber, a visit to our Flying Angel Club, and a further one to dedicate the house we had just purchased for our new Lay Reader, Robin Northen. It was a memorable visit. He arrived at our home at 9 p.m. to spend the night with us before beginning his visit to the Fish Quay at 6 o'clock the following morning. We were joined at the Fish Quay by his chaplain, The Revd. Michael Turnbull (later to become Bishop first of Rochester and later of Durham). The Archbishop took a keen interest in the lively fish market and then in the merchant shipping docks, which he toured with officials of the Docks Board. At 10 o'clock Mrs Coggan joined us and we went on board the *J. H. Haworth*, the buoy yacht of the Humber Conservancy Board, for the six-hour round trip to the Spurn and Bull lightships. At the Bull lightship the captain and crew proudly showed him the television set which had recently been presented to them by Muriel Bird, Chairman of our Women's Auxiliary, who also came with us on the trip. At the end of an enjoyable and fascinating voyage, during which the Archbishop's flat cap was blown overboard, we made our way to The Flying Angel Club, where he was able to see for himself the difficulties we experienced working in an unsuitable building. We told him about the compulsory purchase notice and about our plans for a new building. He promised to help in any way he could, and he was as good as his word when the time came. His final engagement of the day was to dedicate the house purchased for Robin Northen and have dinner with us. He left for home a little after 9:30 p.m. and I felt greatly privileged to have spent so long in the company of such a good and godly man. A charming letter of thanks from him two days later completed my satisfaction at the way everything had gone.

## Consolidation

Two years passed from the time when we received notice of the compulsory purchase of the Flying Angel Club till the moment when we laid the Foundation Stone of the new one. It was a busy time. Planning the new centre had to be combined with the continuing provision of a comprehensive service to seafarers in a large and busy port. I spent many hours searching for and examining potential sites, and many more negotiating with the British Transport Docks Board when we found one. I continually pressed officers of Hull City Council to hasten a decision about the amount of compensation we could expect to receive from their acquisition of our building. At the request of our architects I wrote a comprehensive brief for them, in which I set out what I thought were the requirements for the new Flying Angel Club.

Most of my time, though, was spent in the port, at The Flying Angel Club, and in places where shipping business was talked and transacted. I became increasingly knowledgeable about the port; about the cargoes handled; about the difficult industrial relations which prevailed at the time; about life at sea as it affected seafarers from a wide variety of backgrounds, nations and races; about the Church, and how it was perceived; and about people. I came to know the shipping agents, the dock officials, and the policemen at the dock entrances. I was soon on friendly terms with the chaplains of other organisations serving seafarers, such as Father Hardy of the Roman Catholic Apostleship of the Sea, and the Danish, Swedish, Finnish and German chaplains. I worked closely with the Seamen's Welfare Officers of The Sailors' Children's Society, Bill Throssell, Bill Marshall and 'Ginger' Cole. I was made very welcome at Trinity House and at Trinity House School. I came to know my fellow Anglican clergy in the area by attending Chapter meetings. I loved visiting the ships, from the tankers at Saltend at the seaward end of the port complex, the general cargo ships in the King George and Alexandra Docks, the coastal vessels in the Albert and William Wright Docks, to the ships under repair in Brigham and Cowan's Dry Docks.

In the Alexandra Dock we often had as many as six Russian timber ships at any one time, and they stayed in port unloading for up to three weeks because they had not been designed to handle packaged timber. Packaging timber involved binding together a large number of sections of wood of equal dimensions with thin steel bands, thus permitting large quantities to be handled quickly. Their crew members had a grim life: they had little money to spend; they had to go ashore in groups, never alone; they had to produce their official identity documents each time they went ashore; and the gangway was raised each evening to prevent anyone boarding or leaving. We visited them regularly and there was a predictable pattern to our visits. There was always an armed guard at the top of the gangway, who would ring a bell as we approached and not allow us to pass him until an officer had come to check us over. We often got a brusque reply when we introduced ourselves, and we were sometimes dismissed with phrases like: 'Russian seamen don't go to church.' But it was obvious that they loved playing football (they could often be seen playing on the jetties when work for the day was over) so I learned to say: 'I'm not inviting you to church; I've come to see whether you would like to play football against another ship's crew.' The atmosphere would lighten immediately, and negotiations would begin. Another team, a pitch, and transport would have to be arranged quickly, and sometimes we had difficulty co-ordinating all the details. So with the aid of Len Smith, my secretary's husband, we formed The Flying Angel football team to play matches against ship's teams, and I played in the team myself. We were a motley bunch, coming from a wide variety of backgrounds, but we were all committed to providing a service to seafarers. Soon we were playing fifty matches a year, and after a game we were often invited back on board for refreshments, Russian ships included. Sometimes far-reaching discussions took place at these parties, and it was an effective way of quietly witnessing to our faith. Sometimes the Russians would come to the Flying Angel Club for dance evenings, and they loved the relaxed atmosphere. They also loved having a tour around Yorkshire in the Mission's minibus. On one occasion I took a group of them to Whitby, where we enjoyed a picnic lunch provided by the Russians on the clifftop. On the way there we had passed close to the Fylingdales anti-missile Early Warning station and the political officer was fascinated by it. 'What are those?' he asked excitedly, looking at the huge concrete balls; and he was amused but sceptical when I told him they were giant mushrooms!

As the months passed the reputation of the Flying Angel Club and The Missions to Seamen grew on the waterfront and among the general public. People had noted how we had dealt with the *Sea Gem* disaster, so when a small German coaster, the *Elke*, collided with another vessel and sank in thick fog at the entrance to the Alexandra Dock, it was to the Flying Angel Club that the dock worker who had seen what happened telephoned. I was at the club when he rang, and he told me that at the exact moment of the collision a tug was passing close by the *Elke*. The *Elke* went down very quickly, but her crew were all able to step aboard the tug without even getting their feet wet. They had, however, lost all their belongings. I went to the dock immediately, arriving at the scene at the same time as the emergency services. When the initial formalities had been completed, I drove the seven members of the ship's company to The Flying Angel Club, where they spent the next few hours on the telephone, letting people know they were safe. Later that day the ship's agents drove them away to begin their journey home, and we were able to relax, content in the knowledge that in an emergency people had looked to the Church for help and we had not failed them.

One of the most interesting and rewarding aspects of regular ship-visiting is that you never know quite what to expect when you reach the top of a ship's gangway. When an Israeli ship registered in Haifa berthed in the King George Dock – the first Israeli ship I had ever seen – I went on board with eager curiosity. When I got to the galley, the cook, who was a Hungarian Jew, stunned me by asking if I could get him a complete Bible, Old and New Testaments, in Hungarian. It was then around 11 a.m. and I knew that the ship was due to sail the next day, so time was short. I said that I could not promise that I could get one in the time available, but I could promise that I would try. I went back to The Flying Angel Club and telephoned the British and Foreign Bible Society in London. The girl I spoke to told me that they did indeed have a full Bible in Hungarian, and it cost fourteen shillings. I explained that I needed it that same day, if possible, and why; and I waited to hear what she would say. After a brief pause she asked the times of trains from Kings Cross to Hull; if there was a convenient one she would take the Bible to the station and ask the Guard to deliver it to me on arrival. I checked the times of the trains, and we agreed on a mutually convenient one. At 6 o'clock that evening I met the train and collected the Bible from the Guard. I went straight to the ship and gave it to the cook – and you would have thought I had given him the Crown Jewels!.

There were significant numbers of deep sea ships which came to Hull regularly, and we got to know the people on board really well. Friendships developed between the seafarers and the hostesses, and in due course a number of marriages resulted. The officers and crew members of a Swiss-registered bulk carrier, the *Regina*, were very special; our Flying Angel football team played their team several times and the hostesses were always pleased to see them. On one particular dance evening most of the crew came to the Flying Angel Club just after the ship docked. They had had a terrible voyage across the Atlantic, with gales and mountainous seas; the ship had sustained damage and nobody had had much sleep. But they desperately wanted to come to the club and had rushed to get ready. Within half an hour, in the warm, cheerful, relaxed atmosphere, most of them were fast asleep! The *Regina* was not exceptional. There were regular ships from Italy, Jugoslavia, Brazil, Romania and Poland whose arrival was eagerly awaited, as well as British ships trading in the Far East, the Indian sub-continent, and West Africa. But all were treated alike and everybody was made welcome; it was a basic principle of our ministry.

The docks in Hull were situated some distance from the centre of the city, where the Flying Angel Club was located, so transport to and from the club was important. We made it a rule that every seafarer wanting transport back to his ship at the end of our evening programme would be taken either in the minibus or by one of the male voluntary helpers in his own car. The same practice applied to the hostesses if they needed transport. It made us late home on dance evenings, but it also gave rise to many interesting conversations, some of which could be followed up the next day whilst ship-visiting. The minibus was invaluable, travelling up to 400 miles a week sometimes in the service of seafarers.

Our daily morning service in the chapel came to mean more and more to me as the months passed. It was a time for thanksgiving, confession and forgiveness, intercession, reflection, encouragement and inspiration. It was a reminder that we are an integral part of the world-wide family of the Church. It was a reminder, too, that we should not neglect our responsibilities to share our experience with the wider Church and take our proper place in its life. So I attended the regular meetings of the clergy chapter, acted as secretary to the East Riding Stewardship Committee, and on Sundays regularly preached in the churches of the East Riding.

At one of the churches where I was preaching I was illustrating my sermon with an account of a particularly traumatic recent event. I related how I had been called to the hospital at 10 p.m. on a Saturday evening to talk to a young seafarer's wife whose six-month-old baby son was gravely ill with pneumonia and not expected to live. When I got to the hospital the mother was desperate to get her husband home. He was on a ship currently in port somewhere on the eastern seaboard of the United States; the trouble was that she was not sure which port. I went to my office at The Flying Angel Club, and traced the ship to New York. Then I rang the duty chaplain at the Seamen's Church Institute of New York and explained the situation to him. He promised to get a message immediately to the baby's father, who was the Radio Operator on the ship. By now it was almost midnight. I went back to the hospital and told the mother what I had done. I stood by the baby's cot, watching as he struggled to breathe. All I could do for him was to pray. As I drove home my heart was heavy. I thought of our children and what it would mean to us to lose one. In the morning I went into the hospital on my way to The Flying Angel Club, convinced that the baby would be dead. When I got to the ward the Sister greeted me with the news that he had turned the corner and was going to live. I was absolutely thrilled, and so was his father when he arrived home. His ship had been actually leaving the berth when the chaplain in New York used all his influence to have it stopped and the radio operator relieved. At the end of the service at which I told this story a lady came up to me and said: 'I don't think that I would have believed that story if it hadn't been my grandson you were talking about.'

Inevitably we had our bad moments at The Flying Angel Club. One evening when everything was quiet, a very drunk man claiming to be a seaman came to the reception desk. He asked for a room for the night, but as I had never seen him before, and also because he was very drunk, I asked him to show me his seamen's discharge book. He said that he hadn't got it with him, so I asked him what evidence he had that he was a seaman. He had nothing to offer and I had serious doubts as to whether he actually was a seafarer, so I told him that I would not book him in until he could convince me that he was genuine. It was the signal for a prolonged torrent of abuse and threats of violence. When nothing I could say would stem the tide of his wrath I warned him that if he persisted I would have no alternative but to call the police. Eventually I had to call them and he was still abusing the duty steward and me when the police arrived. He was so worked up that he failed to notice the officers on either side of him. They listened to him for a few moments before one of them tapped him on the shoulder and arrested him. 'But, officer,' he said, 'I was just talking to my friend here.' The policeman winked at me, and then said to him: 'Come on, mate, it'll be porridge and chips for breakfast in the morning!' I hated sending for the police, and I very seldom had to. When that happened it always seemed to me that we had failed.

### The New Flying Angel Club

For most of 1966 until early 1968 there was much to be done in the way of preparing to move from the existing Flying Angel Club to the new one. The immediate tasks included negotiating compensation for the compulsory purchase of our building, acquiring a suitable site for the new premises, writing a comprehensive brief for our architects and identifying sources of funding.

The negotiations for the purchase of our current building proved long and frustrating. We claimed 'equivalent reinstatement', which was the legal provision when Church property is compulsorily purchased, and we estimated the figure to be £58,000. But Hull City Council's Planning Committee refused for a long time to accept that basis and we reached an impasse in the negotiations. So our Committee of Management invited the whole City Planning Committee to visit our building and meet us. They came and were impressed by what they saw – and immediately agreed the basis of our claim. For more than a year I had made a weekly visit to the Council's Solicitor and/or the Valuation Officer to ask if there was any news about our claim. They were always very polite and courteous, but once the Council had agreed the basis of our claim the Valuation Officer said to me: 'Well done! You were a bloody nuisance! You did a good job.' I took that as a compliment!

Writing the brief for the architect was a challenge. I had never done anything like it before, and I thought long and hard. I analysed the trading patterns of the port, with particular reference to new trade which was opening up with the introduction of container ships and the growth of the European Economic Community. I listed the facilities I thought would be necessary. And I spelled out the way I envisaged the building working, and the design features I wanted to see incorporated. My vision was of a building where a seafarer would look around as he entered and see at a glance all the major amenities of the centre, including the chapel, through glass walls. The brief was discussed, amended and approved by our Committee of Management and the General Secretary of The Missions to Seamen in London. I then spent many fascinating and productive hours with our architects; there was time to plan thoroughly and we worked through every small detail.

Early in the process we were offered a site for the new Flying Angel Club by the British Transport Docks Board. After some persistent and impassioned persuasion they agreed to lease the land to us on very favourable terms, and we were able to begin to translate the architect's brief into reality. No praise could be too high for Harold Hollingsworth, who designed the building. The site itself was an awkward shape, and he considered and discarded a number of layouts until he finally came up with the design we adopted. It was bold and imaginative, but very practical.

When everything was costed out, we discovered that we would need at least £110,000, a huge sum in the late 1960's. The compensation which we had negotiated with the City Council for the sale of the old building was £58,400. The Missions to Seamen in Hull had £10,000 in a building fund. The Headquarters of The Missions to Seamen promised to produce £10,000 from all their sources of funding. The balance, of at least £33,000, we would have to raise locally. It appeared to be a huge undertaking, but I was convinced that our planning was good and that the new centre would meet the needs of seafarers in the foreseeable future. I was all for going ahead in faith, trusting that God would meet our needs, and after full discussions, the Committee of Management bravely approved the decision to proceed. Early in 1968 the architect obtained tenders for the building, and a local firm with a good reputation, George Houlton and Sons, was awarded the contract. Building

*Hull, launching appeal, Helen, The Bishop of Hull and The Lady Mayoress, 1968.*

began, and May 22nd 1968 was agreed for the laying of the Foundation Stone by the Archbishop of York.

Once the decision to proceed had been made, fund-raising began in earnest. The Lord Mayor and Lady Mayoress of Hull launched the appeal with a lunch in the Guildhall, which raised £1,500. On the following Sunday 140 people joined in a sponsored walk from Hull to Hornsea, 17 miles away, raising £500. These were big events, and well supported, but as I looked at the total of £2,000 raised, I realised the enormity of the task confronting us. We knew that we needed some very large donations, and it was time to make use of all the skills and talents God had given us. One of our committee members mentioned that Lord Rank had owned his first flour mill in Hull, and suggested that we should submit a request for help to his trust fund; so I prepared a careful presentation. I asked Peter Briggs, our Student Assistant, to go to the Reference Library and obtain the address to which I should send our submission. He came back with the address and was at the same time full of enthusiasm for a book called *The Directory of Grant Making Trusts* which he had seen there. I went to the library myself and soon realised that Peter's enthusiasm was justified. The book cost four pounds ten shillings and I actually asked our Treasurer's permission to spend that sum to buy it! It was the best thing I could have done. I picked out six small funds which I thought might help us, and received fifty pounds from each. Greatly encouraged, I prepared submissions to a number of larger trusts; in the three years of fundraising we received a total of £22,000 from trust funds. One of my treasured memories is of returning from a visit to the lightships in the North Sea on Christmas Eve, 1968, and being told by Doreen, my secretary, that we had received more than £10,000 that day from two trusts. By then the Appeal had been running for nine months, and although many small and medium-sized donations had come in, we were desperately in need of some big ones. I had been waking up at night, anxious about the fundraising and the whole project, and this huge boost to our funds was a major tonic. Deep down I knew then that although there was a long way still to go, we were going to succeed. One of the two trusts whose contribution came on Christmas Eve was the Rank Trust; the other was a local one, whose main trustee was a neighbour of ours. He stopped me outside our house one day and asked if we were still raising funds. 'Write to me,' he said, 'I may be able to help.' I wrote, but as the weeks passed with no reply I put it out of my mind. £5,200 from him on Christmas Eve was a wonderful Christmas present indeed.

While all this fund-raising was going on (and we had no professional fundraisers working with us), the day-to-day ministry to seafarers continued as normal. As work on the new building progressed, the hostesses became more and more enthusiastic about the project, and the seafarers contributed by buying bricks for the building. Our Committee of Management grew progressively more optimistic that we would raise the necessary funds and the voices of the handful of doubters grew less strident.

As the building neared completion, a succession of major events were planned to mark its opening. A huge Maritime Fair, in which almost all the parishes in the large Deanery of Hull participated, was arranged for June 21st 1969. Our Annual General Meeting was scheduled for July 3rd and the official opening and dedication of the chapel by the Archbishop of York for July 21st. Two weeks later, on August 4th, Her Majesty The Queen, His Royal Highness The Duke of Edinburgh and Her Royal Highness The Princess Anne were to visit the club for half an hour as part of a visit to the city prior to sailing from Hull to Norway in the Royal Yacht for a State Visit. An immense amount of hard work went into the preparations for all these events, and everybody connected with 'The Mission' went to work with enthusiasm.

When the time came to move into the new Flying Angel Club, we were all thrilled with our new surroundings. On June 16th 1969 the Hull *Daily Mail* published an article about it from which I quote:-

> Merchant Navy men will in future get four-star treatment at a Hedon Road building, where even the wardrobes have fitted carpets. The building is the new Flying Angel Club of The Missions to Seamen, whose flag fluttered from the flagpole outside for the first time today. It signified that the £100,000 plus premises were open for business...And for the Rev. William Down, Port Chaplain, it was a great step forward. 'It is the realisation of a dream' he said, as with jacket off he tested the long electrically operated curtains in the main hall.
>
> The layout of the building is designed to make a newcomer feel at home as soon as he steps into the entrance, and it achieves its purpose. 'We spent two years planning before a single brick was laid,' said Mr Down. Few of the doors have writing on them. Instead they have symbols – a television for the TV Room, and a telephone over a globe for the overseas telephone. 'This is for the benefit of the foreign seamen who do not understand English,' said Mr Down. In the bar which overlooks the games room built below ground level hangs a ship's bell. It was presented to the Mission by the Swiss ship *Regina*...Above the short flight of stairs leading from the two-tone carpeted entrance to the games room, the life-size wooden figure of the Good Shepherd looks down. It (came from) the Mission's old Posterngate* chapel, where it used to hang over the altar...'

A library, four bedrooms for seafarers, offices for the chaplain, his secretary and the manager, an attractive courtyard, and ample storage space completed the list of the club's amenities.

The Maritime Fair was a huge success, and the Annual General Meeting was a joyful occasion. At that meeting the Sheriff of Hull, Mr J. M. C. Otten, a Roman Catholic, paid glowing tribute to the new building, comparing it favourably with Anchor House, the fine Roman Catholic seafarers' centre at the other end of the city. And our Honorary Secretary, Edward Good, paid me a compliment which I have treasured: 'He always manages to make friends and to inspire people with the faith he has in his purpose,' he said. In his Honorary Treasurer's report Ted Bickersteth was able to say that we had raised more than 90% of the capital funding required for the new building, and he expressed optimism for the future.

The opening of the Flying Angel Club on July 21st was an unforgettable occasion. It was the first time that Archbishop Donald Coggan had seen the

---

*Posterngate.

completed building and he was greatly impressed by it, particularly the chapel. 'It is superb,' he said, 'strong, simple, and central.' It opened off the entrance foyer and was immediately visible through a glass wall. A plain metal cross was suspended over the altar, giving the unmistakable message that this was a Christian centre.

The Royal visit on August 4th was equally memorable. It was impossible to invite everybody who had helped with the project as we had to restrict ourselves to a hundred people. The Chairman, 'Skidder' Watson, conducted The Queen around the building, I accompanied The Duke of Edinburgh and Dr Coggan escorted Princess Anne. It was a happy, relaxed visit, in which the Royal visitors put us all at our ease. It took on a very special significance a few years later when Princess Anne agreed in 1983 to become President of The Missions to Seamen, a position she holds to this day. She has retained a very clear memory of her visit to Hull.

With the official opening and the Royal visit behind us, it was time to concentrate on establishing the new club on a sound basis. For a brief period around the time of the opening there was a marked decline in the number of ships using the port, and we became anxious about the prospects for the use of the club. But this proved to be a passing phase, and we were soon forging ahead. The seafarers loved the building and all its amenities, and within six months an average of 100 seafarers a day were visiting us. There were three full-size snooker tables and a darts alley in the Games Hall; a beautifully furnished TV lounge; a comfortable, well-stocked bar, without spirits; a pleasant library, with a good selection of books for seafarers to take or exchange; four superbly equipped bedrooms (two with full en-suite facilities), each named after generous benefactors; a magnificent hall with a sprung maple floor for dancing; and a chapel that seated 50 people in comfort. At the end of every dance evening a short service was held in the chapel, and it was usually full to capacity. The service was deliberately kept short because there were always seafarers present who had little or no English. There would be one or two verses from the Bible, a prayer for the homes and families of all who were there, the Lord's Prayer said in their native languages, and a blessing. Although the service was so brief, I always wore a cassock for it, to show how important I felt it to be. Often seafarers came to me afterwards to say how much they had appreciated the service; they had found its simplicity very meaningful. There was a table outside the chapel on which we placed Bibles in various languages for seafarers to take, and a steady number were taken.

Although the attendance figures greatly exceeded our expectations, care for the individual was never neglected. A year before we moved into the new club an Irish seaman came to stay at the Flying Angel Club. Paddy was 53 years old and had been at sea on deep sea ships for 35 years. Now he was going to serve

*Hull, Royal Visit, greeting The Queen, The Duke of Edinburgh and Princess Anne*
*with Archbishop of York and Chairman 'Skidder' Watson, 1969.*

on the lightships out in the North Sea at the mouth of the Humber. He
would be spending three weeks at a time on the lightship, where no alcohol
was permitted at any time, followed by a week's shore leave. He had no home
of his own and asked if he could live at the Flying Angel Club when he was
on leave. He was a likeable cheerful man and we were very happy to agree to
his request. Each time he returned from duty, however, with four weeks
wages in his pocket and nobody but himself to consider, he would virtually
disappear for three or four days, returning late at night much the worse for
drink. Then, with his money gone, he would spend the last few days of his
leave recovering. He was no trouble to us, but we were all very worried about
him because his health was obviously deteriorating. No matter what we said
or did, we just could not get him to cut down his drinking, and the outcome
seemed inevitable.

Things came to a head on the day of the opening of the new Flying Angel
Club. Just after the formal proceedings had ended and the Archbishop had
departed, I was standing in the entrance foyer talking to the Lord Mayor of
Hull, Mrs Maud Heath, as she too was preparing to leave. She was still
wearing her chain of office. Suddenly the front door opened, and in rolled
Paddy. As I looked at him, my heart sank. Paddy was drunk, very drunk. His

shirt collar was sticking out under one ear, he had lost a sleeve of his jacket, and he had obviously recently fallen into a ditch. He focused his gaze on the Lord Mayor and staggered towards her. He put his arm round her shoulder and told her how lovely she was. If there had been a trap door in the floor I would have happily dropped through it! The Lord Mayor took it in her stride and the crisis passed. But when he had sobered up, I took Paddy aside and gave him the dressing down of a lifetime. In simple direct forthright terms I told him that there would not be any repeat performances – not with the Queen's visit just two weeks away!

When he returned three weeks later I did not see him on the first evening, and I did not give this much thought. But next morning he was waiting for me when I arrived. 'Padre,' he said, 'I didn't have a drink last night, and I don't want to have one today. For God's sake find me some jobs to do to keep me occupied.' For seven long days I found a succession of jobs for him to do, and every night he went to bed exhausted. So did I! But he did not have that first fatal drink. Next time he came back the same thing happened. When he returned the third time he obviously found things easier, so in a quiet moment I asked him what had happened. 'It's a long story, Padre,' he said, and began at the beginning.

In 1945, he said, he had been at sea on the *Queen Elizabeth*, when she was sailing as a troop ship. When she docked at Southampton he had telephoned home to Liverpool, where his wife was expecting their third child. He learned that she had gone to the hospital for the birth, so he travelled to Liverpool and went straight to the hospital. There he found that his wife had died and so had the baby. He was left with two small daughters to bring up. Relatives and friends looked after them while he was away at sea, and each time he came home there would be a happy family reunion. But after a few days he would start thinking again about the family he might have had but had lost, and he began to drink to forget. As they grew up, his daughters wanted nothing more to do with their father – he was a complete mess. So he drifted from ship to ship, and from seamen's mission to seamen's mission, with no home of his own. 'Now,' he said, 'here among friends I have found a strength greater than my own. I've put my trust in Jesus Christ.'

During the rest of his life he never touched another drop of alcohol, because he dared not. But he rose to become Captain of his lightship. He paid cash for a small house, which he kept immaculate. He was reunited with his daughters and met his grandchildren. And to see him going off to his lightship, erect and smart in his uniform, was to see a new man. He was a living illustration of the truth of St Paul's words:-

> If anyone is in Christ, he is a new creation;
> the old has gone, the new has come.
> *(2 Corinthians 5[17], NIV)*

*Hull, 'Paddy' Kirwan, 1971.*

When he gave up drinking Paddy asked me to 'manage' his financial affairs. His wage packets were sent to me, and I set up a bank account in his name, with our Honorary Treasurer (who was also a bank manager locally) as co-signatory of his cheques. His needs were simple, and he soon accumulated a healthy bank balance. When I left Hull the bank manager, Bert Marsh, continued to look after him, and he was as thrilled as I was when Paddy was able to buy his own house. Friends at the Flying Angel Club helped him to furnish it, and he remained a firm favourite with everybody until his death. At his memorial service the chapel was packed.

The Flying Angel Club went from strength to strength. There was a wonderful group of hostesses, some sixty in all, ranging in age from 18 to 50, and the Flying Angel football team continued to play up to fifty games a year against ships' teams. Some of the voluntary helpers were prepared for Confirmation, as were a number of seamen. The highly unusual step was taken of issuing marriage registers to a non-parochial church, our chapel, and it was a great joy to conduct the wedding services of several of our hostesses to seamen there. Deanery Synod meetings were held in the Club. Seafarers and their families came to the chapel for their children to be baptised. In addition parties of visitors came from far and near to have a tour of the docks and see our work at first hand. Seafarers brought gifts from far-away places to decorate the club, and within eighteen months of opening, all the bills had been paid. We had raised more than £40,000 ourselves, without professional assistance, and among those who did so much to make the new club possible were the dedicated members of our Women's Auxiliary. These wonderful ladies, mostly of mature years, worked away behind the scenes raising funds for our work, and I have happy memories of a trip to Holland with them in the minibus. The Flying Angel Club won a Civic Trust award as one of the three best new buildings in the north of England, which was a richly deserved recognition of the work of our architect and builders. The Flying Angel Club in Hull was on the map!

## Family

We were very happy as a family in Hull. We liked our house, and we had wonderful neighbours. There were a number of young families in the houses near us, and the children and parents all got on well together. We were all in the early years of our professional lives and we enjoyed doing things together. In due course Andrew and Helen started school at the excellent local authority primary school, and in this way we met other parents. Our Vicar, Les Erving, was a strong character and much loved by everybody. He spoke his mind like the true Yorkshireman he was, and he was kindness itself to us. I helped him at the parish church as and when I could, and we became good friends. He called on us when we first arrived, and while he was with us he noticed that we had no TV set. In his bluff way he asked why we did not have one, and we were forced to admit that we just didn't have the money available. Nothing more was said, but a few days later he telephoned to say that a parishioner had died, the house was being cleared, there was a television about to be given away, and he had asked the family to give it to us! It was a kind thought on his part, and we were very grateful to him. Andrew and Helen went to the Sunday School at the church, and Sally worshipped there too.

Christmas 1966 was overshadowed by Sally having a miscarriage a few days before the festival. It happened while I was out at sea making the Christmas visit to the lightships with the Bishop of Hull. Doreen, my secretary, stepped into the breach magnificently: she sat with Sally until the doctor arrived, looked after Andrew and Helen, and got a message to me when Sally was taken to hospital. As we came off the buoy yacht at the end of the lightship visit, the Bishop said that he would call in on Sally on his way home. I went home to relieve Doreen and then went to the hospital as soon as I could. Sally was in a four-bed ward, and as I entered an elderly lady in one of the beds opposite her looked at me and exclaimed loudly: 'Oh God, not another one!' It transpired that I was the third clergyman within an hour who had visited Sally, and the old lady thought it was a bit excessive! She was acutely embarrassed when she discovered that I was Sally's husband, but good relations were soon established.

In September 1968 our daughter Julia was born. Andrew was then six years old and Helen four and a half. Arrangements had been made for the baby to be born at home and in the early hours of September 11th I telephoned the midwife to let her know that labour had started. She came at once and all the last-minute preparations got under way. Progress was slow and just before 7 o'clock Sister Taylor told me that she did not expect things to speed up until midday; she was therefore going home to prepare her elderly mother's breakfast. 'Ring me at once if there is any change,' she said. A quarter of an hour later Sally said that the baby was coming and that I should alert Sister Taylor. I rang at once and told her that Sally had said the baby was coming. 'Nonsense!' she replied, 'she's panicking,' and put the phone down. I went back to Sally and faithfully repeated the message. 'Get back on the phone,' she said, 'and ask her to tell you what to do if she's not coming herself.' By this stage I was really alarmed and rang again, explaining what was happening and asking what I should do. 'Put the flat of your hand on the baby's head, and don't let it come too fast,' she said. I went back to Sally to report, and then rang our nearest neighbour to tell her what was happening and ask if she would give Andrew and Helen their breakfast. She agreed at once, and as it was cold and raining I had to spend vital moments putting their coats on and seeing them along the pavement. I went back to Sally and was reassured by her calmness. Soon afterwards the baby's head emerged, and Sally told me to see whether the cord was round its neck. My inspection was inconclusive! At the next contraction the whole baby appeared, yelling lustily. I told Sally that it was a baby girl, and I moved her round in the bed so that Sally would not roll on her. Then I stood for a few seconds wondering what to do next. The bedroom door was suddenly flung open, and there was Sister Taylor. 'Get out of the way,' she snapped; 'you're letting that baby get cold.' 'I've done the work,' I replied, 'you can take the honour and glory!' We all laughed together, relieved that everything was all right and that the crisis was over. I watched her at work with sheer admiration. And I dined out on the story for years afterwards!

We had no shortage of wonderful doting baby-sitters. Some of the hostesses who lived nearby were very willing to come and look after the three children, and several of the mothers of hostesses would come too. Cynthia Heron, whose two daughters were hostesses, was marvellous with them; they loved her coming, and she loved them too. Thirty-five years on we are still in touch.*

Sally was a tower of strength to me and to the children. Her Christian faith is strong, simple and deep: she lives what she believes. She gave herself wholeheartedly to the children and to me. She was always there for us all, encouraging, leading, comforting and sometimes scolding. She applied her

---

*Cynthia died early in 2004.

considerable intellectual gifts to organising our family life, and made few complaints that with the children so young, her academic and teaching gifts were necessarily restricted to our family and the parish church. When Andrew and Helen started school, Anlaby Infants and Junior Schools gave them a sound start and both flourished. Julia showed at a very early age that when the occasion required it, she could hold her own with both of them.

Throughout our time in Hull we needed to keep a close watch on finance as clergy salaries were still very low. It became even harder to manage when the Appeal for funds for the new mission was running, because there were events at which I could not avoid expense. It all came right, however, when I asked the Chairman, 'Skidder' Watson, to attend a particular function because I was going to be elsewhere. It cost him £5, and he asked how I managed to pay such expenses. So I told him and he immediately arranged a discretionary fund for me. We never got into debt but we did struggle. We were glad of handed-down clothes for the children; all our holidays were spent with our families; and Sally worked wonders with small resources.

## Moving On

Once the new Flying Angel Club was open and obviously flourishing, we were faced with the need to make a decision: should we stay put in a place where we were very happy, or should we accept a fresh challenge? It was not an easy decision. I was coming up to thirty-six, we had children aged eight, six and two, and a fresh challenge with The Missions to Seamen was likely to be overseas. We wanted the children to be with us wherever we went, so education was a major consideration.

Early in 1969, six months before the opening of the new Flying Angel Club, I was asked to consider an appointment to Wellington in New Zealand. It would have meant leaving Hull before the new Club opened and leaving my successor with a building whose planning needed to be vindicated by use and experience, and with a significant amount of money still to raise. Sally and I both felt that we could not leave in such circumstances, so with some reluctance I refused the appointment. I was glad, though, that I could see the task in Hull completed. Sir Francis Drake's prayer has always been a source of encouragement, inspiration and strength to me, and I prayed it regularly at that time:-

> O Lord God, when thou givest to thy servants to endeavour any great matter, grant us also to know that it is not the beginning, but the continuing of the same unto the end, until it be thoroughly finished, which yieldeth the true glory; through him who for the finishing of thy work laid down his life, our Redeemer, Jesus Christ. Amen.

In 1970, with the Flying Angel Club up and running, and with the teething problems behind us, I knew deep within myself that I was ready for a new challenge. So when the General Secretary asked me to consider appointment to Fremantle in Western Australia, I was ready to give it serious attention. Sally and I thought long and hard about the impact on our children and our parents, and we decided to accept if all the details could be worked out satisfactorily. The appointment was that of Senior Chaplain of The Missions to Seamen in Fremantle and State Secretary for Western Australia, with overall responsibility for the stations in Albany, Bunbury, Geraldton and Port Hedland. Fremantle and Port Hedland operated under the joint auspices of The Missions to Seamen and The British Sailors' Society, so I had to be interviewed by the General Secretary of The British Sailors' Society before I could be appointed. The British Sailors' Society (or The British and International Sailors' Society as it is now styled) is an inter-denominational Christian organisation with a long and distinguished history, and its way of operating was very different from what I was used to. Direction from Headquarters, rather than a two-way partnership between Headquarters and the chaplain, was its way of working, and I hoped that there would be no conflicts of interest.

Slowly everything fell into place and I was duly appointed. Our furniture went into store, we said a very affectionate farewell to our many friends in Hull, and we left for a three-month stay with our families before flying to Australia. By then I had served with The Missions to Seamen for nearly eight years. I had begun to have a comprehensive knowledge of the shipping scene. I had grown in confidence, and I realised that under God's constant guidance I could trust my own judgement. I looked forward to Western Australia.

# CHAPTER FIVE

# A Welcome Opportunity:
# Port of London, Victoria Dock Road,
# April/May 1971

WE LEFT HULL in February 1971, expecting to go on to Australia two months later. In the event it was more than three months before we actually flew out.

It was both an exciting and an unnerving time for our family as we moved out of the comfortable home we had enjoyed for more than five years and prepared to travel 12,000 miles to a place where none of us had been before. We planned to spend the first month with Sally's parents at Great Shelford, near Cambridge, and the second with my parents at Teignmouth in South Devon. Andrew and Helen would attend local schools on a temporary basis. We would then return to Great Shelford prior to departure. The move proved particularly traumatic for Julia, then two and a half years old, as we discovered later. She had been taken out of the security of the familiar surroundings and cherished possessions of the only home she had known, and many of her toys, clothes and belongings had been packed for shipment to Australia. It was only when she had become thoroughly accustomed to being in Australia that we learned how much she was looking forward to being reunited with a certain pink rabbit, which, with her apparent agreement at the time, had been given away. It was a heart-rending moment.

I had been looking forward to this period of rest, relaxation, family life and re-orientation. I was feeling emotionally and spiritually drained after the intense activity, excitement and stresses of spearheading the building and establishing of a new and costly seafarers' centre for which I had been largely responsible, and I needed time to adjust. I also wanted to spend some time reading while we were staying near Cambridge.

For three weeks I spent the mornings in the Reading Room of my old college, St. John's. Early on I casually picked out a large book on alcoholism published by Alcoholics Anonymous. The rehabilitation of Paddy in Hull was fresh in my mind, and I read the 600 pages avidly. Some of the personal histories in this *Big Book* (as it was referred to in Alcoholics Anonymous circles) were very moving, and my understanding of alcoholism was broadened and deepened.

I learned that alcoholism is an illness, with physical causes and mental and spiritual concomitants; that it is a condition which cannot be cured once and for all, although alcoholics can be helped to come to terms with it and keep it in check; that complete and permanent renunciation of alcohol by the alcoholic is the long-term aim of treatment; that alcoholics should be treated with understanding, compassion, patience and firmness, as circumstances require; that the alcoholic has to have a real desire to overcome the problem if he/she is to be helped effectively; that the process of rehabilitation is long and includes the understanding and active support of others; and that relapses can and do occur. Unbounded compassion and perseverance are demanded of those who care for alcoholics.

As I rejoiced over Paddy's continuing success in his struggle with alcohol, I contrasted his outlook and progress with that of his friend and workmate Eric. Like Paddy, Eric was a pleasant man, a good seaman, and an alcoholic. I did my best to help him face up to his addiction, but he simply had no desire to abandon drinking. The most that we at 'The Mission' could do for him was to try to keep him out of trouble.

In the last few weeks before we flew to Australia, Prebendary Tom Kerfoot, General Secretary of The Missions to Seamen, asked me to help out in an emergency situation at the Victoria Dock Road seafarers' centre in the Port of London. I agreed willingly. I had heard and read a lot about this huge building with its 130 bedrooms and unusual history, and I welcomed the opportunity to see it for myself. L.A.G. Strong's book, *Flying Angel*, which was published in 1956 to mark the centenary of the founding of The Missions to Seamen, contained this illuminating and cautionary passage about the centre:-

> What happens here, [he wrote], is not characteristic of the work as a whole... Because of the conditions which the nature of the port imposes, The Mission in Victoria Dock Road has more in common with a transit camp whose residents are continually changing than most others; and this makes its work unique, and perhaps more difficult than that of any other station...In the heart of London's dockland it is difficult to find the hostesses and voluntary workers who, at most other stations...help to make the atmosphere welcoming and friendly.
>
> Because London is a terminal port, and most British seamen who can get to them have homes to go to, those to whom the institute has most to offer tend to be the homeless and the social misfits. Among these are a small proportion of men who are neurotic and who, because drink and misfortune have made them all but unemployable, can hardly be called seamen at all. Bums and scroungers are a traditional element in any dockland, and it is fatuous to pretend that they do not exist.

With this picture in my mind, I arrived in mid-morning to take up my duties. I was greeted at the door by Victor, the chief porter. 'Can I help you, sir?' he asked. I said who I was and why I was there, and asked to be taken to my room. 'Nobody has told me anything about you, sir,' he replied, making it apparent that he thought I was probably a conman. After some increasingly forceful explanations he grudgingly led me to the office, where thankfully it was made clear to him that I was expected and that I was most welcome. By now suddenly very affable, Victor then accompanied me to the room on the sixth floor I was to occupy for the next three weeks. I quickly unpacked my bag and returned to the entrance foyer.

As I emerged from the lift, I was given an immediate introduction to the life of the centre. Victor was engaged in a heated exchange with a man he was trying to escort from the building. Seeing my clerical collar, the man turned to me and said:

'Isn't that right, Padre?'

'Isn't what right?' I inquired.

'I've got no money,' he said, 'and the Church should give me some!'

'No,' I replied, 'of course it's not right.'

'Oh,' he shouted, 'you're another bastard like the rest of them!'

'Right,' I said. 'Outside! And I'm coming out with you.'

He watched me very closely as we went out.

'You go that way,' I said, pointing along the road.' I'm going this way,' and I went back in.

He went like a lamb, but I could see that my stay was going to prove eventful.

Most of the men using Victoria Dock Road were genuine sensible down-to-earth seamen, and it was a joy to serve as a chaplain among them. They were men of varying ages, many of whom had been around in the shipping world for a long time and who could tell much about the places where they had been. They had experienced physical danger at sea, long separations from home, family and friends, and the frustrations and limitations of shipboard social life. I discovered the values they considered to be important, particularly honesty and truthfulness with each other, qualities essential when living in close proximity and in restricted space for long periods of time. I heard much about the problems of seafaring and shipboard life. It was good to meet up with some of them again when I arrived in Australia, and it was always pleasing to note their surprise at our meeting again so soon.

At Victoria Dock Road a disproportionate amount of time was spent by the chaplaincy staff dealing with requests for a handout. After a few days I resolved to try to bring some sort of order to these constant requests. I discussed with the excellent Club Manager, Dion Leach, what I was suggesting we should do. We would offer help if they would offer work in return. We would put up a notice stating that we would be in the office to deal with personal and financial problems at 10 a.m., 2 p.m., and 6 p.m. every day. We would not deal with problems of this kind at any other time except in cases of dire emergency. Dion welcomed the suggestion and I asked him to prepare a list of jobs in the building needing attention. So late next evening we put up the notice and awaited the reaction.

By 9:45 next morning there was a long queue outside my office. At 10 o'clock Dion called the first man in. I asked him what his problem was and why he needed help. He explained that he had been expecting to join a ship that day, but that it had been delayed and he was not now to join it until the next day. He had no money left and nowhere to spend the night. I asked him if he was prepared to work around the building in exchange for his meals and a room for the night. He said that he was, and Dion allocated him his task. Conversations with the next two men followed similar lines, and they too were allocated jobs. There was a long pause after the third man had left. Nobody knocked on the door. Dion got up to call the next man but I asked him to wait a few moments. In due course he opened the door and found nobody there. The deal we were offering was obviously not palatable to some. But during the remainder of my stay the problem assumed manageable proportions.

With all the 130 bedrooms regularly in use, there were inevitably some difficult moments. One occurred on my first dance evening, when a small group of men appeared dressed in women's clothing and heavily made up. They sat down together at one of the tables and were obviously waiting to see what I as a newcomer would do about it. For half an hour I ignored them, pondering furiously what I should do. I did not want to rush in hastily, but eventually I came to the conclusion that they could not be allowed to stay like that. So I walked across to them, smiled and said politely; 'The game's over, gentlemen. Please go and dress properly. NOW!' As one they got up and left, and returned dressed normally a few minutes later.

It soon became clear to me that it would be easy to stay in the building all the time in order to be on hand to deal with the endless succession of queries and minor problems which occurred. It was also clear that my task as chaplain was to be on the ships, in the hospitals and in places where decisions affecting the lives of seafarers were being made, as well as in the centre. So I encouraged Dion Leach to exercise the authority of his position and not be afraid of making decisions, even if they were sometimes mistaken. He was a splendid person. He lived with his wife and young daughter in an apartment on the premises, and he welcomed the encouragement to assume a more prominent role. He had the priceless gift of being able to combine firmness with understanding and compassion. Some years later he was appointed Club Manager of the Port Hedland Seafarers' Centre in Western Australia, where he did a superb job.

With Dion firmly in charge at the centre, I was much freer to catch a glimpse of the vastness of the Port of London and the extent of the work of The Missions to Seamen there. I visited Athlone House (our centre in

Tilbury), our Chinese Seafarers' Centre close to Victoria Dock Road, and the Dreadnought Seamen's Hospital in Greenwich. I had long talks with Peter Kao, our Chinese chaplain, and Neville Overitt, an Anglo-Indian lay reader who specialised in ministry among seamen from the Indian sub-continent. I toured the docks and visited ships. I realised what a huge task confronted the Senior Chaplain of The Missions to Seamen in the Port of London, and what a challenge working out his priorities would present.

This brief interlude at Victoria Dock Road lasted just three weeks, and was fascinating, challenging and humbling. It taught me some valuable lessons and reinforced some growing convictions. It became apparent, in unfamiliar surroundings and among people I did not know, that I had matured. I no longer felt that I was inexperienced and ignorant of the ways of the shipping world. I was finding that I could speak on equal terms with senior ship's officers and shoreside staff. I had discovered that I could trust my own judgement in major matters where I had time to think seriously and prayerfully. I was learning more about how to witness effectively to my Christian faith. I had learned to balance the ability to think on my feet and respond quickly and sensibly to sudden and unexpected situations with the need to think carefully before acting in potentially explosive circumstances. And I saw that I must aim at combining firmness with compassion, justice with kindness, and caution with spontaneity. I still had a lot to learn.

# CHAPTER SIX

# Western Australia 1971-1974: Senior Chaplain, Fremantle

## Arrival in Australia

WHEN MAY 21ST 1971, the day arranged for our flight to Australia, finally dawned, we were ready to go. We were travelling under the Australian Government's Assisted Passage for Migrants scheme, and we had been asked to report and check in at the British Overseas Airways Corporation terminal at Victoria. About 170 people were due to travel on that flight, most of them parents with young children, and many family members and friends came along to see them all off. Sally's mother and father accompanied us, and it was a poignant moment when we said goodbye to them.

The flight was long, and at times tedious, but as only I had ever flown before, the novelty of it all kept us alert. The aircraft was a Boeing 707, and we had refuelling stops at Beirut, Delhi and Singapore. The clock advanced steadily as we flew eastwards, and our body clocks became progressively more disorientated. We ate meals at unusual times, and we did not sleep for very long at a time. Julia, a little over two and a half, was particularly unsettled: she was wide awake throughout the long night stages from London to Beirut and Delhi, and then went fast asleep on my lap as we approached Delhi; she woke as we touched down in Singapore! When we finally landed in Perth, twenty-four hours after leaving London and at around midnight local time, we were thoroughly exhausted but wide awake. Nearly two hours passed while we completed Immigration formalities and waited for our luggage to arrive, and then we were free to move out to the Arrivals Hall.

There the Chairman of the Committee of Management of the Fremantle Flying Angel Club, Hugh Rudderham, the Assistant Chaplain, Michael Dean, and one of the Assistant Bishops of Perth, Brian McDonald, were waiting to greet us. It was so good, and such a relief, to see them. They made us feel very welcome, and we deeply appreciated their being there in the middle of the night. Bishop McDonald informally welcomed us on behalf of the diocese and told me to ring him if we had any problems. Hugh and Michael accompanied us to our new home – 29 View Terrace, East Fremantle – and saw us safely installed. We had a quick tour of the house, a bungalow with four bedrooms, before falling into bed just before 4:00am. When the door bell rang at 12 noon we were all still fast asleep. The caller was Michael Dean, who had come to see if we had everything we needed. It was good to see him, and to ask him a host of practical questions about the house, the school, the shops and The Flying Angel Club.

During the first afternoon we took stock of our surroundings. Situated at the top of a hill, our house commanded superb views of Fremantle, Fremantle Harbour and the Swan River. It had been built in the 1930's for the first Chaplain of The Missions to Seamen in Fremantle, Wilfred Clift, and he had chosen the site himself. There were no other houses in the area at that time, and his choice of location could not have been bettered. By the time we arrived, streets and houses had been built all around ours; there was an infant and junior school two blocks away; there were shops within easy walking distance; and a bus service to Fremantle passed the bottom of our drive. The drive up to our house was fearsome: it was steep, narrow and uneven, with high concrete walls on each side. It was a source of great satisfaction to me that I never once scraped the paintwork of the car going in and out! It was a pleasant, comfortable house, typical of the 1930's style, and we were soon happily settled, a few minor but important problems, such as the almost complete absence of cutlery in the house, being speedily resolved. The Flying Angel Club was a mile away, and the centre of Fremantle a further mile beyond.

Three things particularly struck us on that first afternoon. One was the brightness and the clarity of the light: everything stood out in such sharp relief. Another was the toughness of the grass in our garden: we soon discovered that it had to be tough to survive the long dry scorching summers. The third was the friendliness of our neighbours. Jan and Arthur Ballingall and their daughters Janine and Debbie lived next door, and they made a point of coming over to visit us as soon as they saw us outside the house. Janine and Debbie were close in age to our Andrew and Helen. They attended the nearby Richmond School, where Andrew and Helen were due to start immediately, and they made sure from the outset that our children were not without friends. Our other neighbours were also helpful and kind.

**Early Impressions**
On our first full day in Fremantle I began my ministry at the Flying Angel Club. It was a magnificent building, completed four years previously. Situated no more than a hundred yards from the nearest berth in the Inner Harbour, and on the main road from Fremantle to Perth, its location was ideal. The facilities were superb. On the ground-floor, the entrance area of which was dominated by a copper fountain sprinkling water over copper outlines of every continent, constructed as a map of the world, there was a well-stocked shop, restaurant, dance floor, games room, the Reception Desk, the Senior Chaplain's and the Club Manager's offices, and a lovely simple chapel. On the first floor there were twelve bedrooms, a committee room, and two light, airy

and beautifully furnished bars, the Chain Locker Bar and the Chain Locker Club Bar (the latter a legal requirement). And on the lower ground floor, which opened on to a stairway leading down to the harbour, were the vast and well-stocked book room, the barber's shop, the toilets and the shower rooms. At the rear of the building was an open area where it was hoped one day to build a swimming pool. I was greatly impressed by the excellence of the whole set-up, and when I was asked later that morning at a meeting of the ladies of the Flying Angel Guild of Service how I liked Australia, I replied by saying that if I could not enjoy it, the fault would be mine.

On that first day I had my first taste of Australian hospitality. At lunchtime I made my way up to the Chain Locker Club Bar; as I walked in I was greeted cheerfully by an Australian Master Mariner, Tony Fletcher, who was also a shipping agent.

'G'day, Padre!' he said. 'Would you like a drink?'

'Oh,' I replied, 'that's a lovely idea.'

'What'll you have?' he asked.

'A glass of beer, please'.

'A glass?' he queried.

'Yes, please,' I said.

'Give the Padre a glass of beer,' he said to the barman.

Almost immediately a small glass holding a quarter of a pint of beer appeared.

'What's that?' I asked, taken aback by its diminutive size.

'That's a bloody glass,' he said. 'That's what you asked for. That's what you've got!'

Embarrassed by my ignorance, I drank it all in one long swallow. It was icy cold. My throat felt paralysed, and for a moment or two I felt frozen solid. Tony looked at me and grinned.

'Serve you bloody right!' he said.

I soon learned that in Western Australia there were three sizes of beer glasses: a glass, containing a quarter of a pint; a middy, holding a third of a pint; and a pot, holding half a pint. The measures were deliberately small, because in the heat the beer soon got warm and lost its fresh flavour. I learned, too, not to drink it too fast!

In the midst of all the excitement and uncertainty of settling into a new home in an unfamiliar land, and into a new challenge in my ministry, I thought about my most immediate priorities. These were to get to know my colleagues at the Flying Angel Club as quickly as possible; to make a comprehensive tour of the port in order to familiarise myself with its layout; to visit the ships, and to ensure that as far as possible every ship coming in to port was visited; to get to know the members of the shipping community; and to piece together in my mind's eye a picture of the whole scene. I also needed to arrange visits as soon as convenient to the other centres of The Missions to Seamen in Western Australia, in order to meet my colleagues and see where they operated. There was plenty to get on with.

It was soon apparent that the staff at the Flying Angel Club were hard-working, cheerful and committed to their work. At the time of our arrival approximately a thousand seafarers a week were using the Club. Twenty full-time and part-time staff were employed to cover the vast amount of work involved in the various departments, and there were more than a hundred dedicated voluntary helpers, without whom the Club just could not have coped with the sudden and unpredictable arrivals of large numbers of seafarers. The Club's finances were not strong, mainly because efforts had been concentrated on raising the funds needed to pay for the new building; however, the excellent Club Manager, a canny Scot named Jim Traill, was carefully and systematically establishing them on a sound basis. The Assistant Chaplain, Michael Dean, had been assigned to a fundraising and public relations venture, The Miss Endeavour Quest, which involved the voluntary activities of a number of very attractive and personable young ladies, and during my first six months his availability for ship-visiting was limited.

The responsibility for carrying out the ship-visiting was therefore plainly mine, and I undertook it with enthusiasm. The port of Fremantle has an Inner Harbour situated at the mouth of the Swan River, and an Outer Harbour in Cockburn Sound. The Inner Harbour has berths stretching for about a mile on both sides of the river; they were designed and built by a brilliant engineer, C.Y. O'Connor, early in the twentieth century, and with routine maintenance and some extensions, have been in use ever since. There is sufficient water alongside to accommodate large ocean-going passenger vessels and huge modern container ships. O'Connor died in tragic circum-stances. He designed and supervised the construction of a three hundred-mile-long pipeline to carry water from Perth to Kalgoorlie. When pumping started, it took a week for the water to reach Kalgoorlie. Fearing that his project had failed, O'Connor took his own life; the next day the water started gushing through. The Outer Harbour lay to the south in Cockburn Sound, and consisted of a number of separate terminals. There were iron ore, bauxite, oil and grain terminals. Ships carrying explosive materials berthed at a secluded jetty. The West Australian Meat Company had its own wharf. And a yard for building oil and natural gas rigs was also being planned. The furthest jetties were almost twenty miles from the Flying Angel Club and I always enjoyed the journey to them. In the first six months I visited more than seven hundred ships.

Getting to know the shipping community turned out to be relatively easy. On Fridays a smorgasbord lunch was held in the Chain Locker Club of the Flying Angel Club, and it had become a regular meeting place for ships' agents, shipping company executives, and officers. The Chain Locker Club had come into being because of the requirements of the licensing laws. Non-sea-going members of the shipping community had to pay a membership fee to use the premises, and so two bars had had to be installed. Seafarers could use both bars, but members were restricted to their own. Forty to fifty people usually arrived for lunch on Fridays, and they lingered over their meal. In such a relaxed atmosphere it was not difficult to get to know them, and to keep in touch with what was happening. Some of the officers from *H.M.A.S. Leeuwin*, the nearby shore establishment of The Royal Australian Navy with a complement of 1,000 personnel, were also regular visitors to the Chain Locker Club, and I soon got to know them too.

A few days after our arrival, the Chairman of The Committee of Management, Hugh Rudderham, suggested that I should ring the office of the State Premier, The Hon. John Tonkin, to ask for an appointment to call on him. I was very dubious about this; but Hugh insisted that it was the usual practice, so I duly telephoned his office. 'Sure! You'll be most welcome,' came the immediate reply. 'When would you like to come?'

I said that I was sure that the Premier's diary was very crowded, and that I would fit in with him.

'No', the secretary said, 'you tell us when you're free, and we'll work around that.'

A week later I arrived at the Premier's office, and exactly on time I was shown in.

'Good morning, sir,' I said.

'Don't call me sir, call me John!' he said.

And so began a very happy relationship. He was a man of great integrity, a retired schoolmaster approaching seventy. He had an easy manner with people and was blessed with a phenomenal memory. I came to have a great admiration for him, and when his party was defeated at the next election of the State Parliament he accepted the decision of the electorate with great dignity. For my part I learned that in a huge State with a small population (a million and a quarter people in a million square miles!) you soon became acquainted with the decision-makers. And I liked the way everybody used Christian names.

Also within a few days of our arrival I received a phone call from the Archbishop of Perth, Geoffrey Sambell. He told me that there was soon to be a meeting of all the Bishops of Western Australia, and invited me to coffee on one of the mornings of the meeting so that I could be introduced to them all. It was a kind and thoughtful gesture and one which I greatly appreciated. Geoffrey was a former Senior Chaplain in the Australian Army, a bachelor, and, as I discovered for myself, a very caring pastor. He did not suffer fools gladly, and was accustomed to call a spade a spade. When I arrived at the meeting he greeted me warmly. 'Welcome, Bill,' he said. 'I don't know much about you, but it's good to see you. Come and meet the Bishops.' I felt welcome, and it was a great way to start my work as State Secretary of The Missions to Seamen in Western Australia. In that capacity my task was to be the liaison officer between all the Society's stations in Western Australia and the representative of its headquarters.

My first port visit as State Secretary, three weeks after our arrival, was to Port Hedland, a thousand miles north of Perth and 21° south of the Equator. A year previously The Revd. Paul Gribble and his family had moved there from Queensland to establish a ministry to seafarers in this rapidly growing iron ore port, under the joint auspices of The Missions to Seamen and The British Sailors' Society and with the strong support of the Diocese of North West Australia. He had established a temporary centre in the old Rectory and was busy planning a permanent purpose-built facility. It was important for me to meet Paul and to see the set-up if I was to play my part in developing the ministry there, and I had been looking forward to the visit. Our aircraft took off from Perth airport for the two-hour direct flight at six o'clock in the morning, and I looked down at the landscape below with keen interest. Twenty minutes or so into the flight the Captain spoke to us over the public address system:-

'Good morning ladies, and gentlemen,' he said, 'Welcome aboard this MMA* flight to Port Hedland…Look down on either side. What do you see? M.M.B.A. – miles and miles of bugger all! Or miles and miles of bloody Australia!'

It set the tone for a marvellous day.

In our early weeks in Fremantle I visited some of the new container ships sailing between the United Kingdom and Australia. These vessels had a cruising speed in excess of twenty knots and made the journey from Fremantle to Tilbury in just over three weeks. I could picture the container terminal at Tilbury very clearly after my spell of duty in the port of London, and there were times when I felt suddenly very homesick as I thought of those ships arriving 'home'. The feeling usually passed quickly, but it was very real while it lasted. I was glad that I had told Andrew and Helen at breakfast on their first day at school that home for us all was now here, in Australia, where we were all together, and that they should try not to compare Australia with 'back home'.

In those early days everything around us was new and exciting. On days off we explored the National Parks: we were fascinated by the kangaroos, koalas, goannas and other animals; by the multitude of different species of birds, wildflowers, trees and shrubs; and by the landscape. We began to recognise

---

*MMA are the initials of The MacRobertson Miller Airlines, now Ansett of Australia.

landmarks. We took note that some words and phrases had different meanings and connotations in Australia, that the laws of the land were different from the United Kingdom, and that we were registered as electors, with a responsibility to vote at all elections, within days of our arrival. We found a widespread willingness among Australians to meet newcomers halfway if we were prepared to be open and friendly, and we certainly encountered no hostility just because we were 'Poms'. People welcomed us into their homes and we soon became part of the community. A significant moment for me came when I realised after three or four months that I was saying to migrants arriving on ships that 'in Australia we do this or that' instead of 'In Australia they do this or that'. I found, too, that I was beginning to speak like an Australian.

## Senior Chaplain in Fremantle

We arrived in Australia at a time when the Fremantle Port Authority was successfully coming to terms with many far-reaching changes in the merchant shipping world.

The introduction of containerisation in the late 1960's revolutionised the handling of dry cargo. The concept was breathtakingly simple. Dry or refrigerated cargo was stowed in standard size metal containers at inland terminals. The containers were then closed and sealed in the presence of Customs officers, and transported by road or rail to the port of departure. On arrival within the port complex, they would be stacked ready for loading on to specially designed container ships; refrigerated containers were plugged into electric power supply points. When the ship berthed at the container terminal, the containers were brought alongside on railway wagons or motorised transporters, and lifted into their allotted position on the ship by special cranes (portainers) which locked on automatically to the top corners of the containers. At the port of arrival the process was repeated in reverse. The whole operation was simple and efficient: from the outset one container crane operated by one man could handle between fifteen and thirty containers in an hour, and techniques improved all the time.

While the concept of containerisation was simple, its implementation was phenomenally expensive. New terminals inland and in port complexes had to be designed and constructed. New ships had to be built. Purpose-built road and rail transporters, and a vast quantity of containers, had to be constructed. Sea-going and shoreside personnel had to be trained. A significant number of ports were involved, and each had to be fully equipped. Shipping companies formed large consortia to finance the operation, and in 1969 a fleet of twelve fast new ships came into service to carry containers between Europe and Australia. Within three years a similar service between Europe and the Far East was introduced. Cargo handling methods had begun to change dramatically, comprehensively and irreversibly.

The advantages of containerisation to the shipowner were immense. Cargo could be moved much more rapidly. Pilferage was largely eradicated. Loading and unloading were dramatically accelerated. Ships spent much less time in port. The number of port workers required to handle a ship was greatly reduced. Fewer seafarers were needed to crew the ships. And fewer ships were required. When containerisation was introduced, it was estimated that one container ship of 28,000 deadweight tons carrying 1,400 standard size containers (20 feet long, 8 feet wide, 8 feet high) and with a crew of 30 would do the work of four and a half conventional cargo ships of 15,000 deadweight tons and each with a crew of up to 60. It proved to be an accurate estimate.

To many dockworkers, accustomed to traditional long-established ways of working, these changes were anathema. Enormous job losses were inevitable, and a fundamental review of the future role of dockers was forced on them. The new container terminal at Tilbury lay idle for two years while protracted negotiations over its operation dragged on. But the impetus for change was unstoppable. Containerisation had arrived.

Fremantle was among the early ports to have a container terminal, and by the time of our arrival it was firmly established. The teething problems had been sorted out, industrial relations were reasonably satisfactory, the ships were turning round swiftly and smoothly, and a revolutionary change had been effected.

Containerisation, though, was just one of a number of major developments taking place in the maritime world at that time. Bigger oil tankers were being built. Liquid Natural Gas Carriers were being designed. Roll on/Roll off cargo vessels were dramatically speeding up the handling of non-containerised dry cargo. Bigger bulk carriers were on the stocks. Experiments were being carried out with Lighter Aboard Ship vessels, which transported barges that could be floated off to facilitate cargo handling in shallow water ports. Sophisticated oil rig tenders were coming into service. New ships were becoming increasingly automated, thereby reducing the number of personnel required to crew them. Large, fast passenger jet aircraft were replacing passenger liners for inter-continental travel; the passenger liners were becoming cruise ships. Ships were spending less time in port, and seafarers had fewer opportunities for shore leave.

It is not to be thought for a moment that these changes came about overnight. For a number of years traditional shipping patterns existed alongside new ones, but it was apparent that the innovations were not going to be temporary. It was an exciting and challenging time to be a seafarers' chaplain, and it was clear that The Missions to Seamen would have to make bold and far-reaching changes in its ministry to the seafaring community if it was to continue to have a significant role. Chaplains undertaking the vital task of ship-visiting would need to take into account the increasingly rapid turnaround of ships and consequent inconvenient times of their arrivals and departures. They would need to keep abreast of the changed and continually changing patterns of shipboard life. And large seafarers' centres might become uneconomic and need to be replaced by smaller operations.

Our arrival in Fremantle coincided with a four-month season of visits to the port by ships of the Royal Navy. The long-established base at Singapore was about to be de-commissioned, and the ships which had been based there were making a round of farewell visits to the ports and regions they had served for so long. Frigates, destroyers, cruisers, Royal Fleet Auxiliary vessels and aircraft carriers all visited us. When the aircraft carrier *H.M.S. Eagle* called, she had more than three thousand personnel on board; she berthed a hundred yards away from The Flying Angel Club, and throughout her stay we were at full stretch coping with the influx of visitors. A feature of these naval visits was the generally exemplary behaviour of our visitors; the few incidents involving unruly behaviour were due to high spirits fuelled by alcohol. Another welcome feature was the substantial boost to the finances of the Flying Angel Club!

With so many naval vessels calling, my early months in Fremantle were hectic. Day after day the Flying Angel Club was busy from early morning till late at night, with the shop, bar, restaurant and residential accommodation all doing a roaring trade, and I felt that I had to be available there most days. I visited ships, spent time with individual seafarers, visited sick and injured seafarers in hospital, arranged outings for seafarers to the national parks and vineyards, all the while familiarising myself with life in Australia. I was acutely conscious of the need to devote time to the merchant ships as well as to the naval vessels, and I made sure they were not neglected. On board I met ships' agents, Customs officers, Port Health officials, Port Authority staff and Seamen's Union officials; there was genuine goodwill among us all, and it was good to see many of them again in the relaxed atmosphere of the Chain Locker Club.

During my early months in Fremantle I was visiting more than a hundred ships a month, and it soon became clear that our particular Flying Angel Club enjoyed a wonderful reputation among seafarers. It became clear also that I would need to be very disciplined myself if I was to be able to maintain a satisfactory balance between the many demands on my time as both Senior Chaplain in Fremantle and State Secretary for Western Australia. I became aware of changes in the pattern of my ministry to seafarers in Australia compared with what I had been doing in England. I was now spending more time on each ship I visited; I attributed this mainly to the fact that with Fremantle being the first and last port of call in Australia for ships crossing the Indian Ocean, the concerns of seafarers assumed a greater urgency. I was now working very closely on a daily basis with the whole shipping community; this was smaller and more cohesive than I had previously experienced, and I was discovering that I had my own particular role in it. I was finding that with greater experience I was now relating more deeply to seafarers at all levels. And I was being called on frequently to assist with problems arising on board the ships. There was a sixteen-year-old English Galley Boy on his first voyage on a container ship, who deliberately missed his ship in Fremantle; he could not get on with the Chief Cook, who was making his life a misery, and he had not dared tell anybody. The law required that he should be held in detention before being repatriated. Through the combined representation of the ship's agents, the shipping company and ourselves, the Department of Immigration was persuaded to allow him to stay at the Flying Angel Club (where he was thoroughly spoiled by our female staff!) until the next company ship could pick him up. There was an eighteen-year-old British seaman who was talking of committing suicide just before the ship sailed; the Captain rang to ask if I would go immediately to talk to the young man and see if I could find out what was troubling him. In the end we had to take him ashore to hospital, and I visited him regularly until he was able to return home. There was a young Russian seaman who spoke no English and who was hospitalised in Fremantle for surgery; his ship had to leave without him, and we looked after him at the Flying Angel Club until he could be repatriated. There were weddings, baptisms and confirmations to arrange at short notice, and, sadly, funerals; often I spent hours on a ship where a seafarer had died or been killed, just being with the crew members and praying with them. And there was a ship with a West Indian crew whose wages had not been paid for several months; a telephone call to the Seamen's Union representative soon dealt with that.

At the beginning of 1972, seven months after our arrival in Western Australia, a quiet spell on the waterfront afforded an opportunity to review the work of the Flying Angel Club in Fremantle. It was clear that the changes in cargo handling and ship operating which were taking place all over the world would have a significant long-term impact on our work. Seafarers would be in port for less time, and there would be fewer of them. Visits to naval vessels, which in the past had provided a welcome boost to our finances, would decrease in number dramatically. The bigger ships of the future would need new terminals and the deeper water of the Outer Harbour. The role of the Inner Harbour would change, with fewer large cargo ships being handled there. And there was also the very real problem that the Flying Angel Club and the Stella Maris Club of the Roman Catholic Apostleship of the Sea were only half a mile apart. In the mid 1960's, when the new Flying Angel Club was being planned, it had not been possible to bring together under one roof the work of The Missions to Seamen, the British Sailors' Society and the Apostleship of the Sea, and the result was that two really excellent seafarers' centres existed close to each other serving the same clientèle. It was apparent that serious thought would need to be given to this problem, and it was encouraging that the Roman Catholic chaplain, Father John O'Shea, was really keen for all three societies to work together in Port Hedland. It seemed clear that there would continue to be a long-term need for the Flying Angel Club, but also that financing its operation would become increasingly challenging. We would need to respond to change.

My ministry in Fremantle was very satisfying. Because there was an excellent Club Manager at the Flying Angel Club, Jim Traill, to whom I could entrust the daily running of the club with absolute confidence, I was able to spend a lot of time on the ships. I had time to listen to people on board, and I heard many personal stories. I knew that I was trusted in the shipping community, and good working relationships and many lasting friendships were established. Two incidents among many illustrate this.

At lunch one day in the Chain Locker Club I saw one of our shipping agents, Thom Dercksen, having lunch with two ships' officers. At the end of lunch Thom called me over and introduced me to his two guests. They were the Captain and Chief Engineer of a Russian Ship. We talked for a few minutes, and then the Captain surprised me by asking when I would visit his ship. The Cold War was at its height, and chaplains' attempts to visit Russian ships were usually met with a blunt refusal or outright hostility.

'How long will your ship be here?' I asked.

'Two days,' replied the Captain.

'I'll come tomorrow,' I said.

'What time tomorrow?'

'Tomorrow morning,' I said

'What time tomorrow morning?' he asked.

It was always difficult to be pinned down to a particular time when ship visiting, because it was impossible to predict situations which might arise and require immediate attention, but after a moment's thought I said that I would come on board at eleven o'clock.

'You come too,' the captain said to Thom.

Exactly at eleven o'clock next morning we arrived at the ship and were escorted to the Captain's cabin. The senior officers were all there, and a party had obviously been in progress for some time: there were bottles and glasses all over the main table. The Captain welcomed us, introduced us to the other officers, and invited us to help ourselves to a drink. I poured myself a glass of white wine, promising myself that it was going to last a long time. The Captain had a bottle of Gordon's Gin in front of him, from which he poured himself a very generous helping. After a few minutes a glass of Vodka appeared before each of us, and at the Captain's request we all stood to drink a toast to world peace. A few minutes later we drank a toast to the brotherhood of mankind. Other toasts followed. Half an hour or so later all the officers except the Captain were asleep. Looking round at them all he then said to me, 'Come up to the bridge'.

I got up to follow him, and so did Thom.

'You stay there,' he said to Thom.

On the bridge the Captain shut the door. Then he said:

'Father, I am a Christian. I want to make my confession.'

I was stunned. I heard his confession, and at the end he said:

'In my gin bottle I had water. I knew I could only make my confession safely if I got them all so drunk that they would not remember anything. Please forgive me.'

I never saw him again, but I was left pondering the evil nature of a regime which forced a good man to act as he had. And although I knew that Thom was curious to know what had happened on the bridge, it was many years before we spoke about it.

The second incident was equally moving, though in a different way.

Early one morning, as I was dealing with the mail, I received a telephone call from a shipping agent, Tony Fletcher. He told me that a British seaman was being held in the Detention Centre at Woodman Point just outside Fremantle and was to be deported later that day. He was very distressed, and it would be good if I could visit him as a matter of urgency. I went at once, and at the Detention Centre I met a young seaman aged about thirty. We sat down together, and his story poured out.

Several years previously he had left his wife and baby daughter at home in England when he went to join a ship. The ship's sailing date was delayed, so he returned home. He arrived to find his wife in bed with another man. The lover escaped, and in anger he struck his wife, who hit her head as she fell awkwardly, and died. He was convicted of manslaughter, and was jailed for a year. A few days before his release his two year-old daughter was killed in a road accident. After the statutory probationary period he returned to sea, and during the present voyage to Australia he had met a young lady to whom he was very attracted. The ship's captain, who was aware of his background, granted him shore leave while the ship was calling at a number of ports on the Australian coast so that he could develop the relationship, and when he returned to the ship he and the young lady were engaged to be married. They were planning to live in Australia, so he went to the Immigration authorities and told them his story. When the ship berthed in Albany he was arrested and detained by the Commonwealth Police as a prohibited visitor, and then ordered to be deported. Hence his presence in the Detention Centre as he waited for his flight back to the United Kingdom.

I was incensed by the apparent injustice of his treatment. He had paid the price of a moment's understandable anger and his rehabilitation had been thorough. His captain spoke highly of him and the ship's owners were prepared to support him. There was no time to lodge an appeal with the Immigration authorities before his deportation, but I promised that I would take up his case and keep in touch. After a long campaign, the ban on him was lifted, and he was free to return to Australia. Then, tragically, before his return, his fiancée was cruelly murdered. I shall never forget the depth of his grief and despair as he told me about it later, and my heart went out to him. Words seemed so inadequate.

★   ★   ★

More than a thousand seafarers visited the Flying Angel Club every week, and in addition to the excellent and varied amenities provided there – including the well-stocked shop, comfortable bar, canteen and restaurant, television, snooker and pool tables, table tennis, library, dance-floor, barbecue area and chapel – we also ran a comprehensive programme of social activities. Minibus tours around Perth, to the Yanchep National Park, and to the vineyards, proved very popular, and informal picnics on these trips often gave rise to serious discussions or conversations. Dance evenings were popular, and we had an excellent group of hostesses.

In a centre as busy and thriving as the Flying Angel Club it was inevitable that there were occasional unsavoury incidents. The worst was when an Asian seafarer picked a quarrel with the son of one of our staff members. He was asked to leave, and went. But he waited along the road, and when his adversary appeared he jumped on him and fatally stabbed him. I could not blame myself personally, since I had not been in the club at the time of the incident, but I felt responsible. Next morning I sat in my office, dejected and depressed. In mid-morning the captain of a container ship came into my office. 'I know what's happened,' he said, 'come over to the ship.' I thanked him, but declined: I felt that I could not face anybody. But he insisted, and was very persuasive, and eventually I roused myself and went with him. On board his ship the officers and crew members came up to his cabin to tell me how much the Flying Angel Club meant to them. It was very moving, and very humbling, to be on the receiving end of such kindness and understanding; they did more for me that day than I could ever do for them.

Weekends at the Flying Angel Club were always busy and lively. Early on a Saturday morning most of the eight hundred Junior Recruits at *H.M.A.S. Leeuwin*, the shoreside training establishment for sixteen year-olds signing on for service in the Royal Australian Navy, were given shore leave until ten o'clock on Sunday evening. These young lads spent a year at the training base. They arrived in intakes of two hundred four times a year, and at the weekends when they had shore leave they came to the Flying Angel Club in great numbers. Among the many facilities we offered was a sub-branch of the

*Fremantle, Julia presents bouquet to Princess Margaret, 1972.*

Commonwealth Savings Bank, which handled the banking of all Junior Recruits, whose wages were paid directly into their accounts. As we ran the only branch of the Bank open at the weekend, we transacted a huge amount of business; every Friday the Bank delivered a substantial cash sum to enable us to cope with demand. When they had withdrawn their spending money, many of the Junior Recruits spent much of the day, and much of their money, in the Club. They played table tennis, snooker and pool, ate huge meals in the restaurant, and consumed milkshakes in unbelievable quantities.

During our years in Fremantle there were many memorable moments and incidents. There was a most enjoyable visit to the Flying Angel Club by Princess Margaret, President of the British Sailors' Society, at which our four year-old daughter Julia was due to present a bouquet; she had last-minute qualms, and had to be firmly propelled into action! There was a visit by The Duke of Edinburgh to the Town Hall in Fremantle, at which he spotted my

Flying Angel lapel badge (he was a former President of The Missions to Seamen) and came across to talk, followed closely by the Mayor. After greeting me he said, with a wide grin, 'Do you need anything from the city for the Flying Angel Club? Ask now. He can't refuse!' There was a seaman on one of the Overseas Container Line ships, Bill Blaker, who, I discovered, had been taught at Infant School by my father's sister. He lived in Exeter, just twelve miles from my parents in Teignmouth, and during his leave periods he often went to visit them. He provided a lovely link with home.

There was the wedding of the Purser of the Blue Funnel passenger liner *Centaur*, Jack Higgins, on a Thursday evening during the 1972 Olympic Games. It was 12:30pm when Jack and his bride-to-be Joanne approached me to ask if they could be married that same day. I had to pull out all the stops. But by three o'clock all the special permissions had been granted and we were free to proceed. The wedding took place in the chapel of the Flying Angel Club, which was packed to the doors, and next morning the newspapers carried banner headlines calling for an Olympic Gold Medal for the Padre for the speed with which he had arranged the marriage! There was a visit by a Japanese whaling mother-ship on Easter Sunday morning. She had a crew of five hundred, and they had been at sea for many months. They were homeward bound, and they arrived at the Club in droves. In a few short hours they bought virtually everything in our well-stocked shop.

There was a very moving, informal Christmas Carol Service on board a South African ship. Officers and crew members stood side by side, with no trace of apartheid, and with our ten year-old daughter Helen accompanying the carols on her recorder. There was a Confirmation Service of a seafarer in the chapel arranged at twenty-four hours notice during Holy Week. I had telephoned the Archbishop to ask whether one of the Bishops might be available to conduct it. After a short pause he said: 'I'll come myself. The others will be with their families.' There were just four of us for the service, which the Archbishop conducted with great simplicity and dignity.

And there was the Friday when the Archbishop came to lunch in the Chain Locker Club. I had phoned him early in the week to invite him, and I had told him that there was no business to discuss, I did not want anything, and that it was just a friendly invitation. He loved the company of shipping people, and he accepted immediately. On the day he enjoyed his lunch, and afterwards sat in a corner of the bar relaxing. Suddenly he said:

'Tell me, Bill, why are there so many people here?'

'It's Poet's Day, Your Grace,' I said, without thinking.

'Poet's Day? Poet's Day? What's Poet's Day?' he asked.

I drew a deep breath, because I realised that either he was going to laugh or I was going to be out of a job. I replied:

'It means, Piss off early, tomorrow's Saturday.'

*Fremantle, Ecumenical Wedding Service, 1974.*

For a split second everything hung in the balance. Then he started to laugh, and he laughed till tears rolled down his cheek.

'Well,' he said, 'if you ask a bloody fool question, you get a bloody fool answer!'

And I survived!

# CHAPTER SEVEN

# Western Australia 1971-1974:
## State Secretary of
## The Missions to Seamen

THE MISSIONS TO SEAMEN established its work in Western Australia in 1920 in the port of Bunbury. In 1931 a seafarers' centre was opened in Fremantle, in 1938 another in Geraldton, and in 1965 a fourth in Albany. Each station had its own constitution, and chaplaincy activities were co-ordinated by the Senior Chaplain in Fremantle, who at the time of my appointment was usually given the extra title of State Secretary.

My appointment to Fremantle, as Senior Chaplain at the Flying Angel Club and State Secretary of The Missions to Seamen for Western Australia, had to be agreed by the Seafarers' Trust in London as well as by the Archbishop of Perth. The Seafarers' Trust was a new body, legally constituted in England. Its function was to own property and monitor operations in ports where The Missions to Seamen and The British Sailors' Society worked in partnership. It came into being in the 1960's primarily because of the situation in Fremantle, where both Societies had out-dated premises and had agreed to finance jointly and operate together a new seafarers' centre. Its jurisdiction now included the seafarers' centre at Par in Cornwall and the newly established centre at Port Hedland in Western Australia. The day-to-day management of the Fremantle centre, which was to be named the Flying Angel Club, was delegated to a locally constituted committee, and the Senior Chaplain/State Secretary was responsible for submitting a monthly report to both Societies in England.

In 1970 Father Paul Gribble, an Anglican priest from the diocese of Rockhampton in Queensland, was appointed by the Seafarers' Trust to pioneer and establish a ministry to seafarers in Port Hedland. It was an inspired appointment. Paul, his wife Val, and their three young sons were ideally suited to the challenge; there was a pioneer spirit in the whole family, and they had boundless energy and enthusiasm. Port Hedland, a thousand miles north of Perth and on the north-west coast, was expanding rapidly as a port with the establishment of a vast iron ore terminal in addition to its sea salt and general cargo wharves. It was also growing rapidly as a centre of population. Paul and his family moved into a State Housing Commission home and transformed the old Rectory into a temporary Seafarers' Centre, which was immediately very well used. A permanent purpose-built centre was obviously essential. In London I had been told that the Roman Catholic Apostleship of the Sea was very keen to be a partner in the project, and I had been asked to liaise about this with Paul and with Father John O'Shea, National Director of the Apostleship of the Sea and chaplain of the Stella Maris seafarers' centre in Fremantle. So a visit to Port Hedland was a top priority, and I flew up there just three weeks after our arrival.

It was an unforgettable visit. It was extremely hot and humid. A thick layer of red iron ore dust covered everything. When the wind blew, particles of iron ore dust adhered to your skin and your clothing. The huge stockpiles of iron ore were regularly damped down to reduce the amount of dust flying around. Clouds of iron ore dust rose from the holds of ships that were being loaded. Out of town there was a large sea salt plant. Here sea water was pumped into a number of vast man-made ponds, and allowed to evaporate in the intense heat of the sun. The thick layer of salt thus deposited was harvested by bulldozers, and then crushed and cleaned ready for shipping to various parts of the world. The port itself was still being developed, with the channel to the open sea being blasted and dredged to a depth of sixty-three feet to cope with the big bulk carriers. It was a tough place in which to live and work, but a vibrant progressive attitude was apparent everywhere and I was excited by it.

Paul Gribble and I got on well together from the outset. He was a straight-speaking, down-to-earth, energetic Anglo-Catholic priest, with a clear vision of his ministry. His day began very early with a long time of private prayer and devotion, and he was uncompromisingly sincere. People knew where they stood with him. He would tell me plainly if he disagreed with me, and I would do the same with him, without any fear of damaging our relationship. He had a lively sense of humour, and he dearly enjoyed a glass of Bundaberg rum from his native Queensland.

During that first visit he told me about iron ore mining in Western Australia. It was just ten years since the West Australian government had issued the first licences for the commercial exploitation of the truly enormous reserves of high grade iron ore in the North West. A three hundred-mile-long railway had been built to convey the iron ore from the open cast workings at Mount Newman to the sea at Port Hedland. Ten trains a day, each one and a quarter miles long, with three engines at the front and two at the back pulling and pushing some one hundred and eighty five trucks, each containing a hundred tons of iron ore, made the journey in each direction. To a newcomer it was mind-blowing.

Paul also told me that at Dampier, 120 miles South West of Port Hedland, another huge iron ore exporting operation was coming into service; and there was yet another at Port Walcott/Cape Lambert, between Port Hedland and

Dampier. There were plans to harness vast reserves of natural gas in the Indian Ocean off the North West coast. Multi-national companies were pouring enormous sums of money into these developments, with Japanese involvement considerable. In the sweltering heat, harsh living conditions, and the remoteness of North West Australia, industrial relations tended to be volatile and long strikes were not uncommon.

I returned from my visit to Port Hedland with much to think about. The need for a purpose-built seafarers' centre in Port Hedland was clearly urgent, and I had a long meeting with Father O'Shea to sort out practical details. We agreed to go to Port Hedland together to discuss everything with Paul and Val (Val acted as manageress of the seafarers' centre). The development of the ports and the necessary infrastructure was not as far advanced in Dampier and Port Walcott as in Port Hedland, but we would need to keep a close watch on both since there might well be a need to establish a ministry to seafarers there later.

The way leading to the building of the Port Hedland Seafarers' Centre proved to be rocky at times. Father O'Shea wanted his architect to design the building, but the British Sailors' Society did not like his plans. We experienced difficulties in raising funds from the Japanese companies involved in the development of Port Hedland. Paul and I became impatient with the delays, and eventually the Chairman of the British Sailors' Society, Hugh Brackett, made a visit to Port Hedland during a business trip to Australia. He arrived by air late in the evening and he, Paul and I stayed up all night discussing the project. At about three o'clock in the morning we all agreed that the project should go ahead. As dawn broke, we took Hugh on a tour of the port and the town, so that he could have a clear picture of what was being planned. When the Port Hedland Seafarers' Centre opened in September 1973, it was immediately a spectacular success; situated within easy walking distance of the iron ore berths, it provided all the necessary amenities for visiting seafarers. And Paul's attractive personality brought in a good crowd of willing voluntary helpers.

In December 1975, a year after we left Western Australia, the Port Hedland Seafarers' Centre lost its roof in a cyclone, which also demolished the brand new hospital. Cyclones pose a constant threat in tropical North West Australia, and there are a significant number of them in most years. In 1972 I happened to be in Port Hedland when one struck. Twelve inches of rain fell in twelve hours, mostly during the hours of darkness. The windspeed exceeded 100 miles per hour. An hour or so before the storm reached its peak, at 3 a.m., the electric power supply was switched off. Sleep was impossible because of the howling of the gale, the lashing of the rain, and the thunderous roar of the waves on the beach. There was a sudden complete calm as the eye of the storm passed over us. It was eerie, and lasted for twenty minutes. Then the storm renewed its battering with unabated ferocity. Gradually the wind dropped, and it was possible to doze. At daybreak the landscape was barely recognisable. Huge areas were flooded, some of the buildings were wrecked, and there was debris everywhere. It was announced on the radio that sixteen miles of the Mount Newman to Port Hedland railway track had been washed away, some businesses had been put out of action, and there had been damage to ships at sea. Yet by mid-afternoon the airport was open and aircraft were flying in and out!

An amusing incident occurred after that particular cyclone, although when it happened there was much local anxiety. At that time there were no road bridges over the main river beds in the remote North West. For most of the year the beds were dry and you simply drove across them. But when cyclones deposited vast quantities of rain in a short time and the rivers started to flow, it became impossible for vehicles to get across; you waited for the river to subside, and you could be marooned for days. The main road between Dampier and Port Hedland crossed a watercourse at Whim Creek, where there was a hotel/petrol station – and nothing else. When the cyclone struck, a number of vehicles were stranded there. It proved impossible to establish radio or telephone contact with the hotel for several days, and there was uncertainly and anxiety about who might or might not be there. But everything was cleared up when on the fourth or fifth morning a radio message requesting help was received in Port Hedland from the hotel.

'What help do you need?' asked the radio operator in Port Hedland.

'We've drunk the bloody pub dry,' came the response. 'Can you send a helicopter with some supplies?'

★   ★   ★

Seven hundred and fifty miles south south-west of Port Hedland, and two hundred and fifty miles north of Perth, lies the port of Geraldton. It exports grain, mineral sands and iron ore, and handles a small amount of general cargo. The population when we were in Australia was around 15,000, and about 150 ships a year called at the port. The Missions to Seamen commenced operations there in 1938, and its premises were a converted engine shed close to the port and just a few yards from the beach. Bob Shinn was the Lay Reader-in-Charge, and I paid a twenty-four hour visit to Geraldton to meet him and familiarise myself with the set-up a few weeks after our arrival.

Bob was a wonderful Christian, and a great character. He was in his early sixties, and had led an interesting and eventful life. He was born in England, and before the Second World War was chauffeur to a well known film star. He served in the Army during the war, and was posted to the Far East. He was captured by the Japanese and was a prisoner-of-war for three years. He was badly ill-treated by the Japanese, and was partially deaf as a result. By mistake he was reported 'Missing Presumed Dead.' On his return to England at the end of the War in 1945 he found that his wife had married again, believing him to be dead, and he emigrated to Australia. He worked at the rocket base at Woomera in South Australia, and eventually married again. He served a prison sentence for debts incurred by his family, and on his release the Rector of his parish, The Revd. Howell Witt, took him under his wing. When Howell was elected Bishop of North West Australia, he took Bob with him to run The Missions to Seamen in Geraldton. The seafarers' centre opened during the evenings and at weekends, and Bob combined a daytime job at the Public Works Department with living at the centre and running it.

Bob was a sturdy, friendly man, and on my first visit to Geraldton two Japanese seamen came into the centre. Bob got up to greet them and serve them in the shop. They played table tennis for a while and then watched television. When they left, Bob got up again and wished them well. I can picture him now with his arms around their shoulders and a happy smile on his face. It was not until much later that I learned of his ordeal in the prisoner-of-War camp, and I marvel still at the depth and completeness of his forgiveness and love. He did a very good job in Geraldton, and I was delighted when two years after our arrival he transferred to Fremantle to become our resident Lay Reader.

★   ★   ★

At Bunbury, a small port handling bauxite, mineral sands and general cargo, The Missions to Seamen operated from a superb modern centre built in 1967. The chaplain was The Revd. Ernest Scrivens, and he had gathered a fine group of voluntary helpers around him. He carried on his ministry faithfully and effectively. He was a keen gardener, and his beautiful garden was a joy to behold. His wife Lily had been seriously injured in a road accident soon after their arrival in Bunbury, and Ernest cared for her devotedly. As Bunbury was only a two-hour drive from Fremantle it was perfectly feasible to fit in a visit in half a day.

★   ★   ★

The port of Albany lies on the south coast of Western Australia, 250 miles south-east of Fremantle. About 150 ships a year used the port, the main export cargoes being grain and wool. In the 1970's there was also a flourishing whaling station, and I have vivid memories of watching a seventy-five feet long blue whale being cut up there with large sharks lurking nearby, attracted by the blood and offal. In 1965 The Missions to Seamen opened a seafarers' centre in the old post office, and a lovely old couple in their late seventies, Harold and Dora Kesper, were appointed to run it. Harold was a Lay Reader;

he had retired from his paid employment, and he took to the ministry to seafarers like a duck to water. He and Dora were gentle, kind, humble people. They were devoted to each other, and there was a moving serenity about them. They were genuinely pleased to be able to help, and they were the salt of the earth. It was a very sad day for The Missions when Dora died suddenly. Soon afterwards Harold's health failed and he too had to give up. He was succeeded by Tony Gadd, a young English-born electrician who was exploring a calling to the ordained ministry of the Church. The Albany seafarers' centre continued to flourish under his leadership.

The monitoring of these four stations, and the need to investigate the possibility of establishing new centres of The Missions to Seamen in Dampier and Port Walcott, involved me in extensive travelling around the State, and I had meetings with people from many different walks of life as I pieced together a picture. There were also other ports handling small but significant numbers of ships, such as Esperance, Cape Cuvier and Broome, which could not be ignored. Our Archbishop, Geoffrey Sambell, was keenly interested in, and supportive of, the ministry among seafarers, and he set up a commission to examine the scope and financing of this work and to make recommendations for the future. He appointed as Chairman the Bishop of Kalgoorlie, The Right Reverend Denis Bryant.

Denis was a distinguished bomber pilot in the Royal Air Force during the Second World War, and had emigrated to Australia in 1961 after ordination in 1958 and two curacies in the diocese of Guildford. His first appointment in Western Australia was as Rector of Esperance, and having served as Archdeacon of the Goldfields and then as Bishop of Kalgoorlie, he was well qualified to chair the commission. He was a lively, friendly, approachable man – a man's man, with an infectious sense of humour. He had had a dramatic conversion experience, and his simple but profound faith was an inspiration. When it became clear that he and I needed to make a visit to the North West to take a good look at Dampier and Port Walcott, a member of the commission, Dr. Jim Goldacre, a partner in the Fremantle Port Medical practice and a volunteer with the Royal Flying Doctor Service, offered to fly us there in his single-engined aircraft. We accepted his generous offer gratefully, and arranged to fly north on New Year's Day 1973.

We planned to fly to Geraldton in the morning, re-fuel the aircraft there, and make a visit to the new Reader-in-Charge of The Missions to Seamen, Frank Weber, and his wife Clare. In the afternoon we would fly on to Carnarvon, a further three hundred miles north, and spend the night at the Rectory. Next day we would fly to Karratha, a new town, and drive to Dampier. The first part of the journey worked out perfectly, and we duly headed north from Geraldton after lunch. Two hundred miles north of Geraldton, and a hundred miles south of Carnarvon, the single engine of the aircraft began to misfire badly. Immediate checks revealed that we had plenty of fuel and that there was no remedial action we could take. We put out a Mayday call. We were at a height of six thousand feet, following the coast road, and we were over an area of wild country. Below us in the bright sunlight we could see one solitary homestead. The map told us that it was the Yarringa homestead, and when we put out our Mayday call, the Department of Civil Aviation came on the air asking for details of our problems. The engine was still misbehaving, and we were losing height. We reported our position, and the D.C.A. advised us that there was some sort of track near the homestead, and that we should try to land on it. 'Just give us a call when you're safely down,' came the final message. 'Good luck!'

Denis and Jim were sitting in the front of the aircraft, busy with the controls. I was sitting behind them, fascinated but terrified. I knew that in a few moments we could all be dead, and I said a prayer: 'Lord, please get us out of this safely.' Then I sat on the edge of my seat, keeping quiet: I realised that both God and our pilots had enough on their minds without me saying anything! We headed for the track by the homestead. It was very bumpy and uneven, but there was no alternative. We landed with a mighty bump and a great leap forward, but we stayed the right way up and eventually came to a stop. For perhaps thirty seconds we just sat in our seats, stunned by the suddenness of it all, and thankful to be alive. Then we saw a car driving towards us from the homestead, half a mile or so away. As it got nearer we could see that there were two very attractive young women in it. Denis rubbed his eyes. 'I don't know if I'm dead and in Heaven,' he said, 'but if I am, I like it!'

We got out of the aircraft and introduced ourselves. The ladies told us that they had just returned with their husbands from a New Year's party with their neighbours, ninety miles away, when the Department of Civil Aviation had contacted them, telling them to expect visitors! An examination of the engine of the aircraft revealed that an exhaust valve had sheared off and that no further flight would be possible till a replacement valve was brought up from Perth. We were well and truly stranded. 'Never mind,' said one of the ladies, 'Come back to the house; we'll have another party!' During the impromptu party Denis and I, mightily relieved to have survived, made good use of the generous hospitality. Jim sat quietly in a corner, keeping his own counsel. Next morning he said to me, very quietly. 'I think we'd better find a church, to say thank you. There's obviously someone up there who shuffles the scenery for you fellows.'

We visited Dampier and Port Walcott at a later date, and in due course seafarers' centres were established in both ports, as will be seen in a later chapter. Our commission duly reported to the Archbishop and Bishops, and I felt that we were now more visibly an integral part of the Anglican Church of

Western Australia. And there was a lovely sequel to our flying escapade. The following Christmas I received a card from the people at the Yarringa homestead: 'Do drop in again!' was the message.

# CHAPTER EIGHT

# Western Australia 1971-1974: Ministry in the Anglican Church of Australia

## Royal Australian Naval Reserve Chaplain

WITHIN A YEAR of arriving in Australia I was appointed as a chaplain in The Royal Australian Naval Reserve, to serve at *H.M.A.S. Leeuwin* in Fremantle, and it became a part of my ministry which I both enjoyed and found deeply satisfying. It was demanding and challenging. In addition to regular 'Padre's Hours', the chaplains ran four Character Guidance courses a year, one for each intake of Junior Recruits as they neared the end of their year's training. Two full days were allocated to each of these courses, the aim of which was to encourage the young men to work out and develop a sound and realistic philosophy of life. The Navy laid down a rough framework for the courses based on the content of the Ten Commandments. We showed high quality films covering a variety of themes, such as the wonders of creation, human reproduction, *Singapore Story* (a moving film portraying the treatment Bishop Leonard Wilson of Singapore received in a Japanese Prisoner-of-War camp during the Second World War), and the treatment of Prisoners-of-War in the Korean War. The Chaplains introduced the films, initiated discussions, answered questions, delivered lectures and were available for one-to-one interviews.

It usually fell to me to give the sex morality lecture, and it was a real challenge to maintain a disciplined atmosphere and get the message across to a group of up to ninety 17 year olds. My first lecture did not go well, and I sat down to try to work out a more effective method of presentation. I decided to start the session with the film on human reproduction, and go on to tell them how I had delivered our daughter Julia in emergency conditions. I would then spell out the Biblical teaching about sex and marriage, and follow this with some practical teaching about contraception, as required by the Navy. It proved to be a good formula, and the sessions were always lively, and the questions not always predictable. On one occasion a Junior Recruit stopped me as I was talking about contraception:

'Sir,' he said, 'you said sexual intercourse is for within marriage, right?'

'Yes,' I replied, 'I told you that that is Christian teaching.'

*Fremantle, Chaplain Royal Australian Naval Reserve, 1974.*

'Well, sir,' he went on, 'why is it then that they issue us with contraceptives every weekend?'

There was an expectant hush as they waited for my reply.

'No,' I said, 'that isn't quite right. The situation is that if you want a contraceptive you go to the Sick Bay and ask for one. That isn't the same thing as being issued with it.'

'It's all the same to me, sir,' he said. 'Why do they do it?'

By this time I had had time to think:

'There are two reasons,' I said. 'The first is to protect you from contracting a venereal disease. The second is to protect the general public from young so-and-so's like you!'

It brought the house down, with the youngster who had asked the question being the first to laugh. But the point had been made, and it showed me that it was perfectly possible to combine serious teaching and frank uncomplicated replies to questions with an element of humour.

Being a chaplain in the Naval Reserve was a great asset in dealing with the hundreds of Junior Recruits who descended on the Flying Angel Club every weekend. They became accustomed to seeing me in uniform on the base and in civilian clothes at the club; in the relaxed atmosphere of the club I often had long conversations with some of them. Years later, when I was visiting Australia regularly as General Secretary of The Missions to Seamen, young men would come up to me in airport lounges and ask whether I remembered them from their time at *H.M.A.S. Leeuwin*. Occasionally one would talk about how he had valued his Character Guidance Course, and that gave me great satisfaction.

When I was appointed as a chaplain I was told that I should attend a Basic Training Course, and so it was that in a very hot January I reported to *H.M.A.S. Cerberus*, thirty miles outside Melbourne, for the fourteen-day course. There were 36 of us: 24 young doctors starting their National Service, 4 dentists, 4 schoolmaster instructors, and 4 Reservists from various walks of life. I was the sole chaplain. In intense heat we were drilled on the Parade Ground, put through a swimming test, given fire-fighting training and a simulated sea rescue by helicopter, and other basic training. The day came when all of us were assigned to particular departments for specialist training, and I was surprised to learn that it had been decreed that I should be taught sword drill. It was in vain that I protested that no chaplain ever carried a sword under any circumstances, so I duly proceeded to the Parade Ground, accompanied by my Chief Petty Officer instructor. Just before we commenced the session the C.P.O. said very quietly; 'Sir, I know that chaplains never carry swords. But we've got to show willing. After a few minutes, sir, please order me to dismiss you. I shan't want to see you for the rest of the morning!' Fifteen minutes later I was back in the comfort of my cabin.

I really enjoyed the course. It was everything I had hoped it would be, and it made me realise that I would have enjoyed life in The Royal Navy if I had not suffered from tuberculosis twenty years previously.

## The Anglican Church of Western Australia
I look back gratefully for the warm, no-nonsense welcome I received from the Anglican Church in Western Australia when we arrived. Bishop McDonald welcomed us at the airport in the middle of the night, the Archbishop telephoned within a few days to greet us and to invite me to meet the Bishops of the Province at their next regular meeting, and Archdeacon Ralph Thomas, Rector of the parish church of Fremantle, came to meet me at the Flying Angel Club very early on. I could not have been made to feel more welcome, yet all without any fuss; it seemed to be a case of 'We're glad you are here. Get on with your job. Shout if you need any help.' Throughout our years in Western Australia, and in subsequent later visits as General Secretary, I was made to feel a valued partner, despite being a Pom! The Bishops became friends to whom it was acceptable to speak frankly and freely; the parish clergy were welcoming, and grateful for any help we could

give; and the staff in the Diocesan Office were helpful and considerate. We were all on Christian name terms, but this in no way undermined our respect for our leaders.

Our Bishops were strong characters, with very diverse gifts and personalities. Archbishop Geoffrey Sambell, a bachelor, never shrank from frank and forthright comment when he felt it was necessary. He had the priceless gift of being able to go directly to the heart of a problem and then deal with it firmly. He was thoughtful, kind, generous and considerate, but uncompromising in his attitude towards slackness and what he perceived as low standards. He was painfully shy with women, yet he was a wonderful host at the lunch he gave for the clergy wives during Synod – even if he did quietly slip away to the kitchen when everything was proceeding smoothly! Brian McDonald, one of the two Assistant Bishops, was a perfect foil to the Archbishop. Quietly spoken, down-to-earth, shrewd and kind, he unobtrusively provided strong support and sound commonsense; clergy turned to him naturally for advice. The other Assistant Bishop, Alfred Holland, was a gentle, deeply spiritual man. He always had time for people, and tragedy in his own life, when a much loved son was killed in a road accident, only seemed to deepen further his empathy with people.

In the diocese of Bunbury Bishop Ralph Hawkins was renowned for his ability to raise enormous sums of money for diocesan projects. If in the course of a conversation he suddenly addressed me as 'Father' instead of the usual 'Bill,' I knew that fund-raising was next on the agenda! In the diocese of Kalgoorlie Bishop Denis Bryant struggled heroically with chronic financial difficulties. And in the diocese of the North West Bishop Howell Witt was one of the great characters of the Church. Blessed with an irreverent and irrepressible sense of humour, which transformed meetings at which he was present, he was greatly loved in his vast diocese of 670,000 square miles, with a population of fewer than 70,000 people. Fifteen priests served this enormous area, and as I got to know a few of them I was impressed by their dedication; the Church was a vital part of life in the outback.

In the diocese of Perth, where I had been licensed and commissioned by the Archbishop, I was included in many aspects of diocesan life. I served as one of the Archbishop's selectors of candidates for the ordained ministry of the Church. This involved interviewing and assessing potential clergy during residential selection conferences, and reviewing, with other selectors, their abilities and vocation. I assisted with the training of the ordinands. The Archbishop arranged that all the ordinands should spend a full day with me, and I took them ship-visiting, round the harbour, to shipping offices, and to the Port Authority. They had lunch in the Chain Locker Club Bar of The Flying Angel Club, mixing with the seafarers and shipping personnel who were there. When they returned home, they had had a very full day. I also attended clergy chapter meetings, diocesan Synods and clergy summer schools. I felt very much part of the Anglican Church of Western Australia.

## Family

The move from Hull to Fremantle involved a massive upheaval for our family. Andrew and Helen had to be uprooted from a school where they were happily settled. Julia was old enough at two years of age to be aware of big changes and to be unsettled by them. And we would not be seeing our parents and our families for a considerable time.

Sally and I had discussed at length the factors for and against the move, and I was very thankful for her level-headed approach. She thought it through from all angles. She was aware of her love of England, home and family, and she had no great desire to 'see the world'. Her prime concern was the best interests of the whole family, and we talked about the children's education, my own long-term future, and the health and well-being of our parents. She had a clear view of her own role, which was also very humbling. She was a graduate teacher with a very good Honours degree from Cambridge, who was also the mother of three young children. She felt strongly that she should be at home for them while they were small. She was also the wife of a priest, whose calling might lead almost anywhere. She sacrificed a huge amount for our family and for me. When we decided to accept the appointment it had been a thoroughly considered decision, and we went to Australia with a positive attitude.

Andrew was nine, Helen seven and Julia two years and eight months when we arrived in Fremantle. Andrew and Helen attended Richmond School, the local State primary school, and both settled in well. They received an excellent balanced education, with due emphasis placed both on basic learning requirements and on social and sporting activities. Both were soon fully involved in the life of the school. Academically they were very capable; Andrew was showing promise of being a very good mathematician, and Helen had real literary talents. They were involved in the wider community, too: Andrew played soccer with a local boys team, and Helen was a keen Brownie. They were well prepared for a return to the English educational system when the time came, although Andrew had to cope with a very different way of teaching mathematics, the transition from primary to secondary education, and having no knowledge of French. Julia attended kindergarten, and later the first year at Richmond school, and she too was given a good grounding in basic skills. She had no trouble adjusting to an English school on our return. Sally too was much involved with the school and the community. She assisted in a voluntary capacity in the school library and the canteen, and with teaching religious instruction. She and the children were active members of the congregation of our parish church, St. Peter and St. Mark's, Palmyra. She also helped one evening a week at the Flying Angel Club.

A feature of our time in Western Australia was the family holidays we enjoyed in Geraldton and Albany. They gave us an opportunity to appreciate the vastness of the country, the beauty and incredible range and variety of the wildflowers, the unique wildlife, the richness of the farmlands, the majesty of the lofty trees in the forests of South West Australia, the desolate appearance of the bush, the smallness of the population in relation to the size of the State, and the warmth and generosity of Australian hospitality.

A wonderful bonus for us all was a two-months' visit from Sally's parents. Her father had retired as County Treasurer of Cambridgeshire not long after we had left for Australia, and they decided to come and spend a holiday with us. They had never previously been out of the United Kingdom, and we welcomed them eagerly. We took them to see places of interest and to meet our friends, and it gave them an insight into Australia. We were sad to see them go when the time for departure arrived.

## An Exciting Challenge

Early in 1973 all the chaplains of The Missions to Seamen received a letter from the Chairman of the Council of the Society advising us of the retirement of the General Secretary, Prebendary Tom Kerfoot, at the end of 1974. Advertisements for his successor would shortly be appearing in Church publications, and any chaplain who wished to be considered for the appointment was invited to indicate his willingness to the Council. Sally and I gave this serious thought. I was thirty-eight, had served with the Society for ten years, was enjoying a challenging and responsible posting in Western Australia, and was beginning to feel that after Fremantle I would need a change of emphasis in my ministry. I genuinely loved ministering in the maritime world, and I felt that I would like to be considered for the post. In my heart of hearts I thought that my comparative youth would be a drawback, but at least I knew at first hand what was happening on the shipping scene. So after much thought and prayer I wrote to the Chairman asking to be considered.

Some weeks later I received a telephone call from Tom Kerfoot. He told me that I was on a short list of four people who would be interviewed for the post, and that the interviews would be held in London in mid-June, three months away. I was to book a return flight, and not tell anyone the real reason for my trip; I was to say that Headquarters wanted me to attend a conference. In due course I flew to London and attended the interview. I was the last of the four to be interviewed and by the time the moment for my interview arrived, I had convinced myself that all the others were far more high-powered and able than I was and that there was very little likelihood of my being appointed. I actually enjoyed the questions I was asked; many were about the current shipping scene, and I really did know what I was talking about on that subject. I also admitted freely that there would be a huge amount to learn, and that I would approach the task with that in mind.

My interview lasted less than half an hour, and then the candidates and the interviewing committee had lunch together. After lunch the committee retired to make their decision. Tom Kerfoot came to me and said that no announcement would be made that day, and asked me to return to the Merchant Navy Hotel where I was staying. I did not know what to think. I had been given no inkling of what was happening, and I had nothing to tell Sally. I spent a long and lonely evening in my room. Early next morning Tom telephoned. He told me that he was not supposed to say anything, and that no public announcement was imminent, but he felt that he could not leave me in complete uncertainty. 'You had better start thinking worldwide,' he said. He went on to swear me to silence until an official announcement was made. Incredibly, it was five long months later when I received a handwritten letter from the Chairman of the Council, Bishop Neville Welch, inviting me to accept the post of Deputy General Secretary for one year with the prospect of becoming General Secretary at the end of it. It was a slightly unsatisfactory arrangement, but as I felt that I could escape with dignity if I proved to be totally unsuited to the task, and because I was aware of my relative youth, inexperience and inadequacy, I accepted.

So after two and a half years in Western Australia I had to start thinking of a future a year or so ahead and of a return to England. When the time came to tell the children of the move they were sad to be leaving Australia but excited to be returning to England. For my part I was genuinely sorry to be leaving, but excited and apprehensive about my new role. I was glad that with my new responsibilities, I would certainly be returning to Western Australia at regular intervals.

Sally and the children flew back to England in September 1974, and I followed them by sea two months later. Just before she left Australia we discovered that Sally was expecting another baby, and that we would certainly have something very tangible by which to remember Australia! It had been a wonderful three and a half years.

# CHAPTER NINE

# The Voyage of a Lifetime:
## From Fremantle to Tilbury on
## *Discovery Bay*, November/December 1974

EARLY IN SEPTEMBER 1974 Sally and the children flew back to England so that the children could enter school at the beginning of the academic year. I needed to stay on in Fremantle, both to await the arrival of my successor, The Revd. Angas Murray-Stone, an Anglican priest serving with the British Sailors' Society in Ghana, and also to attend the triennial conference of The Missions to Seamen in Australasia, which was due to be held in Melbourne in November. After that I would return to the United Kingdom as soon as possible.

For a number of reasons I was keen to travel back to the United Kingdom by sea. I needed some time alone to prepare for my new responsibilities. I was ready for a break after a prolonged period of working at full stretch. And I felt that since I had never made a long sea voyage, it would be of great value to gain some first-hand experience of life at sea. So I enquired whether Overseas Containers Limited (OCL), whose ships I visited regularly in Fremantle, would be kind enough to give me a passage to England. To my great delight they agreed willingly; they said that I would be welcome to travel on any of their ships, provided that there was accommodation available. The first ship leaving Fremantle after the Melbourne Conference was the *Discovery Bay*, and accommodation was available on her. Captain John Cosker was the Master of the ship, and he assigned the Owner's Suite to me for the voyage.

The voyage was one of the most memorable experiences of my life. We sailed from Fremantle early on a Sunday morning in mid-November, with dozens of helpers from the Flying Angel Club waving goodbye from the quayside following a final farewell party on board. An hour out of port John Cosker came to my cabin and handed me a beautiful leather wallet with an inscribed plate inside. It contained a hundred Australian dollars 'for expenses on the voyage,' and was a gift from the shipping agents in Fremantle. He said that he had had orders not to give it to me before the ship sailed in case I tried to give it back! He made me very welcome, and I settled down to enjoy the voyage.

The Owner's Suite was magnificent. It was situated on the top deck and faced aft. There was a small entrance lobby, with clothes pegs, a large mirror and a fridge (already stacked with twenty-four cans of beer!). The day cabin was large, carpeted bulkhead to bulkhead, and with huge stern-facing windows; it had a comfortable settee, armchairs, bookshelves and a big writing desk and chair. The night cabin, also with stern-facing windows, had two single beds, cupboards, fitted wardrobes and two large wash hand basins. There was a separate bathroom, with bath, shower and toilet. As soon as I arrived on board, a notice was pinned to my door, announcing simply: *The Vicarage.*

I already knew most of the officers and crew members from their regular visits to Fremantle, but I got to know them all much better as the voyage progressed. I was invited to move freely through all parts of the ship, and I took care not to abuse the privilege. I spent time on the bridge, in the engine room, in the crew bar, in the officers' bar and with the Captain. He and I often talked for an hour or so after dinner in the evening, and I learned much about life at sea from him; our conversations were always full of interest, and we got on together very well.

The ship was a 28,000 deadweight ton container vessel, carrying 1,400 standard size containers. Her cruising speed was around 20 Knots. There were 35 of us on board, including myself and one other supernumerary. Our projected course took us across the Indian Ocean, round the Cape of Good Hope, up the west coast of Africa, and through the Straits of Gibraltar to the new container terminal at Fos, forty miles West of Marseilles, where we were to discharge 400 containers and load some empty ones. We would then return through the Straits of Gibraltar, sail round the coast of Spain, Portugal and France to Vlissingen in Holland and Bremerhaven in Germany, and then cross the North Sea to the Thames and Tilbury.

The first stage of the voyage, five thousand miles and ten days across the Indian Ocean, was endlessly fascinating, doubtless because it was all so new to me. We were out of sight of land the whole time, and for nine days we did not see another ship. But we did see some of the wonders of Creation: a great whale swimming close to the ship, spouting water high into the air; an albatross, which followed us for three days and nights and flew close to the windows of my day cabin, its fourteen feet wingspan covering the width of the windows; and shoals of flying fish skimming over the surface of the waves. I spent time gazing at the ceaseless motion of the sea. I familiarised myself with the ship. I talked to members of the crew, who seemed to find many small jobs to do in my cabin and enjoyed a long chat in the process. I read a lot. It was a peaceful, relaxing change of pace and surroundings. Meals were highlights of the day; the food was excellent, and I enjoyed the half hour before lunch and dinner having a drink with the officers or crew.

A week into the voyage, on the first full Sunday at sea, I held a church service in one of the cabins which was not in use. The suggestion to hold the service came not from me but from Captain Cosker. Seven people were present, some of whom were Roman Catholics who had checked with Father O'Shea, the Apostleship of the Sea priest in Fremantle, that it was in order for them to attend. The service lasted fifteen minutes, of which five were allotted to an informal talk about how I had come to the ministry of the Church and how I came to be on the ship. After the service the congregation adjourned to *The Vicarage*, where a lively discussion went on until lunchtime. On the following Sunday the congregation numbered twelve; we followed the same format, and as it was 'Bible Sunday', I talked for a few minutes about what the Bible meant to me. Afterwards we again repaired to *The Vicarage*. On the third Sunday there was a congregation of fourteen, which represented just about everybody who was not on duty.

As we approached the coast of South Africa, we ran into a fierce storm. The smooth gentle regular motion of the ship gave way to a violent tossing. The whole ship shuddered and shook. Booming crashes followed the bows butting into the waves. Moving about the cabin became hazardous. Although it was early in the day, the sky was very dark, rain was lashing down, and a howling gale was raging. I inched my way up to the bridge, clinging tightly to the handrails. From there I looked forward to the ship's bows, six hundred feet ahead. It was an awesome, spectacular and intimidating sight. The bows ploughed into the huge waves. The ship then seemed to stop in its tracks, shuddering from stem to stern as tons of water thundered over the bulwarks. Slowly the bows rose out of the sea, and the ship's hull flexed with the strain. The whole sequence was repeated again and again. It was my first experience of a real storm at sea, and all sorts of scary thoughts went through my mind. We were 500 miles from land: could I remember the lifeboat drill if it came to that? Would we be picked up? Would we even survive? For a while I knew what it was to be really frightened, as indeed has every seafarer at some time in his career. Gradually the storm abated, and next day, on a perfect spring morning, we sailed into Table Bay, Cape Town, and I had my first view of that magnificent panorama dominated by Table Mountain.

We slowed down to pick up the stores and the mail, and then resumed our course north up the west coast of Africa. The Chief Steward, Pat O'Hara, brought round the mail, and everybody grabbed their letters eagerly. Everybody, that is, except Sam. Sam was an Assistant Steward, a large, quiet, shy man. There were no letters for Sam, and he turned away sadly. I learned that he had not received a single letter at any port during the voyage, and his loneliness and disappointment were palpable.

As we approached the Equator the ship's tiny swimming pool was freshly filled each day, and off-duty officers and crew enjoyed lounging beside it. So did I, and when we crossed the line I was ceremonially thrown in to be ducked by King Neptune. On fine evenings we enjoyed deck games, and on other evenings we had quiz nights or other informal activities. As we rounded the north-west coast of Africa and approached the Straits of Gibraltar, Captain Cosker was on the bridge most of the time. He was keeping a watchful eye on the hundreds of small fishing boats, many of which displayed no lights while fishing at night; being built of wood, it was almost impossible to pick them up on the radar. It was an anxious time for John, and I was impressed by his calm vigilance and great skill. We passed through the Straits of Gibraltar early on in the day, and I had my first view of the massive Rock as we headed for Fos.

At that time Fos was a newly-developed port, about forty miles west of Marseilles in a flat and remote location. High winds prevented our entering the port for twenty-four hours, and there was nothing to do but wait at anchor. It was frustrating, and I experienced the boredom that is an integral feature of life at sea: out of sight of land one stretch of water looks very much like another; when the ship is tossing about in rough weather, or vibrating at speed, it is difficult to write or undertake delicate work with your hands; and waiting for a berth to become vacant can be tedious in the extreme. The problems are compounded if there is not a plentiful supply of good reading matter on board.

When we entered port early next morning, we were due to stay for just twelve hours. It was a miserable December day, cold and raining. There was no public transport system linking us to the nearest centre of population, the small town of Port St. Louis du Rhône, nor were there any taxis. After three weeks at sea a small group of us felt that we would like a brief change of scene, and the ship's agent drove us into the town. There was not much there to see. It was raining hard. I was the only one who could speak French. Nobody took any notice of us. We went into a bar to keep out of the rain and to try to get warm. We walked back to the ship, and were soaked to the skin when we arrived. I had learned the hard way what it is like to be a stranger in a strange place where nobody seemed to care. I thought of St. Paul's words when he was shipwrecked on the rocky shores of Malta:-

> The rough islanders treated us with uncommon kindness; because it was cold and had started to rain, they lit a fire, and made us all welcome.
>
> *(Acts of the Apostles, chapter 28, verse 2).*

There was no seafarers' chaplain and no seafarers' centre in Fos, and I resolved to try to rectify that as soon as I could. In the event it took ten years before a seafarers' centre was opened, but we had a chaplain there much earlier.

We sailed that evening for Vlissingen in Holland, arriving early on Sunday morning. The first visitor on board after Customs, Immigration and Port Health, and the ship's agent, Tony Driver, was the Lay Reader from The Missions to Seamen. He did not know that I was on the ship, and it was lovely to see him when he came up to my cabin on his way round the ship. He told me that there would be a church service in the Mission Chapel that evening, and that he would come to collect us in his minibus. It was another cold, wet and miserable day, and the eight or nine of us who went to the Mission that evening were very grateful for the lift. The Mission, another Flying Angel Club, was situated close to the dock gates about a mile from where we were berthed, and it would not have been a pleasant walk.

The Flying Angel Club was buzzing with activity when we arrived. There were more than a hundred seafarers from many parts of the world in the building. They were playing table tennis, snooker, and other games; watching television; sitting in groups, chatting and having a glass of beer; reading; making purchases at the shop or the canteen; exchanging money; and making telephone calls. About forty seafarers attended the short service in the chapel. It was a pleasant, lively, happy evening, and I enjoyed experiencing it as a seafarer. Tony drove us back to the ship at the end of the evening, and as I reflected on the visit the overwhelming feeling I had was that I had been a stranger in a strange place and had been made very welcome. It made me realise more fully than ever before how much the ministry of the Church means to the seafarer.

We spent twelve hours in Vlissingen, unloading and loading 400 containers, before sailing on to Bremerhaven. In Bremerhaven we berthed a long way from the dock entrance, and as there was no transport available, I stayed on board during our brief stay. By now everybody on board was very excited about going home. It was just over a week before Christmas, and the ship had been away for three months. Everybody was due for leave when the ship docked in Tilbury. We crossed the North Sea in stormy conditions, and in the morning entered the Thames Estuary. As we were making our way into the estuary, we received orders to anchor off Southend. The lock-keepers at Tilbury had come out on strike, and nobody could tell us how long we would have to wait before coming alongside our berth. Three long days and nights dragged by, and we all had visions of still being aboard over Christmas. Some very unchristian sentiments were expressed about those lock-keepers! But the shipping company was marvellous. They arranged a tug to bring out the relief crew, and took us ashore in the same way. I went down the side of the ship on a rope ladder and in a strong wind, but I did not mind in the least. I was going home to my family, and I was going to be there for Christmas! When I arrived at our new home later that day, the reality of coming home exceeded even my fondest imaginings: it was wonderful. We had been apart for more than three months, and it was lovely to be back with Sally and the children.

During the days that followed I often found myself thinking about the voyage and about what all those new experiences had taught me. I had seen the sea in many of its moods. I now had a better understanding of the heavy responsibility a ship's captain carries for the safety of his ship, his officers and crew, and for other seafarers. It had been good to live for a prolonged period with the same group of men and to cope with their individual idiosyncrasies. I now knew at first-hand what loneliness and boredom could mean for seafarers. I was more aware of the ever-present dangers of seafaring. I had come to appreciate more clearly the strength and depth of the intangible but very real bond of fellowship and support that links seafarers of every race and background in a common concern for each other. I also had a better idea of how the Church should carry out its ministry to seafarers.

My voyage on *Discovery Bay* had given me a far more comprehensive view of the maritime scene than I could otherwise have had, and I was, and am, most grateful to Captain Paul Ogden, General Manager of Container Fleets, for inviting me to make the voyage, and to Captain John Cosker and my shipmates for making me so welcome.

# CHAPTER TEN

# London 1975-1990:
# Deputy General Secretary 1975

## Settling In and Reorientation

WHEN WE RETURNED to England for me to become Deputy General Secretary of The Missions to Seamen, our whole family had to adjust to major basic changes.

Sally was almost three months pregnant when she flew to London with the children early in September 1974. She was faced with moving into a house which we had never seen and sorting out furniture which had been in store during our years in Australia. She had three children to see established in new schools; and Andrew, aged twelve, had a difficult first term at Watford Grammar School, because he was a whole year behind his contemporaries in French, and had followed a different Maths course in Australia. She knew nothing about the local Church life. She needed to register herself and the children with a doctor, and also to make contact quickly with the ante-natal clinic. She did not hold a United Kingdom driving licence, and there were a number of necessary journeys to make. It was all fairly daunting, but she and the children coped magnificently. Her parents were a tower of strength. Her father drove her to many appointments, helped with the installation of the furniture, and was generally available and helpful.

The house they moved into was in Bushey Heath, just on the Hertfordshire side of the boundary with Middlesex. It was owned by friends of my family, Alan and Beryl Peebles, who had just retired and were about to move to Teignmouth, near my parents. They had been intending to let the house as a source of income, but when they learned that we were returning to England, and that we would need to live within easy reach of central London, they offered us the use of the house, rent free. They further promised to give us good warning if or when they wanted to dispose of it. It was a wonderfully generous offer, and we accepted gratefully. It was ten years before Alan's widow Beryl decided to sell it, and by a happy arrangement The Missions to Seamen bought it from her so that we could continue to live in it. It was a detached house, with four bedrooms and a spacious garden, and located in what estate agents would describe as a 'highly desirable area.' In the garden, about twenty yards away from the house, there was a large single-room cedar hut, which was affectionately known as 'the Ranch House'; it was initially a playroom, but eventually became my study.

When I arrived home in Bushey Heath four days before Christmas, there were just two weeks before I was due to take up my new appointment. We spent Christmas at Teignmouth with my parents, who had not seen Sally and the children for nearly four years; it was lovely to be with them again, and we all enjoyed it. Soon, though, it was time to return home, for the children to start a new term, me to start a new job, and Sally to prepare for the baby's arrival in addition to running the home.

A good domestic routine had already been established by the time I arrived, including settling into the life and activities of St John's church, Stanmore, two miles away. Sally and the children had worshipped once at both St Mary's, Watford, and St Peter's, Bushey Heath, before one day she walked down to Stanmore. She looked at the parish church notice board, and saw to her joy that the Rector was Michael Bowles, whom we had both known at Cambridge. The next Sunday she and the children attended a service there and were all made welcome. Sally introduced herself to Michael, and the children were gathered up by one of the Junior Church leaders, Phyllis O'Leary, and shown round the Sunday School. The two girls, Helen aged ten and Julia aged six, wanted to join Junior Church there, and Andrew and Sally were impressed by the atmosphere of the church. I was equally delighted with it when I arrived, and Michael Bowles and I enjoyed a happy friendship and partnership for the next fifteen years. It was unusual for us not to worship in our parish church, but we established a very good relationship with George Austin, our parish priest in Bushey Heath. I assisted him occasionally with services, and our families were good friends.

One immediate decision I had to make was how I would travel to the office each day. The Headquarters of The Missions to Seamen was St. Michael Paternoster Royal, a Wren church at the north end of the Southwark Bridge in the square mile of the City of London. Limited car parking space was available there, but as it was a sixteen-mile journey from Bushey Heath involving negotiating more than fifty sets of traffic lights, and which would have to be undertaken during or around the rush hour, I was not keen to drive more often than I needed to. I decided instead to drive to Stanmore, park the car in the station car park, and travel to the city on the Underground. I experimented with this for a few days and decided that this was my preferred means of travel. I left home every morning at 7 a.m. and reached Embankment Station at around 8 o'clock. On fine mornings I walked the two miles to St Michael Paternoster Royal along the Embankment, arriving in the office by 8:30, and this became my routine throughout my fifteen years in London. I normally left the office between 5:30 and 6:00 p.m., and it was 7 o'clock before I was home. I became a regular commuter when I was not travelling overseas.

An unexpected aspect of my re-orientation was that I had not realised how

Australian I had become in my speech. On my very first full day in Bushey Heath I went to the Public Library to obtain a borrower's ticket. After I had asked for it the Librarian looked up and said, 'Do you come from Australia, sir?' Without a moment's thought or hesitation I replied, 'Too right, mate!' – and then realised how I had answered. A few weeks later I took Andrew, Helen and Julia to the London Zoo one Saturday. As we sat in the cafeteria eating our lunch, a very pleasant man leaned towards us from the next table and asked, 'Excuse me, could I borrow the Tomato Ketchup?' 'Go for your life, sport!' I immediately replied, much to the amusement of the children. They too had Australian accents. When Julia started school in Bushey Heath she asked her teacher, 'Can I do some pineting (painting)?' The teacher asked her to repeat the question, not because (as she told us later) she had not understood, but because she wanted to hear her say it again!

### Headquarters – St Michael Paternoster Royal

St. Michael Paternoster Royal was an ideal location for the Headquarters of The Missions to Seamen. Situated within the square mile of the City, where many important shipping companies and shipping-related businesses had their offices, it was two minutes' walk from the Mansion House and Cannon Street Underground stations, five minutes from the Bank and seven minutes from St Paul's Cathedral. It was very convenient for our many visitors from overseas.

The church itself has a long history. The first recorded mention of it was in 1219, and in 1423 Dick Whittington, the famous four-times Mayor of London, rebuilt the church and established a college of clergy there (hence College Hill, the name of the street in which the church is located). Its full title originated from its proximity to Paternoster Lane, where there were a number of rosary makers, and from its connection with the wine trade (it lies within the Vintry Ward) and the trade's link with the town of Réole, near Bordeaux. It was destroyed in the Great Fire of London in 1666, and rebuilt by Sir Christopher Wren between 1686 and 1694. During the Second World War it was badly damaged by German 'doodle bug' flying bombs, and only the space under the tower could be used. It was closed in 1955, and the diocese of London considered disposing of it; but its historical and architectural importance led to a decision to restore it and make it available to one of the Anglican Church's outreach organisations. Around that time, the mid-1960's, The Missions to Seamen was actively seeking new premises for its Headquarters. The lease of its premises in Buckingham Palace Gardens was nearing expiry, so after selling the remainder of the lease, office space was rented in a building at Norbury, a fifteen-minute rail journey from central London. This move proved deeply unsatisfactory, and another move became imperative. When the Society was offered St Michael Paternoster Royal, it accepted gratefully and moved in late in 1968. I was privileged to attend the re-hallowing and dedication of the church in the presence of His Royal Highness The Duke of Edinburgh.

The restoration of the church was magnificent. The fine reredos and pulpit had been removed before the bombing, and both were restored and replaced in their original positions. All the woodwork, old and new, was oak. At the east end three superb new stained-glass windows by John Hayward fittingly complement the dignity of the altar. On the south side another Hayward window portrays Dick Whittington and his cat; it is a striking window, although irreverent visitors have been heard to liken the illustrious Lord Mayor to Sherlock Holmes, or even a gamekeeper! At the west end, underneath the tower and separated from the church by an oak and glass screen, is the Whittington Hall, a lovely oak-panelled room which can accommodate fifty people in comfort at a function.

The tower was imaginatively converted into three floors of offices. The first floor was allotted to the Ministry Department; there were three individual offices, and a large open area for the secretaries. The second floor was the Administrative Department, with one individual office and open areas for the secretaries, the Filing Department and the copying machines. On the top floor were the Finance and Public Relations Departments, each with one individual office and open space for the assistants. In the basement (formerly the crypt) there was a small kitchen and dining space.

One of the conditions of the lease from the Diocese of London was that the church should be open to the public throughout normal office hours five days a week but that no Sunday services should be held. This was a wise decision, because there are thirty-nine active Anglican churches in the square mile of the City, and at that time very few residents at the weekend. The churches had full, varied and busy ministries in midweek, and some had flourishing weekend congregations. At St. Michael Paternoster Royal our Chinese chaplain in the Port of London conducted a weekly Chinese language service for Chinese seafarers and the resident Chinese community; a number of City Livery Companies worshipped in the church once or twice a year; Morning Prayer was said daily; there was a weekly lunchtime celebration of Holy Communion; the Annual Service of The Missions to Seamen was held there; there were baptisms, marriages, funerals and memorial services; people from many walks of life popped in to enjoy the peace and quiet of the church; and some came out of sheer curiosity. In all, more than five thousand people a year worshipped in the church.

## Deputy General Secretary

When I was appointed Deputy General Secretary, the intention was that I should spend the early months 'getting my feet under the table' at

Headquarters. I was young (just forty), and there was much to learn. I would become acquainted with the staff, familiarise myself with the office set-up and routine, sit in on the various committees, read background information, make visits to chaplaincy staff and Regional Directors (the fundraising staff), and prepare myself for the greater task ahead. But 'the best laid schemes o'mice and men gang aft a-gley'!*

At the end of 1974 The Revd. John Rowlands, Personnel Secretary of The Missions to Seamen, left to become Rector of Woodbridge in Suffolk. The decision was taken not to seek a replacement for him before my arrival, since it was felt that as I would be working closely with whoever was appointed, I should be consulted. There was therefore no Personnel Secretary when I arrived in January 1975, and I was asked to undertake the work involved until a permanent appointment could be made. So for six months I interviewed potential chaplains and student assistants, dealt with the day-to-day problems of chaplains and lay readers all over the world, acted as Secretary to the Pastoral Committee, read the monthly reports from stations around the world, and quickly learned how the office functioned.

I soon experienced some of the frustrations of the job. One of the chaplains was leaving a port in Australia for one in New Zealand, and his personal effects, which would fill a standard-size container, needed to be transported. I advised him to take no action about this while I sought to arrange free carriage. I had good contacts with shipping personnel in Australia, and I had no difficulty finding a company willing to carry the container free of charge. I was about to give the chaplain the good news when I received a letter from him saying that he had obtained and accepted a quotation from a forwarding agency to transport the container at the commercial rate. I was furious, and in the privacy of my office I threw his letter on to the floor and kicked it around until my wrath subsided.

After eleven and a half years as an active port chaplain, the change in my daily pattern of work took a lot of getting used to. I was accustomed to making an early start: a short morning service, a brief staff meeting, dealing with the mail and administrative matters, and then out to the ships from 10 a.m. until lunchtime, was my regular routine. The afternoon was the time for paperwork, appointments and 'home time', because ships in port are normally quiet in the afternoons, when officers and crew members not actually working are either ashore or resting. On four or five evenings a week I was usually on duty at the Flying Angel Club and used to arrive home between 11 p.m. and midnight. Now I was working in an office, where the day began officially at 9:30 a.m. with our daily service. A number of us came much earlier, and this provided a golden opportunity to write papers or dictate

---

*Robert Burns 'To a Mouse'.

letters before the others arrived. The reason for the late start was the distance many staff members had to travel and the time involved in travelling; commuting into London is time-consuming, often frustrating, and tedious. A fair degree of latitude was allowed as to how we all worked our hours. But by 10:30a.m. I was usually getting restless, feeling that it was time to be on the ships. It was several years before I lost that feeling.

I set out to be as efficient as possible in the office. In South Shields I had learned the hard way that it is counter-productive to try to do other people's jobs as well as my own. In Hull I had admired the way our Honorary Treasurer, Ted Bickersteth, administered his office and drew out the best from his staff, and I had tried to work out how he did it. In Fremantle I had had to determine my priorities carefully, and stick to them firmly, in order to accomplish what really mattered and to avoid becoming bogged down by trivia. At Headquarters I was going to need to dictate letters to a machine rather than to a secretary: if the telephone rang while I was dictating a letter, one of us would be wasting time; I might wish to dictate letters before my secretary arrived; and complex letters require careful expression and revision. But initially I found it hard to talk to an impersonal machine, and I struggled until one day I decided to write to a number of people I knew well. As I dictated the letters, I pictured the person to whom I was writing in my mind's eye, and I found it much easier. It was not long before I was happily dictating letters into the machine, and this training proved invaluable later when I was producing reports on my overseas visits.

As the weeks became months, I came to the conclusion that despite my comparative youth and lack of first-hand knowledge of much of the Society's work, I was ready and willing to assume the position of General Secretary, daunting though it was. My appointment was ratified by the Society's Council, approved by the Archbishop of Canterbury, and announced at the Society's Annual General Meeting in the middle of the year. I was to take up the appointment on January 1st 1976. I was happy and excited by the prospect, but under no illusion that it would be easy. Tom Kerfoot, the retiring General Secretary, spared no effort to help me. We had always got on well together, and although I realised that my way of working was very different from his, I knew that I would always be able to count on his support.

In July 1975 Tom accepted appointment as the first General Secretary of The International Christian Maritime Association. It was a part-time appointment, and he was the ideal person for it; he had played a key role in the founding and establishing of the Association, and he had the knowledge and experience vital for the task. He also had the trust and affection of everybody concerned. I was delighted when he accepted the appointment, and we made available an office for him at St Michael Paternoster Royal. People told me that I was foolish to offer him an office on our premises, but I had no qualms; he was not the man to take advantage of the situation. It was good to have him around and it worked out very well.

Early in my time as Deputy General Secretary Tom and I discussed the appointment of a new Assistant General Secretary with responsibility for Ministry to replace the Personnel Secretary. His advice was to appoint Jimmy Wilson-Hughes, Senior Chaplain in Durban. Jimmy was 62, and would be retiring three years later. He was a very experienced chaplain, and Tom felt that he would be easy to work with. So we invited him to consider the appointment, and he accepted willingly. It was a very happy appointment. He settled in quickly and well, and he was a tower of strength to me. He had a delightful sense of humour, and I was richly blessed in having him as one of my closest colleagues.

The Assistant General Secretary with responsibility for Administration was Neville Barwick, a former District Officer in the Colonial Service in Nigeria, and more recently the Society's Regional Director for the Midlands. Neville was a delightful character. He was a good administrator, and he related easily to colleagues and the general public. We became firm friends, and I valued highly his ability to offer frank and constructive criticism in a pleasant and acceptable way. I knew that there was a good team to support me.

## Family
As I settled into my new responsibilities, and Andrew, Helen and Julia all made good progress at school, we looked forward to the new arrival. Early on the morning of April 29 1975 I drove Sally to the Maternity Hospital half a mile away, and then went home to wait. At around 1 p.m. Timothy Paul came into the world. He weighed 9lbs 3ozs, and brought great joy to us all. I was so excited and thrilled that I telephoned the school and asked them to give Helen and Julia the good news! But I did not ring Andrew's school: I thought it would be too embarrassing for a twelve year-old boy to receive the news in the presence of his classmates! When he arrived home and I gave him the news, he was as delighted as we all were.

Sally and I realised that because of the extensive travel overseas I would be undertaking as General Secretary, and because when I was not overseas I would be working in an office sixteen miles away, I would not see as much of Tim in his early years as I had of our other children. We were sad about this, and I determined to make the most of every opportunity of being with him.

## General Secretary Designate
With my appointment as General Secretary having been formally ratified with effect from January 1st 1976, I could begin to make firm plans for the future.

*London, family picture, Helen, Sally, Julia, Timothy, myself and Andrew, 1975.*

There were still six months to run of my appointment as Deputy General Secretary, and I wanted to make the best use of this time.

One of my first major engagements was to attend the second triennial conference of the International Christian Maritime Association (ICMA) at Elsinore in Denmark a few weeks later. The ICMA was the direct result of a very significant and emotional international consultation on the welfare of seafarers held in Rotterdam in 1969. The consultation brought together representatives of all the major Christian agencies serving seafarers with representatives of secular organisations with similar objectives; they were the 'movers and shakers' of the maritime welfare scene at the time. Its aim was simple and straightforward: how could the needs of seafarers be met most effectively? The conclusion was similarly simple and straightforward: by all the organisations working together. A working party was constituted with the aim of 'studying the manner in which a permanent association of Christian voluntary agencies…may best be brought into being.' The purpose of the association would be 'to foster collaboration and mutual aid among constituent bodies, and to further common interests,' and 'to be the collective and respected voice of the association within the industry and outside it.' The association was then formally established, its full title being The International Christian Maritime Association. In 1970 it was granted observer status at the International Labour Conference in Geneva: it had arrived on the international scene.

The Elsinore Conference of 1975 was my first experience of a large international and ecumenical gathering of Christian leaders in the maritime world, and it was challenging and exhilarating. I had valued my contacts with chaplains of other denominations in the ports where I had served, and we had got on well together. Now I was also moving among those who made the decisions on behalf of their various organisations, and I was glad that I was not yet in the 'hot seat' of The Missions to Seamen: I was on a steep learning curve, and I needed time to become acclimatised to the more rarefied atmosphere!

There was a definite air of purpose about the Conference, and the goodwill on all sides was genuine. We had broken, and were continuing to break, new ground, with chaplains and lay staff of different denominations coming together and working under one roof in a number of ports. One of the earliest instances of this was in Antwerp, where in 1970 the Roman Catholic Apostleship of the Sea, the Anglican Missions to Seamen and the inter-denominational British Sailors' Society had combined to build a new centre, the Antwerp Mariners Club, in the heart of the docks. With the completion of that project the chaplains of the three Societies, Father Alphonse Laureys of the Apostleship of the Sea, Ken Good of The Missions to Seamen and Arthur Kenworthy of the British Sailors' Society, engaged in discussions about working together from one centre. They agreed that the most suitable centre was the Stella Maris Club of the Apostleship of the Sea, and with the agreement of all the relevant authorities, it was decided to proceed. The Missions to Seamen sold its building; the British Sailors' Society rented out theirs; and the Stella Maris Club became the Antwerp Seafarers' Centre. The chaplains were equal partners in the ministry, and they prayed, planned and co-ordinated their daily work together. I was thrilled to hear at first hand about this, especially since I was about to visit Buenos Aires to talk with the chaplains and committees of The Missions to Seamen and the Apostleship of the Sea about bringing together the work of both organisations under one roof in that port.

I made many new friends at the conference. The General Secretaries of the British Sailors' Society, the German and Dutch Seamen's Missions, and the Scandinavian Seamen's Missions were helpful and considerate, and it was good to see how they all worked together on the Standing Committee. I met chaplains of various denominations who were previously just names or unknown to me, and I caught a glimpse of how effective a body like the ICMA could become.

I also learned much. With inter-confessional collaboration becoming a reality, it was clearly imperative that our relationships with each other should be open, frank and honest. It might be said that there should be no need to make such a statement in Christian circles, but the fact is that the history of the Church has been tarnished at times by deviousness and half-truths. I determined that my yes would be yes, my no would be no, and that if I was not sure of something I would say so. I came to appreciate the importance of loyalty to my own ecclesiastical tradition, and of respect for the traditions of others whose emphases were different. I saw that what unites us as servants of our Lord Jesus Christ is far greater and more important than what separates us, and that working happily together is not totally dependent on everybody agreeing about everything. My horizons were broadening, old attitudes were being questioned, and new challenges were appearing and being faced.

After the ICMA conference and a family summer holiday, I embarked on an autumn programme of overseas visits. It was an ideal time for this, as Jimmy Wilson-Hughes had started work as Assistant General Secretary (Ministry), thus relieving me of the Personnel Secretary's responsibilities, and Tom Kerfoot was due to spend most of his remaining months in office in London preparing to hand over.

My first visit was to South America in September. The Missions to Seamen had seafarers' centres at Santos in Brazil, Buenos Aires and Rosario in Argentina, and Valparaiso in Chile, and I planned to visit the stations in Argentina and Brazil and to return to the United Kingdom via Port of Spain, Trinidad, where we also had a station. I would visit Valparaiso on my next tour. There were various reasons for visiting South America at that time, the most pressing being an attempt to secure the agreement of all concerned to the proposed partnership of The Missions to Seamen and the Apostleship of the Sea in Buenos Aires.

My visit to Buenos Aires was quite literally a baptism of fire. Two years previously Juan Peron had been returned to power as President of Argentina, and the country was now in turmoil. Guerrilla organisations were undermining the processes of law and order. A state of emergency had been declared. The Army and the Police had been invested with sweeping powers. Inflation was rampant, spiralling at a rate of 25% per month. In the capital tanks rolled through the streets, their guns depressed to pavement level. Roads passing police stations had been blocked off following bomb attacks from passing vehicles. Cars were being hi-jacked at traffic lights at night. Assassination squads drove through the streets in cars with no registration plates. Everybody had to carry their identification papers at all times. In the banks armed guards monitored proceedings from transparent bullet-proof vantage points. Innocent people had been killed in the violence. A significant number of civilians had 'disappeared'. Ambassadors had been kidnapped. One of our Missions to Seamen hostesses had been shot and badly injured while going home in a taxi. All this I saw for myself, as well as witnessing a long-running gun battle round an Army Headquarters close to our Missions to Seamen building.

Yet incredibly life in the city went on. The streets were crowded, the shops were doing business, and there were cars everywhere. Our chaplain, The Revd. Eric Casson, a Master Mariner with many years sea-going experience behind him, and his wife Doris coped with it all quite admirably. He continued to visit the ships, took sensible precautions to avoid dangerous situations, and went about his work as normally as possible. He knew that the possibility of being shot was very real. It was in this atmosphere of tension and violence that we were to attempt to forge a partnership in the ministry to seafarers between the Roman Catholic Apostleship of the Sea and the Anglican Missions to Seamen, and I was greatly impressed by the way everybody involved made real efforts to attend the various meetings.

With Eric Casson I visited the Stella Maris Club of the Apostleship of the Sea and met the chaplain, Father Alex Dalpiaz. His enthusiasm for the proposed partnership was as great as ours, and it was clear that the two chaplains had already established a good working relationship which would blossom further through working together under one roof. It was also clear that for good practical reasons the Stella Maris Club building was more suitable for the future than our Flying Angel Club. The Roman Catholic hierarchy were sympathetic to the proposal, but there were some members of the Committee of Management of The Missions to Seamen who either needed to be convinced of its rightness or were actually opposed to it. Eric and I called on the British Ambassador, Mr. Derrick Ashe, who was the Patron of The Missions to Seamen in Buenos Aires, and spent forty-five minutes with him outlining the issues involved. He was very encouraging and supportive, as was the Chairman of the Committee of The Missions to Seamen, Peter Godwin, when we called on him.

When the crucial meeting of the Committee of Management of The Missions to Seamen began, I was thoroughly prepared. Peter Godwin opened the meeting by reminding everybody of the steps that had led up to this moment, and gave a clear indication of his own support for the proposal. He then asked me to speak. It was my first experience of a meeting with such ecumenical significance, and I was nervous. But I was also convinced of the rightness of the proposal, and spoke for twenty minutes about already existing ecumenical projects in the maritime world. In my report, which I wrote the next day, I said that 'I made a point of putting no pressure on the meeting; I had hoped that by love and enthusiasm and reasoned thinking we might reach a common mind.' The decision to proceed with the proposal was taken without a formal vote being necessary, and there was genuine delight at the future prospect. Four months later the proposal became reality when the two organisations began working together from the Stella Maris Club.

As I flew out of Buenos Aires, I gave a huge sigh of relief that I was still alive. My experience there made me think very seriously about the conditions in which our chaplains and their families lived and worked, and I realised that I could never ask anyone to serve where I would not be prepared to serve myself. It also had a profound effect on my spiritual life; it added an urgency to my prayers and a deeper appreciation of my responsibility for my colleagues.

While the visit to Buenos Aires marked a critical moment in the progress of inter-confessional collaboration in maritime ministry in South America, my visits to the other stations were also significant in different ways. At Rosario on the River Plate, thirty hours sailing upstream from Buenos Aires, I heard about important port developments and the deepening of the shipping channel. At Santos, in Brazil, I learned of the formidable obstacles which the authorities placed in the paths of clergy ministering in the port, such as refusing to issue dock passes. I had long discussions with the Bishop about the possible ordination of our Lay Reader, Frank Snedker. I checked the title deeds of our property, which had recently been deposited with the Bank of London and South America. I visited the German Lutheran Church and the Norwegian Seamen's Mission, and I met the members of the Committee of The Missions to Seamen at a social gathering.

At my final stop in Port of Spain, Trinidad, The Missions to Seamen was having to come to terms with the unpalatable fact that our excellent Mariners' Club was now too big because of the changed and changing pattern of shipping using the port. I had long discussions with the Committee of Management and with the Bishop, and we decided to keep a close watch on developments. For a brief break of a few hours I was taken for a swim to the celebrated Marraccas Bay, which was marvellous. However on the return journey to Port of Spain we ran into a torrential tropical rainstorm which rendered the road temporarily impassable. We came to a halt close to a hotel, so we dashed into the bar and there, perched on high stools, with water up to our knees and a rum and coke in our hands, we waited patiently for the flood to subside!

So my first overseas tour came to an end. I had been faced with physical danger in Buenos Aires, with exciting challenges to move forward into the relatively little known and uncharted waters of inter-confessional collaboration, with routine administrative matters, and with complex pastoral issues, notably over the ordination of an English Lay Reader in the Episcopal Church of Brazil. I found it all immensely exciting, challenging and satisfying. I discovered that I was able to cope with the new responsibilities despite the mistakes I inevitably made. I learned also that it was essential to write full reports of all visits as soon as they took place, and to confirm decisions in writing to all concerned.

After six weeks back in the office, during which time I reflected on my fresh experiences, I set out again on a thirty-day tour of the Far East which was to include visits to Bangkok, Hong Kong, Pusan, Kobe and Yokahama, Jakarta, Singapore, Colombo and Dubai. As the tour progressed, I became increasingly aware both of the individual nature of each port operation and ministry and also of the wonderful family atmosphere of The Missions to Seamen, which seemed able to bridge cultural and operational differences and link everybody together in a strong but free fellowship.

In Bangkok the Honorary Chaplain of The Missions to Seamen was Canon John Taylor, Rector of Christ Church and formerly chaplain of The Missions to Seamen and Archdeacon of Dar es Salaam. John and his wife Rose were a dynamic couple: enthusiastic, efficient, charming and with a down-to-earth, commonsense, and a deep spirituality, they complemented each other wonderfully. John was a first-class priest, with boundless energy and unquenchable optimism, and Rose, who had served as a secretary in the Headquarters of The Missions to Seamen before her marriage, was a brilliant organiser. Christ Church, Bangkok, flourished under their leadership, and John made a huge impact on the community. There was no Missions to Seamen centre in Bangkok, but there was a magnificent seafarers' centre operated by a secular organisation. John had become closely involved with this, and his presence and assistance were warmly welcomed. Now he was asking The Missions to Seamen to appoint a priest to serve as chaplain to the seafarers and Assistant Curate of Christ Church. When I had seen the range of daily activities at Christ Church, including the housing and teaching of some Cambodian refugee children, I knew that we had to help.

Hong Kong has two fine seafarers' centres owned by The Missions to Seamen and operated since 1969 in partnership with the Roman Catholic Apostleship of the Sea. The Mariners Club in Kowloon was built in the 1960's and is one of the biggest and finest in the world. Its amenities include five floors of residential accommodation, a lovely chapel, first class restaurant, swimming pool, ten pin bowling alley, shops, ladies' and mens' hairdressing salons, and residential accommodation for the chaplains and the manager. It operated a well-equipped launch, *Dayspring*, for ship visiting. It had a paid staff of more than 100 Chinese men and women. The second centre, at Kwai Chung in the heart of the container terminal, had just opened when I visited in 1975. Among its facilities were medical and dental practices, an imaginative provision in a remote, newly developing part of the port, where ships had an extremely rapid turnaround.

My visit happened during a protracted smouldering dispute between the chaplains and the club manager. The chaplains believed that the manager was seeking and acquiring power in areas that were plainly their responsibility. I sat down with them for several hours, and studied the ordinance governing the affairs of The Mariners' Club. It was clear that the chaplains had a valid point, and I accordingly raised the matter with the chairman of the Committee of Management, David Newbigging, who was Chairman and Managing Director of Jardine Matheson, Hong Kong. Our meeting was both friendly and frank, and with his full agreement I interviewed the club manager and reported back to him. The situation was then firmly and decisively resolved in line with the provisions of the Ordinance. David and I became firm friends: I appreciated his willingness to listen, his searching questions, his incisive thinking and his considered actions. We remain firm friends to this day.

At Pusan in Korea I witnessed the encouraging early stages of the establishment of an important ministry to seafarers in a busy and growing port. I visited the new and immensely impressive shipyard in Ulsan. I saw the early signs of the dynamic life of the Church in Korea, which blossomed gloriously in the next decade.

At Kobe in Japan I was present at an historic occasion when the Anglican and Roman Catholic bishops visited the Kobe Mariners' Club to sign a Letter of Exchange formally initiating interconfessional collaboration between The Missions to Seamen and the Apostleship of the Sea in a building owned by The Missions to Seamen. Before the signing ceremony, the Bishops, Chaplains and all present went into the chapel for a short service, which culminated in the two Bishops standing together behind the altar to pronounce the blessing. It was a moving moment: it was thought to be the first time in Japanese ecclesiastical history that an Anglican and a Roman Catholic bishop had worshipped together in public. The new partnership was a tribute to the vision, drive and humility of the three chaplains, Ken Good of The Missions to Seamen, and Michel Connon and Michel Renou of the Apostleship of the Sea. I went on from Kobe to Yokohama, where I saw our magnificent new seafarers' centre, and met the Primate of the Nippon Sei Ko Kai, the Anglican Church of Japan; and from there to Jakarta in Indonesia.

During the long flight from Tokyo to Jakarta a young Japanese woman, travelling with her two small children to join her engineer husband in Indonesia, questioned me at length about the Christian faith. She had noticed my clerical collar, and finally plucked up the courage to talk. She had been receiving English lessons from a Pentecostal minister, and was worried about Heaven and Hell. I did my best to answer her questions, and I noted, not for the first time, the value of travelling in a clerical collar. People often open their hearts to a priest they think they may well never meet again.

At Jakarta the German Seamen's Mission was actively considering establishing a seafarers' centre in the port of Tanjung Priok, and had invited The Missions to Seamen and the Apostleship of the Sea to be partners in the project. My task was to make an exploratory visit on behalf of The Missions to Seamen to assess the situation. I spent four days there, and discovered just how frustrating life can be in a huge city where the local telephone network did not seem to function. I had been given the telephone numbers of a number of people I should meet, and early on the first morning I failed to get through by telephone to any of them. Hot, perspiring freely in the humidity, and thoroughly depressed, I went to the Swissair office to reconfirm my onward flight. The office was not busy, and I poured out my frustration to the manager. He gave me excellent advice. 'Hire a taxi for the whole morning,' he said. 'Visit the offices of all your contacts. If they're not available, make an appointment to see them tomorrow. That's what we all do!' For the next five hours I did just that, and on the following day I met all my contacts. I met the leader of the Roman Catholic Church in Indonesia, Archbishop Leo Sekoto, and senior members of the shipping community. During the next two days I followed up my contacts, gathered the information I needed, and produced a full report. But had it not been for the sound practical advice of the Swissair manager, I might well have floundered helplessly and wasted a wonderful opportunity. It took seven years to achieve the building of the seafarers' centre, but when it was finally completed it proved its value immediately.

From Jakarta I went on to Singapore, one of the largest ports in the world, where The Missions to Seamen was operating from rented premises as a result of the Singapore Government compulsorily purchasing our centre for redevelopment. Peter Ellis, our new chaplain, had made an excellent impression in his first six months, and it was clear that the long-term future of our ministry had to be secured as soon as possible. This was not going to be easy, however, because of the increasing hostility of the Singapore Government to expatriate seamen's missions. I met the head of the National Maritime Board, the Bishop, the Committee of Management of The Missions to Seamen, and preached in the Cathedral on the Sunday morning. As I departed for Colombo, I knew that dealing with the Singapore situation must be a top priority.

I flew from Colombo to Dubai in the United Arab Emirates. I arrived thirty hours late, because Pakistan International Airlines had overbooked the flight from Colombo. Although I had twice re-confirmed my booking, and my name appeared at number 15 on the passenger manifest, I was told that the first fifteen passengers had been put off the flight to make way for a party of pilgrims travelling to Jeddah. I managed to obtain a copy of the passenger manifest, and it proved invaluable in subsequent conversations with the airline! I was learning very quickly about the dubious practices of some airlines and to cope with the frustrations of air travel.

In Dubai our chaplain, The Revd. Philip Sturdy, was also chaplain of the inter-denominational Holy Trinity church. Philip was carrying out preparatory work for the possible establishment of a seafarers' centre, and he had done his work methodically and well. Leading people in the expatriate community were keen to play their part in setting up and running a centre, and an historic meeting took place on the day after my arrival. In the space of an hour and three quarters we agreed that there was a real need for a seafarers' centre, set up a Steering Committee to take the project forward, and looked ahead to a meeting with the Ruler, Sheikh Rashid al Makhtoum, two days later.

The meeting with the Ruler was fascinating and eventful. There were four people in our party: Bill Duff, the Ruler's Chief Financial Adviser; George Chapman, Chairman of Dubai Port Services; Philip Sturdy; and myself. We waited for a long time outside the Ruler's reception room, and when we had been received we explained what we had in mind. We showed him photographs of some of the best seafarers' centres in the world, such as The Mariners' Club in Hong Kong and the De Beer International Seamen's Centre in Rotterdam. He was keenly interested, and said that he would like to have a seafarers' centre in Dubai. I explained that The Missions to Seamen and the shipping companies could not finance the whole project, but the Ruler brushed aside all talk of money. He called in one of his land advisers, and then through the interpreter told us that he would make available to us a building right outside the Dock Gate. The building was the club premises of the Dubai Petroleum Company, which was about to move to a new site. Five months later, when the building was duly vacated, the Ruler handed over the keys to the Steering Committee.

So an important and very satisfying tour came to an end. In all the ports I visited significant decisions had been made, good relations had been established, my cautious confidence in my ability to cope with new demands and fresh challenges had been confirmed, and I knew that I could cope with the travel. I realised that I was taking over an organisation in good heart and in good shape. I was about to be tested, however, as never before. A few days before my tour ended I received a message from Tom Kerfoot, the retiring General Secretary, asking me to make an emergency visit to Vancouver before Christmas. I was due back in England on December 9th, and would fly on to Vancouver on the 15th, staying there for a week.

The need for me to go to Vancouver was indeed urgent. Ten months previously The Revd. Joe Parker, Senior Chaplain of The Missions to Seamen in Belfast, had been appointed Senior Chaplain in Vancouver in succession to Canon Stanley Smith, who had recently retired after a long and distinguished ministry in The Missions to Seamen. Joe had met the President of the Board of The Missions to Seamen in Vancouver, Bill Baxter, in Ireland, and they had got on well together. But when Joe and his family arrived in Vancouver they found that the arrangements agreed for their housing were not in fact in place,

and there was a major row between Joe and the Board. Another storm arose
when Joe strongly disagreed with the content of an application, prepared by
the Board, for a funding grant from a charitable trust. There was yet a further
serious disagreement when Joe proposed the introduction of a souvenir shop
in the seafarers' centre, and the Board rejected his proposal. Tempers on both
sides were at boiling point, and three months after his arrival Joe submitted
his resignation to the General Secretary, copying his letter to the Bishop. His
resignation was not accepted, as it was felt that because he had been there for
so short a time the situation might well be satisfactorily resolved. The Bishop
was due to visit London later in the year, and it was agreed by all the parties
that no final decision should be made until the Bishop and the General
Secretary had met and discussed the situation face to face. When they met, the
Bishop (by now Archbishop of New Westminster) made it clear that he had
decided that he wanted Joe to stay. The General Secretary made it clear that he
considered Joe to be an excellent chaplain, and that despite his problems with
the Board, it would be right for him to stay if an acceptable modus vivendi
could be achieved. Since it would be I who would be responsible for The
Missions to Seamen side of arrangements in the future, it was agreed that I
should visit Vancouver as soon as possible to attempt to resolve the situation.
The General Committee of The Missions to Seamen authorised me to act as I
deemed best.

So just five days after arriving back from the Far East, South East Asia and
the Gulf, I was on my way again, still slightly jet-lagged. My condition was
not improved by a thirty-hour wait at Heathrow because of dense fog, and
when I finally reached Vancouver it was to discover that because of a mistake
at the check-in desk in London, my suitcase had been taken off the aircraft at
Edmonton. So for the second night running I had no change of clothes and
no pyjamas; it was not an auspicious start to my visit! I was met at the airport
by Bill Baxter, President of the Board of The Missions to Seamen, and as he
drove me to my hotel, he put me fully in the picture as he saw it. I said that I
would be available to talk to all the members of the Board individually at their
convenience, and then at a full meeting of the Board. I fell into bed that night
utterly exhausted and very conscious of the weight of responsibility on my
shoulders.

Next morning Joe Parker came round to the hotel to talk to me. It was
more than eleven years since we had first met, and I had enormous respect
and admiration for him both as a chaplain and as a personal friend. Two years
previously his younger son Stephen had been killed by an IRA bomb in
Belfast while trying to warn others of the danger, and Joe, his wife Dorothy,
and Roger and Karen, their other children, were devastated. In their grief and
anguish, and in a heartfelt desire to help bring about an end to the continuing
violence, they set up an organisation called 'Witness for Peace'. The Missions

to Seamen had granted him eighteen months compassionate leave to pursue this, and at the end of that time had offered him the appointment in Vancouver. It was good to see him again, and I listened for a long time to his account of events.

For the next thirty-six hours I met the members of the Board individually, held discussions with some of them in small groups, lunched with a number of them together, and then had long discussions first with the Archbishop and then with Joe and the Archbishop together. The Archbishop told me of his personal agonising over the problems, and that it was his considered view that Joe should stay. He accepted that many members of the Board would resign if Joe stayed. I replied that it was also my considered view that Joe should stay. I outlined my thinking as follows:-

- The members of the Board had served together for many years with the same chaplain, and had become accustomed to a particular way of working.
- I liked the members of the Board I had met, and would be very sorry indeed if they resigned.
- There was a very serious breakdown in the relationship between Joe and the Board, and after hours of listening I doubted if the damage could be repaired.
- Joe had probably been tactless in some of his dealings with the Board, but he had done nothing to warrant removing him from office.
- In the major disputes between Joe and the Board Joe had not been shown to be in the wrong, although his handling of the disagreements had been open to criticism.

I said to the Archbishop that I was quite prepared to say all this to the Board, and that I would really appreciate his support when necessary. He said that he would give it.

As the time of the Board meeting approached, as a matter of courtesy I told Bill Baxter, the President, of my decision. I wanted to give him time to assimilate it. I also told him that I hoped that the members of the Board would feel able to make a fresh start with Joe. When the meeting began Bill asked me to speak first. I did so for no more than five minutes, giving them my decision as tactfully as possible, and appealing to them to make a fresh start. My short address was greeted by a prolonged silence. I then turned to the Archbishop, and said: 'Your Grace, no chaplain can continue in office without the backing of his bishop. Would you give us your view, please?' The Archbishop looked Joe full in the face. 'I would like Joe to stay. I want you to stay, Joe.' There were gasps of astonishment and dismay around the table, and Bill Baxter adjourned the meeting for fifteen minutes.

When we reconvened the President offered the Archbishop and myself the opportunity to add to what we had already said, and then went round the table asking those present for their responses. Most, but not all, resigned. One who did not was a Master Mariner, who said: 'My loyalty is to The Missions to Seamen and to the chaplain, and I'm proud to stay.' As the Board members left one said to me: 'This may be your first major decision as General Secretary. It will certainly prove to be your biggest mistake.' Another, a lady, was even less complimentary! The Archbishop, the Archdeacon, Joe and I retired to the Archbishop's office, where the Archbishop said: 'Well, the walls came tumbling down. But they were going to tumble anyway.'

Before I flew back to London I had long talks with Joe about every aspect of what had happened. He assured me that he would press on with his ministry there, and that I need not worry about him. As I flew home I felt that I had been through a wringer!

## The Year in Retrospect

As I looked back over my year as Deputy General Secretary I was grateful for the opportunity it had afforded me of establishing myself in the office, familiarising myself with the routine, absorbing the atmosphere, becoming acquainted with my colleagues, assimilating facts and impressions about the stations around the world, and making my first overseas visits – and all without bearing the ultimate responsibility for it. When I flew to Vancouver in mid-December I was well and truly conscious of the fact that 'the buck ended here with me.'

I had had the invaluable experience of acting as Personnel Secretary for nearly six months. I had visited port chaplains and regional staff in the United Kingdom. I had been confirmed in my appointment as General Secretary Designate. I had enjoyed my introduction to the International Christian Maritime Association. I had been the 'midwife' who delivered the first interconfessional collaboration partnership in South America. I had met Bishops and Archbishops, political leaders and Government ministers, seafarers, key people in the maritime world, and most recently the Ruler of Dubai. It was exciting, challenging, and demanding.

At the end of the year I could see how important my visit to Vancouver had been. It was a defining moment for me. I could have taken the easy route, and backed the Board of Management. But in my innermost being I was convinced that Joe Parker had to stay. I had to back my judgement, realising that a number of people would very properly be monitoring events in Vancouver to determine whether or not I had made the right decision. I just had to live with the questions and get on with the job. In the event it worked out wonderfully well. Joe served there for nearly twenty years, and became a highly respected and influential figure on the waterfront. Some years later I received a letter from the Vice Chairman of the Board at the time of the crisis;

he did not resign then, and he told me that my action had been right at the time and vindicated by subsequent events.

I was now as ready as I would ever be to assume the role of General Secretary.

CHAPTER ELEVEN

# London 1975-1990:
# General Secretary 1976-1990
# First Time Round 1976-1978

## My Inheritance

I TOOK UP MY DUTIES as General Secretary of The Missions to Seamen on January 1st 1976. I had served with the Society for twelve and a half years and in five ports. I had visited more than 10,000 ships, been a chaplain in the Royal Australian Naval Reserve, travelled from Australia to England on a container ship and worked at Headquarters for a year. I was aware of the magnitude of the task I was facing, but believed that by the grace of God I could cope.

I inherited a Society in good shape and in good heart. We had 85 seafarers' centres in ports all over the world. We had full-time chaplains and/or lay readers in most of them, and honorary chaplains or lay representatives in some 200 other ports. New work was under consideration or actually being undertaken in Dubai, Pusan, Bangkok and Jakarta. All our operations were being carefully monitored to ensure their continuing effectiveness and viability. A start had been made towards devolving responsibility for the Society's ministry to the Anglican Church locally with the appointment of the Bishop of Natal, Phillip Russell, as Liaison Bishop for The Missions to Seamen in the Church of the Province of Southern Africa. The early ecumenical partnerships which came into being, following the setting up of the International Christian Maritime Association, were blossoming. Financially the Society was on an even keel, though heavily dependent on legacy income.

Tom Kerfoot, my predecessor, had been respected, admired and much loved. He was a wise and prudent man: kind, sensitive, shy, self-effacing, supportive of his colleagues and with a strong streak of determination. He had an encyclopaedic knowledge of the Society and a passionate concern for it. He played his cards close to his chest, however, as I discovered when he visited Western Australia a few months after our arrival there in 1971. He came for a week's visit, which was scheduled to include visits to four other stations and involve two 1000-mile air journeys, five long car journeys and numerous meetings. On arrival he found 30 letters from different parts of the world awaiting his attention. He spent many hours dealing with them all; some involved lengthy phone calls, others long letters. He worked extremely hard, never complained, and fulfilled all the engagements we had arranged for him; but he set me thinking. I wondered why he did not encourage his senior colleagues at Headquarters to make necessary decisions in his absence and thus free himself to concentrate exclusively on the places he was visiting. I thought that that was probably what I would do if ever I was in his place.

The maritime world was in a state of continuing, rapid and far-reaching change. Containerisation was well established and spreading globally. Roll on/Roll off ships were increasing in size, number and in the types of cargo they handled. Bigger tankers and bulk carriers were being built, and new berths had to be constructed to accommodate them. Passenger liner services were being discontinued, and the ships transferred to cruising. Fewer seafarers were required to man the new ships. The turnaround time of ships in port was becoming shorter and shorter, with the result that seafarers had less time for shore leave. More seafarers were being recruited from developing countries because they cost considerably less to employ than their counterparts from developed nations, and unemployment was becoming an increasing problem. Significant numbers of shipowners were falling behind in paying the wages of their crews, and the seafarers concerned were turning to our chaplains for help.

The Missions to Seamen was changing too. The dramatic changes in the shipping industry meant that many of our larger seafarers' centres had become too big for current and future needs, and rationalisation of our facilities was being undertaken in many ports. The need for chaplains to visit ships as immediately as possible after arrival became even more imperative. At Headquarters a new Chairman of the General Committee (the Society's executive committee), Admiral Sir Andrew Lewis, had just been elected. He had recently retired from the Royal Navy as Second Sea Lord, and he had definite ideas as to how The Missions to Seamen should be run. Within the Anglican Communion, the missionary societies were placing a far greater emphasis on partnership with indigenous Churches, and The Missions to Seamen had already taken its first steps in this direction with the appointment of its first Liaison Bishop.

## Taking up the Reins
At the beginning of each new appointment, I have always closely examined and assessed the whole operation before making changes with far-reaching implications. I have worked on the principle that those who preceded me had good reasons for the way they did things, and that I would make significant changes in the early months only as and when a better or more appropriate way of working became apparent. That was how I approached my work as

General Secretary. There were, however, certain matters which needed to be addressed immediately.

A few weeks before I took up my appointment, the General Committee, under its new chairman, had requested a comprehensive review of all the Society's work throughout the world. The review was to include a list of stations which might have to close if our legacy income decreased and a financial crisis occurred. It was a wise and necessary exercise, but it was a difficult one to carry out as thoroughly as I would have liked because I did not have first-hand knowledge of all our stations at that time. It took up much time during my first year in office.

Side by side with this review, I wanted, as a matter of urgency, to consult our chaplaincy staff about the impact which the rapid and far-reaching changes on the shipping scene were having on their ministry, and to encourage them to put forward positive suggestions as to how we might most effectively serve seafarers in the future. We prepared a searching questionnaire which we sent to every chaplain, ordained and lay, and we invited them to consult widely in preparing their response. It proved to be an invaluable exercise; I was delighted by the almost 100% response, which was both illuminating and encouraging.

There were two important practical matters which I wanted to settle immediately. The first concerned the weekly meeting of the Executive Secretaries, which included the General Secretary, the Assistant General Secretaries for Administration and Ministry, the Finance Secretary and the Public Relations Officer. These meetings had been starting at 4 p.m., and frequently went on till well after 6 p.m., and I and others found that a long and important meeting at the end of the day did not receive the attention it required. After informal consultations, we fixed the starting time for 3 p.m. and the finishing time no later than 4:15 pm. It concentrated our minds marvellously, and the practice remained unchanged throughout my 14 years in office.

The second concerned my overseas tours. I was determined to focus my whole attention on each place I visited while I was actually there, and not deal with extraneous matters. I had full confidence in my colleagues, and before I went on my first tour I asked them not to contact me except in a dire emergency. I also wanted the chaplains to know that I had full confidence in my colleagues; they were on top of their jobs and well able to accept responsibility for their actions. I told them that on my return I would back them publicly, and we would sort out any problems privately. They accepted this new responsibility enthusiastically; they were pleased to be trusted. Throughout my years in office, I was contacted in emergencies while on tour just three times.

Another matter which was concerning me was the title 'Headquarters' of the Society. I felt that 'Headquarters' was now an inappropriate way of portraying our role within the Society. In South Africa, full responsibility for the administration and operation of our ministry had already been transferred to a Liaison Bishop and a Provincial Council, and it was working out well. The function of the office in London had ceased to be that of a directing agency and become more of an enabling and liaison body. It seemed clear that this was the way ahead. We would work towards appointing Liaison Bishops and establishing Provincial or National Councils throughout the world, and recognise and affirm the authority and jurisdiction of the Anglican Church locally over the Society's operations. This concept had the wholehearted support of the Executive Secretaries and the Society's major committees, and was enthusiastically received when I outlined the proposal at a United Kingdom staff conference late in 1976. 'Headquarters' would become 'Central Office', and its role would change gradually as more and more Provinces of the Anglican Communion assumed responsibility for our work.

At the beginning of my time as General Secretary I was acutely aware of the large number of our stations of which I had no first-hand knowledge. I therefore embarked on a prolific correspondence during my first year in order to establish contact with as many people involved in our work as possible. For months I dictated up to 100 letters a week, and I planned to visit every station within three years. During those visits I intended to follow up the questionnaire individually and at regional conferences.

In the Society's Annual Report for 1976, written at the end of my first year in office, I summarised my priorities as follows:-

'I came to see that whatever else I did or did not do, I should:-

- get to know at first hand our chaplains, lay staff, voluntary helpers and committee members around the world, and the ports and centres where they exercise their ministry, and do my best to establish a bond of mutual trust and understanding with them,
- maintain and deepen the family feeling among those serving in the Society, and be the linkman between the members of the family,
- keep in touch with seafarers and the changing pattern of the shipping world,
- maintain and extend the Society's links with those who make or influence decisions in the shipping world,
- maintain, widen and deepen the Society's links with the Anglican Church around the world and with other Churches with whom we currently work or might in the future,
- with the Society's Council, General Committee and other committees, ensure that the Society's financial resources are utilised to the greatest advantage,

and

• be available to meet people and speak publicly about the Society's work.'

## At the Office

During my first eight months as General Secretary I spent much of my time in the office at St. Michael Paternoster Royal. I did not travel outside Europe and concentrated on building up a comprehensive picture of my colleagues and of our ways of working. I wanted to get to know the chairpersons and the members of our various committees, make contact with the shipping community in the City of London and around the country, assess the efficiency of our various departments and build up a picture of the Society as a whole.

My senior colleagues proved to be real towers of strength to me in their very different ways.

Jimmy Wilson-Hughes, the Assistant General Secretary with responsibility for Ministry, was a generous-hearted, outspoken bachelor. Formerly Senior Chaplain of The Missions to Seamen in Durban, in his early sixties and with a wealth of experience behind him, Jimmy was a wise counsellor and excellent administrator. He was also a very colourful character. An unashamed smoker, he was rarely without a cigarette in the corner of his mouth; he was the only person I have ever known who could carry on a telephone conversation, cough, and keep on talking – all without removing the cigarette from his mouth!

He could also be very forceful. When a chaplain of mature years was proving difficult over a new appointment, and had already rejected several good offers, Jimmy summoned him to the office. I overheard the first words of the interview. 'John,' said Jimmy,' there are times when the Holy Spirit speaks to you directly through the words of another person: this is one of those times!' I retreated hastily out of earshot, but it was not long before Jimmy appeared to tell me that the chaplain had decided to resign. On another occasion Jimmy had sent for a lay member of staff with the intention of rebuking him for some sins of commission and omission. The man's wife decided to accompany him, 'to see fair play' as she put it. Jimmy would have none of it. 'Just wait outside, luv,' he said cheerfully; 'I won't keep him long!' He didn't. A rocket was duly delivered, the relationship was swiftly restored, and husband and wife went home relieved and satisfied. I came to have a very high regard for Jimmy.

The Assistant General Secretary with responsibility for Administration, Neville Barwick, was very different but equally dependable. Educated at Shrewsbury and Cambridge, he had worked with the Colonial Service as a District Officer in Nigeria for 11 years, and he told some marvellous tales about his time there. He had joined The Missions to Seamen in 1967 as the first Regional Director for the Midlands; this was a new appointment within the Society, and involved representing the Society in the Church and at every level in the community, and raising financial support for our work. It was a job requiring initiative, enthusiasm, personality and energy, and Neville possessed all these in abundance. Previous experience with Planned Giving, a fund-raising company, had equipped him admirably for his task, and he made a great success of the Midlands Region. He was brought on to the Head-quarters staff as Planning and Operations Secretary and was later appointed Assistant General Secretary. He was invaluable in this capacity. He spoke his mind frankly and clearly, but always in a pleasant and acceptable way. He was a man of great integrity and one of his most endearing qualities was his readiness to apologise if he got something wrong. He used to say that he was very good at apologising, because he had had so much experience of it! He had a delightful sense of humour and fun, which was never far below the surface, and he was a capable administrator.

Our Finance Secretary was Jack Freeman. He joined our staff after long and distinguished service in Local Government. He was a gentle, thoughtful man and very good at his job. He went to the heart of a problem quickly and unerringly, his advice was carefully considered, and he had the priceless ability to explain financial situations in comprehensible terms. He was a fine Christian, a convinced Anglo-Catholic, and was happily married with two sons in the ordained ministry of the Church. He was a trusted colleague and a loyal and true friend.

Micheal Jacob was our Public Relations Officer. Young, enthusiastic, outgoing and able, he had galvanised the Public Relations department into a lively progressive unit. He wrote a small book about the Society, and it was good to have his cheerful presence among us. He was clearly destined to progress to bigger jobs, however, and it was a disappointment, but not a surprise, when late in 1976 he moved on. In his place we appointed his new assistant, Gillian Ennis. She too was young, able, determined, charming and enthusiastic. She came from a seafaring background (her father was a Captain in the Royal Navy, and later Deputy Master of Trinity House), and she has served the Society now for 28 years. She has done an outstanding job. She writes with flair and integrity. She thinks clearly, and speaks wisely. She has the great ability to get people to produce what she needs for her publications, and she is very highly respected and loved throughout the Society. I valued her contribution to the Society's life and work and I was always afraid that she would move on to a bigger job.

My Personal Assistant for the first six years of my service as General Secretary was Bobbie Newman. Bobbie and her twin sister Peggy had served the Society throughout their working lives, and they both had a comprehensive knowledge of its personnel and workings. Bobbie was quiet, but had a wonderful sense of humour. She was a superb typist, working at phenomenal speed and with scarcely an error. She guided me gently and unerringly through many potential and actual minefields, and I rapidly learned that I could trust her judgment implicitly. When she retired at the end of 1981 she was a great loss to the whole Society; she was much loved by everybody.

Those first few months in office brought a number of beginnings for me. By virtue of my office, I was a member of a number of important maritime committees. One of these was the Merchant Navy Welfare Board, which at that time was a Government-supported body charged with co-ordinating welfare work among seafarers in the United Kingdom. It had a small, highly efficient secretariat, and ran excellent Merchant Navy Hotels in London and in a number of other ports in the United Kingdom. It also financed the running costs of a number of Asian seafarers' centres around the coast and supplied them with Asian films. The Board received an annual grant from the Government, exactly equal to the National Insurance contributions made by British shipowners in respect of their Asian crews. In addition to its own work, the Board made substantial grants annually to specific approved projects being undertaken by recognised marine charities, and The Missions to Seamen benefited greatly from these. Alas, all good things come to an end, and with the pattern of shipping changing in the 1980's, the Government discontinued the grant.

Another was the Marine Society. This splendid charity, which was established in the mid-eighteenth century, promotes the spiritual, moral and physical welfare of seafarers, gives financial support to young people training for life at sea, and runs a superb library service for ships at sea. I found my involvement in both these bodies illuminating, stimulating and satisfying. Their major committees included influential members of the shipping community, and it was very helpful to have ready access to people who made important decisions affecting the lives of seafarers.

I made visits to the offices of The National Union of Seamen, The Merchant Navy and Airline Officers Association and The International Transport Workers Federation. At each office I was warmly welcomed. I learned more about their activities. I was made aware of the great respect and affection all of them had for The Missions to Seamen. I asked about ways in which we could assist each other, and I made firm and lasting friendships. I was invited to lunch by the Director of the General Council of British Shipping, Jim Rice-Oxley, who was also Director of The International Shipping Federation; and I called on a number of shipowners in the United Kingdom. Wherever I went the welcome was cordial and the work of The Missions to Seamen praised.

As I became established as General Secretary, a clearer picture of the extent of my responsibilities emerged. Within the Diocese of London, my appointment included the title of Chaplain of St. Michael Paternoster Royal: I was responsible for the church. I was fully aware that there were thirty-nine active Church of England churches within the square mile of the City of London, and also that they covered a wide range of outreach and specialist ministry; for instance, our near neighbour at St. Stephen Wallbrook, Prebendary Chad Varah, had started the Samaritan movement at his church. Our responsibility at St. Michael Paternoster Royal, in addition to administering the worldwide work of The Missions to Seamen, was to keep the church open to the public throughout office hours, and we did that faithfully. But we did much more than that. We said Morning Prayer in the church every day, celebrated Holy Communion on Saints Days and regularly once a week at lunchtime, arranged special services on maritime occasions and kept the church immaculate. It was the place where every day we brought our concerns before the Crucified and Risen Lord, and I felt greatly privileged to be entrusted with such a beautiful and historic place of worship.

Across the road from St. Michael Paternoster Royal was the Innholders Hall. The Worshipful Company of Innholders was one of the most venerable of the hundred or so Livery Companies of the City, and their annual service was held in our church. Some individual members of the Company looked on it as 'their church', and baptisms, weddings, funerals and memorial services were regular occurrences. Tom Kerfoot, my predecessor as General Secretary, was their chaplain, and when he died I was invited to succeed him. I gradually got to know the individual members, and found myself dealing from time to time with a variety of personal situations. One involved ministering to a Jewish man suffering from a terminal illness and who wanted to convert to Christianity. I had a number of profound and very moving discussions with him, and we both rejoiced when I baptized him and gave him Holy Communion shortly before he died. In 1978 I became chaplain to the Worshipful Company of Carmen, and in 1981 also to The Worshipful Company of Farriers. I enjoyed the friendship and fellowship of the Liverymen and their families, and I felt that in this way I was making a small contribution to the life of the City.

Weekends at home became very precious. Saturday was my day off, and on Sundays I assisted Michael Bowles, Rector of St. John's, Stanmore, whenever I was not preaching elsewhere on behalf of The Missions to Seamen. I spent an average of 20 Sundays a year at home, and I revelled in our happy family life. We did many things together, such as going to football matches, playing games in our large garden, visiting grandparents and just being together. Sally and the children provided a wonderful calming influence in my sometimes stressful life.

And stresses there were! I was very conscious of my relative youth and inexperience, and for several years I felt that I had to prove myself to the world in general. Part of me knew that I should do my best and leave the worrying to God, and part of me was anxious about how the world might view my performance. I realised that this imbalance was unhealthy, but it took a long time before I rid myself of it entirely. Early on one very senior chaplain serving overseas challenged my authority, and I spent many hours figuring out how to respond to him. Eventually I spent 16 hours putting together a letter which dealt fully and courteously with all the points he had raised, and firmly asserted the role and authority of the General Secretary. He never replied to my letter and no reference was ever made to it whenever we met afterwards. We established a good working relationship, although I never really came to like him. There were stresses when chaplains experienced personal crises or when they were experiencing difficulties with their committees of management. I did my best to be available to deal with problems, and they caused me concern. I was deeply grateful for the way the congregation at St. John's, Stanmore, took our whole family to their hearts and loved us unconditionally.

My working day seldom followed the same pattern on successive days. I made regular visits to ports all over the United Kingdom and Europe. I spent time in their offices with our six Regional Directors in England and the National Directors in Scotland, Wales and Ireland. I welcomed and entertained visitors from the United Kingdom and overseas, including chaplains and lay staff, committee members, voluntary workers, Church leaders and seafarers. I made it my policy to see personally and as soon as possible any staff member who sought an interview. In 1976, my first year in office, we held a special residential conference in order to undertake a thorough review of our work and to look ahead to the future. I could not have accomplished so much without the wholehearted support of our office staff, and I was deeply indebted to them all.

## United Kingdom Ports

While I was settling into so many new experiences, a great deal was happening in ports around the United Kingdom. Some of the large, long-established ports, like London, Liverpool, Hull, Southampton and Glasgow, were experiencing significant loss of trade and income as a direct result of the revolutionary changes in the shipping industry. The changing pattern of shipping had directly affected the work of The Missions to Seamen, and the centres at Victoria Dock Road and Tilbury in the Port of London had been sold, with the chaplains being invited to work in partnership with the Roman Catholic Apostleship of the Sea at Anchor House in Barking and at the Stella Maris Club in Tilbury. In Liverpool, Hull, Southampton and Glasgow a close watch on developments was being kept and changes were being considered. On the east coast of England, Felixstowe and Immingham were expanding rapidly, and a large new dock was being planned at Avonmouth. In all three ports The Missions to Seamen was becoming involved in ecumenical partnerships.

At Par in Cornwall, at the request of the English China Clay Company, The Missions to Seamen took over the management of the seafarers' centre from the British Sailors' Society, with whom we jointly owned the building and who wanted to withdraw as the centre seemed to be in decline. We met representatives of the English China Clay Company, on whose land the centre was situated, and discussed with them the usage of the port and how we could make the centre financially self-sufficient. We agreed that the English China Clay Company should raise a voluntary 'welfare levy' from every ship visiting the port, and this proved to be a spectacular success. It was not long before the centre was operating at a modest surplus.

### Overseas

After spending my first eight months in office establishing myself in my new responsibilities, I made two major overseas tours before the end of 1976. In September I visited most of our African stations, and in November I visited Dubai, Calcutta, Hong Kong, Jakarta and Western Australia.

At the beginning of September I flew to Lagos via Rome. I left London early in the morning, and at lunchtime I was at the Vatican. I had been invited to meet Archbishop Emmanuel Clarizio, Head of the Pontifical Commission for Migrants and People on the Move, the department monitoring the work of The Apostleship of the Sea, and we enjoyed a very positive and enjoyable meeting for two hours over lunch. The Archbishop was much older than I, and infinitely more experienced in the life and ways of the Church, but he treated me with great kindness, courtesy and dignity, and he made me feel that he valued my visit. I was enthusiastic about the interconfessional collaboration that was already taking place, and I raised the question of possible further joint operations in a number of ports. He encouraged me to put forward firm proposals when I had fully investigated the possibilities, and promised that these would be carefully considered. I came away from our meeting greatly encouraged. I now knew who I was dealing with, and a bond of trust had been established. Our meeting was followed by a guided tour of St. Peter's, St. Paul's Cathedral and the Coliseum before I was whisked back to the airport for my flight to Lagos. It was an unforgettable visit.

I had never previously visited Africa, and our Lagos station was experiencing a period of intense frustration. A new seafarers' centre, to be operated in partnership with the Apostleship of the Sea, had been under construction for two years but was still some way from completion. The reason for the delay was the chronic congestion in the port, through which cement for the extensive building work currently taking place all over Lagos was being imported. There was a huge fleet of ships waiting outside the harbour for a berth to become available for discharging their cargo; at one time there were 400 ships there, and some waited a whole year for a berth. Some of the cranes in the port had broken down, and replacement parts were on the ships waiting outside. Ashore, the supply of raw materials for building could not keep up with demand, and the result was utter frustration. The Finance Committee of The Missions to Seamen in London was seriously concerned about the position, particularly since inflation was spiralling upwards in Nigeria, and I wrote a comprehensive report of my visit to set out the situation.

On the Sunday of my visit to Lagos I preached at an Anglican Church in Apapa. It was an unusual and interesting experience for me. The church was simple in design and furnishing, with open sides and a corrugated iron roof. It was filled to capacity by seven hundred people, of whom two hundred and fifty received Holy Communion. My sermon lasted seventeen minutes, and the service two and a quarter hours! The notices occupied a full twenty minutes, and provoked frequent outbursts of laughter. There were four collections! A sudden tropical downpour hammering on the corrugated iron roof drowned all other sounds for several minutes. It was a happy, lively service, with a real sense of joyful celebration, and at the end there was yet another surprise in store for me. The churchwardens insisted that they should pay for me preaching, despite my protestations. The payment was several dozen eggs and two live chickens; and as we drove away, with the friendly farewells of our hosts ringing in our ears, the noisy chickens were a constant and odorous reminder of our visit!

After a brief visit to Port Harcourt, I flew on from Lagos to Nairobi and Dar es Salaam, experiencing all manner of frustrations over airline reservations and obtaining local currency. I found Dar es Salaam intimidating, although I could not be sure that I was not over-reacting. My room at the hotel where I stayed was crudely searched in my absence, and I discovered no fewer than three people listening outside my door as I dictated a report into my pocket dictaphone. Currency regulations were strictly enforced and the country was plainly in an economic crisis. Newspaper reports of the death of Mao Tse Tung eulogised the Chinese leader, and there was an extravagant article praising 'Allende; a revolutionary hero' on the fourth anniversary of the Chilean leader's death.

I was most impressed by our magnificent seafarers' centres both in Dar es Salaam and Mombasa, where I flew on to after my visit to Dar. Both had excellent facilities, including a football pitch, swimming pool, indoor recreational amenities, a bar and restaurant, a shop, and a simple dignified chapel. They were well maintained, well used, and the expatriate chaplains were not harassed by the authorities.

From Mombasa I flew on to South Africa, where I visited our centres in Durban, East London, Port Elizabeth, Cape Town and Walvis Bay, and learned about the early construction work at Richards Bay, which was destined soon to become one of the great ports of the world. It was good to meet chaplains who up till then had been just names to me, and I spent valuable time with Bishop Bruce Evans of Port Elizabeth, the new Liaison Bishop for The Missions to Seamen in the Church of the Province of Southern Africa. At the end of my visit, I spent a day and a half at the South African Chaplains' Conference, which provided a great opportunity for us all to get to know each other better.

My visit to South Africa took place at a time of considerable racial tension there. I arrived in Johannesburg as a mass stay-away-from-work began. For three days no more than 10% of the black labour force went to work, and there were demonstrations in schools and townships. In Cape Province the stay-away lasted a full week: schools rioted, cars were stoned from motorway bridges, and demonstrations were widespread and violent. Reports of police opening fire on demonstrators and schoolchildren were commonplace: The *Cape Times* published a list of 69 people killed in the disturbances, many of them teenage boys and girls described as having 'died from gunshot wounds.' Tension was palpable everywhere, and the white population was extremely apprehensive. A visit from Dr. Henry Kissinger was imminent, and he was widely reported as having greeted Mr. Vorster, the South African leader, with the words: 'The history books tell me that you don't have much time left.'

This was my first visit to South Africa and I resolved to listen attentively, observe patiently and weigh carefully all I saw and heard, and not venture any opinions. Violence was widespread, everybody was talking about the political crisis, and I heard a wide range of opinions expressed. When the case of a black man flogged for robbing a white woman was discussed, a retired white businessman commented: 'Well, 90% of them are savages at heart.' But this was in sharp contrast to the liberal and understanding views of many of the white people I met. I was particularly impressed by the welcome given by a white Rotary Club in Durban to a young black journalist who had been invited to address them on the current racial problems. He was articulate and outspoken. He condemned privilege as enjoyed by white South Africans, and he castigated them for their acceptance of the status quo. But he was passionately committed to peaceful integration, and this shone through all he said. The thunderous applause which greeted the end of his speech told its own story.

I was privileged to visit a vibrant Coloured church in Port Elizabeth with Bishop Evans, and to visit some homes in the parish. I visited a Bantu settlement, and was appalled both by the poverty within a mile of a wealthy white residential area and also by a full-scale fist fight between a teenage girl and a teenage boy. During my two-week visit I had many opportunities to meet and spend time with people of all the different communities, and I wrote in my report that 'throughout my visit I detected tension among Black and White and Coloured communities, yet my overall impression is that there is still time for a settlement of the racial issue.' Over the following 13 years I witnessed the changes taking place in South African society, noted the impact of economic sanctions, and was greatly relieved and cheered by the way the evil policy of apartheid was finally swept away. On that first tour I learned a great deal.

Five weeks later, on November 1st 1976, I was on my way again, this time to Dubai, India, Hong Kong, Jakarta and Western Australia. There were particular and pressing reasons for each of these visits.

In Dubai great progress had been made since my previous visit in December 1975 towards the establishment of the proposed seafarers' centre. The Ruler had handed over the promised building in May 1976. The Steering Committee had made giant steps towards opening the building. Captain Henry Severs, a recently retired Master with the British India Company and latterly with P & O, had arrived to co-ordinate the construction and fund-raising work; and a fund-raising lunch in London hosted by the Chairman of P & O, Lord Inchcape, had raised the magnificent sum of £25,000 towards the necessary conversion work on the building. During a busy two days, I had a good meeting with the members of the Steering Committee in which we reviewed progress, discussed the financial position, amended the Statement of Intent formulated the previous year, and set up a Committee of Management for the new centre. In my report of the visit I wrote that 'my lasting memories will be of the faithfulness and humility of Philip Sturdy as a priest, of the enthusiasm and drive of Henry Severs, of the great goodwill of the shipping community in Dubai towards The Missions to Seamen, and of the eager anticipation for the work of the new centre: and I was thankful that I had been able to reconcile some of the contentious points and people!' It was never going to be sweetness and light all the way!

From Dubai I flew on to Calcutta. There the Honorary Chaplain of The Missions to Seamen was a young Indian priest, The Revd. Father Victor Yardi of the Brotherhood of the Epiphany. He had plans to re-open St. Nicholas church, the former base of The Missions to Seamen in Calcutta. We had received visits in London from clergy from Calcutta encouraging us to concentrate more resources on the ministry to seafarers there, so as Calcutta lay on my route from Dubai to Hong Kong, where I was due to attend the third biennial conference of the South East Asia Chaplains, I decided to pay a brief visit.

During my stay I was the guest of the Brotherhood of the Epiphany, or the Oxford Mission as it is popularly known, and it was the beginning of a happy association for me which has so far lasted for twenty-seven years and which I hope will continue for as long as I live. The Brotherhood came into being in 1880, when the Bishop of Calcutta visited the University of Oxford and appealed for young celibate priests and laymen to go out to Bengal and live, preach and teach the Gospel there. A number responded, and for more than one hundred years there were priests from the United Kingdom serving there in happy partnership with indigenous priests. In the 1960's changes in visa and residency legislation resulted in no further permanent residence permits being issued to expatriate clergy, and it became clear that when the current expatriate Brothers died, the nature of the Oxford Mission would change.

I was immediately impressed by the Oxford Mission. In addition to its work in Calcutta, it is also deeply involved in the life of the Church of Bangladesh at Barisal and Jobarpar. In Calcutta the Brothers' compound covers more than 15 acres and includes a chapel, residential accommodation for the Brothers, a primary school for 750 children, a boys' hostel, an industrial school, Ear Nose and Throat and Eye clinics, a parish church, administrative offices, a superb cricket field, residential quarters for senior staff members, a library, retreat accommodation and two large deep ponds. On the opposite side of the main road outside the compound are the premises of the Sisterhood of the Epiphany, which was established at the beginning of the 20th century. Their compound covers $6^1/2$ acres, and includes a primary school for 130 children, an Old People's Home, the Sisters' quarters and a hostel for teenage girls. Further reference to the Oxford Mission is made later in the book.

My two days in Calcutta flew by, with visits to the new port of Haldia, forty miles downstream from Calcutta; to Cardinal Picachy, the Roman Catholic Archbishop of Calcutta; to the Chairman of the Calcutta docks; to St. Nicholas Church; and to Bishop Amritanand, Bishop of Calcutta in the Church of North India. It was clear to me that Father Victor was doing a good job as Port Chaplain and that we should support him.

Hong Kong was my next port of call. The third biennial South East Asia Chaplains Conference was being held there, and I particularly wanted to be present in order to involve our chaplains in formulating the Society's policy for the future. It was the third regional conference I had attended in seven weeks. The South East Asia conference included chaplains from the Apostleship of the Sea, The Missions to Seamen, the German Seamen's Mission and the Dutch Seamen's Mission. Monsignor Francis Frayne, from the Pontifical Commission for Migrants and People on the Move, was present throughout. He was an inspiration to us all. He brought dignity, enthusiasm for interconfessional collaboration, experience, humility and a rich sense of humour to the conference. He was positive and realistic about what could be achieved together immediately and what would take longer. We all worshipped together every day, although it was heartbreaking not to be able to receive the sacrament of Holy Communion together.

A striking feature of this conference was the extremely high calibre of all the chaplains from the various churches. They were outstanding, and I recalled the words of the Bishop of Selby, Morris Maddocks, a few weeks previously at our United Kingdom Conference, when he had said: 'If diocesan bishops had been asked to give us (i.e. The Missions to Seamen) their best clergy, we could not have found a finer set of men.' Another was the quality of the fellowship; our lives and our faith were enriched by our praying, planning and working together, and there was a universal longing for the unity which our Lord Jesus Christ desires for His Church.

I went on to Singapore and Jakarta to take forward our planning for the future ministry in these ports. In Singapore the National Maritime Board was proving distinctly unhelpful to the Christian organisations ministering to seafarers. They were not only considering phasing out the annual grants from the Port Welfare Fund (money levied on all ships in the harbour loading or discharging cargo on Sundays), but also wanted us all to work from their own Mariners' Hotel. This building, which the Christian organisations considered to be unsuitable for its purpose, was to be the major facility for all seafarers visiting the port. They hoped that the presence and ministry of the chaplains would result in increased attendance of seafarers. Far more attractive to us was the proposal of the Roman Catholic Apostleship of the Sea to renovate and refurbish its former seafarers' centre and invite the other Societies to be guests in the building, and we had a high-level meeting in Singapore between the Societies to discuss this. It was agreed that the Apostleship of the Sea would make definite plans to implement this.

In Jakarta progress had been made towards the establishment of an ecumenical seafarers' centre. A site had been obtained, and it had been agreed that the Indonesian Council of Churches would hold the Title Deeds, since foreign organisations could not own land in Indonesia. A meeting of representatives of the German Seamen's Mission, the Indonesian Council of Churches, the Apostleship of the Sea, The Missions to Seamen and the Embassy of the Federal German Government to formulate a draft agreement between all the parties involved had been arranged, and I was excited by the prospects. I was accompanied to Jakarta and Singapore by the South East Asia Secretary of The Missions to Seamen, The Revd. Ted Matchett, Senior Chaplain in Hong Kong. Ted was a wonderful companion: balanced, wise, supportive and clear-thinking. He was also a first-class chaplain. An Ulsterman in his early sixties, he had spent most of his ministry as a chaplain with The Missions to Seamen in Belfast, Wellington (New Zealand) and

Hong Kong. He was highly respected and greatly loved everywhere he had served, and his eirenic temperament calmed me down on a number of occasions.

My last visit on this important tour was to Western Australia, and I looked forward to it eagerly. I had loved our years there, and when the aircraft landed at Perth I felt as if I was coming home. The purpose of the visit was to monitor progress in our newly-established chaplaincy in the important and expanding iron ore ports of Dampier and Port Walcott; to visit the recently re-built centre at Port Hedland, which had been severely damaged by a cyclone; and to talk to Bishop Witt, in whose diocese of North West Australia all this work lay.

A major concern at that stage was how a new centre at Dampier, a company town and port built by Hamersley Iron, could be paid for. The need was obvious but the cost was high. In North West Australia building materials were very expensive because they had to be transported by sea, and I wrote in my report that I did not see how the necessary finance could be raised unless Hamersley Iron made a really substantial contribution and that I believed a preliminary enquiry to them was a top priority. The Company had already demonstrated its support for the project by making available a magnificent site for the building, and I was cautiously optimistic that we might succeed.

There was still much preparatory work to be undertaken before a firm decision to proceed with building could be made, and when I visited Australia again in 1977, I met Don Stewart, Managing Director, and Brian Coates, the Shipping Manager, of Hamersley Iron at the company's headquarters in Melbourne. I was given a most cordial welcome, and much practical help was promised and given. On his next visit to Japan, Brian Coates spoke to all the leading Japanese shipowners using the port of Dampier and persuaded them to contribute nearly all of the finance needed to build the seafarers' centre. His fund-raising plan revealed a mastery of Japanese business psychology, and I treasure the telex message he sent me from Japan; it included the sentence: 'Please advise the exact sum required so that I can judge my run to the finishing line'! I envied him his powers of persuasion!

★   ★   ★

By the end of 1976 a pattern and routine for my tours and port visits was emerging. On tour I rose very early, washed and shaved, read Morning Prayer and spent time alone with God, and wrote up my reports before breakfast. In this way I could keep the whole day free to concentrate on the place where I was. I spent as much time as possible in informal discussions with chaplains and lay staff, visited the docks, went on board ships if time permitted, and kept abreast of developments in the shipping world. I also made a top priority of keeping in touch with our family. I wrote an air letter to Sally two or three times a week, and sent picture postcards with a full message to each of our children at least twice a week. For her part, Sally, armed with a detailed itinerary of my tour, wrote airletters to me at most of the ports I visited. I looked forward to these and to news of the family as I arrived at each port. We agreed that we would not phone each other while I was on tour unless there was a real emergency.

★　　★　　★

In 1977 I made four overseas tours: to Hamburg and Rotterdam, to the Arabian Gulf, to South America, and to Australia. In all I spent ninety-one days overseas. There were many highlights of these tours, too many to record in detail, but some cannot be omitted.

The tour of the Arabian Gulf began at the recently opened Dubai International Seafarers' Centre. I felt great satisfaction as I looked at the magnificent, but still incomplete, facilities. This was a project in which I had had a key role and I was thrilled to see it becoming a reality. I looked forward eagerly to the building of the swimming pool and the installation of the remaining new amenities. Exploratory visits to Kuwait, Khorramshar and Bandar Shahpour in Iran, made at the request of shipping companies and partner organisations, were fascinating but did not lead on to further action for political reasons, notably the return of Ayatollah Khomeini to Iran.

★　　★　　★

A feature of the South American tour was my first visit to Valparaiso in Chile, where I stayed with Gordon and Lee Cave and their three children. Gordon was Secretary of the Board of Directors of the Valparaiso Seamen's Institute and ran the P and I (Protection and Indemnity) Club in Valparaiso. This was my first close contact with P and I Clubs, one of whose functions is to apportion responsibility in shipping mishaps. During my visit Gordon was dealing with a particularly complex accident involving a tanker carrying several different liquid cargoes, and I was amazed by the extensiveness and intricate detail of his investigation. He worked around the clock, snatching a few hours sleep whenever possible. On two successive days the phone rang at 4 a.m., with a shipowner from Norway, where it was much later in the day, requesting the latest information. I have vivid memories of the conversation on the second morning, when Gordon's patience temporarily lapsed. He reminded the owner of the time of day in Valparaiso and suggested he should ring back later; but he did not express himself quite so politely!

Another important feature was a concerted effort at the highest diplomatic level to resolve the question of the issuing of a dock pass to our lay chaplain in the port of Santos. It involved the Foreign Office in London, the honorary

British Consul in Santos, the British Consul General in Brazil and Her Britannic Majesty's Ambassador to Brazil, and culminated in my meeting the Ambassador in Saõ Paulo. Eventually the situation was resolved and a dock pass was granted.

As I flew out of Chile for Brazil, I had an unforgettable flight over the Andes. The sky was completely cloudless, and as we flew over the mountains, every detail of the crevasses, glaciers, snow-covered peaks and expanses of rich brown rock was brilliantly highlighted in the bright sunlight. The sun's rays heightened the colours of the rocks and cast deep shadows over the valleys, and the effect was quite breath-taking.

★    ★    ★

My last, and longest, tour in 1977 incorporated visits to Colombo, Singapore, twenty ports in Australia, five in New Zealand, Suva in Fiji, Hong Kong, Kobe and Yokohama in Japan, and New York. The entire tour lasted sixty-three days. For fourteen of the ports involved it was my first visit. Memories of all these visits flooded into my mind as I re-read the reports I wrote at the time.

In Australia I had two main aims. The first was to visit each of The Missions to Seamen stations, so as to acquaint myself with their staff and gain an insight into their operations. The second was to prepare the way for the establishment of an Australian Council of The Missions to Seamen, which I felt was highly desirable.

Before my visit, the Chairman of the Society's Council in London, Viscount Leathers of Purfleet, had written to the chairperson of each of the Australian stations proposing that The Missions to Seamen in Australia should assume full responsibility for the conduct of its own affairs, while safeguarding the independence of individual stations and preserving the link through the Central Office in London with the worldwide family of The Missions to Seamen. I was under no illusion as to the size of this challenge, because I knew how much the individual stations prized their autonomy, but I had one priceless advantage in that I had so recently lived and worked in Australia and was known to most of the chaplains.

It was important both to safeguard the independence of each station and also to promote a family relationship between all the stations through the establishment of a national consultative council. This, I believed, was the way to achieve an acceptable balance. The Council would be chaired by a Bishop nominated by the Australian House of Bishops, and include ordained and lay representatives from each State. One of the ordained representatives would act as National Chaplain and Secretary of the Council.

I visited each station and explained carefully what was being proposed. Wherever I went, a cautious welcome for the plan emerged, and when I submitted a Draft Constitution to a full-day National Consultation in Sydney we were able to agree unanimously to establish the Australian Council of The Missions to Seamen along the lines proposed. One of the most important outcomes was that the Society now had its own official representative in the House of Bishops, and a clear-cut hierarchical structure to which the Roman Catholics in particular and other Church organisations could relate. It also had the effect of establishing a soundly-based Australia-wide partnership with Central Office. I was thrilled by what had happened; it opened the door to similar partnerships elsewhere.

From Australia I went on via New Zealand, where I visited our three stations and two potential stations, to Fiji and Hong Kong. In Hong Kong I attended the World Congress of The Apostleship of the Sea as an official observer. It was fascinating to watch the Congress in action. There were Roman Catholic bishops present from many parts of the world, a number of whom presented learned and lengthy papers. Much of the Congress was conducted very formally, but there were many opportunities to meet old friends and make new ones. The six observers from seamens' missions of other denominations were made to feel very welcome, and we played a full part in the group and plenary discussions. But the most poignant moment for me came when we all attended the closing Mass of the Congress. It was officially stated that none of the observers could receive the Sacrament, and when the time came for people to go forward to receive I could not stop tears flowing. I was sitting next to a Roman Catholic priest and close friend, and because I could not go forward to receive he deliberately stayed with me. I felt very aware of the sin of our divisions in the Church.

On my way back to London, after a brief visit to Japan, I stopped over in New York to visit the new Director of the Seamen's Church Institute of New York and New Jersey, The Revd. Jim Whittemore. The Seamen's Church Institute is an agency of the Episcopal Church of the U.S.A. (ECUSA), and had friendly links with The Missions to Seamen. Jim and I quickly established a deep and happy friendship which flourishes to this day. It was an important visit, because in 1978 the triennial conference of the International Christian Maritime Association was due to be held in New York.

So ended the longest tour I ever undertook for The Missions to Seamen. I was away from home for 63 days, travelled 40,000 miles, flew on 30 different aircraft, and posted 17 airletters to Sally and 18 postcards to each of our four children. Throughout the trip I had no physical ailments of any kind other than jet lag. I was loving my work.

★   ★   ★

The two major tours I undertook in 1978 completed the round of first visits to every station of The Missions to Seamen.

In April I spent ten days in Southern Africa, and visited Mozambique for the first time. Memories of that visit are printed indelibly on my mind.

Mozambique in 1978 was aggressively Communist, and that was apparent wherever I went. At the airport in Maputo Immigration procedures were tedious, pernickety and inefficient; one of the forms I had to complete required details of every item of personal possessions purchased outside Mozambique, right down to the last handkerchief and pair of socks! But on departure no reference was made to this document, and I was left wondering about its purpose.

I was met at the airport in Maputo by our Chaplain, The Revd. Christopher Mallangwa. Christopher, a Tanzanian, had been Assistant Chaplain of The Missions to Seamen in Dar es Salaam when European expatriates were expelled from Mozambique in 1976, and we were delighted when he willingly agreed to move to Maputo and accepted the combined appointment of Rector of St. Stephen and St. Lawrence Church and Chaplain of The Missions to Seamen. No problems were experienced in obtaining residence and work permits for him, and he was doing an excellent job. He had endeared himself to the church congregation, but was sorely frustrated in his efforts to minister to seafarers. He was permitted to enter the docks on foot but not in his minibus. He was permitted to talk to seafarers inside the dock area but not to go on board any ships. The seafarers' centre had been taken over by the Government, so he had established a well-equipped centre in a diocesan building. He was trying very hard to carry out his ministry in extremely discouraging circumstances. He was a serene and happy priest, with a strong streak of determination running through him.

He drove me to the Polana Hotel, where I was to spend two nights. The hotel had enjoyed an excellent reputation in the pre-communist Government days, but I found it cold and intimidating. At dinner-time I was escorted to a table where three East European men were already eating, and told to sit there. I was wearing my clerical collar, since I was an approved visitor to the country. One of the men asked me where I came from, and when I said I was British he rudely asked why I was there. 'Probably for the same reason as you,' I replied; 'I'm a guest here.' The rest of the meal passed in frosty silence. There was no choice of food available: you either ate or did not eat what was put before you. I spent a lonely evening in the hotel.

The next morning I waited at the roadside outside the hotel for Christopher to pick me up. A sudden emergency delayed him and I had a long wait. As I stood there enjoying the sunshine, a white man in an open-necked shirt came up to me. 'Shake my hand,' he said, 'as if you have known me for a long time.' I did as he asked, and he introduced himself. He was a Roman Catholic priest, teaching in a seminary. 'Listen to what I say,' he said. 'Check up on what I tell you. Do not write any notes until you are out of the country.' For the next 45 minutes he outlined what was happening in Mozambique. Food was in short supply everywhere; there were long queues whenever bread was available, and many people were starving. It was dangerous to be heard criticising the Government. A significant number of people had 'disappeared', and it was not known whether they were alive or dead or in a concentration camp. The Church was being harshly persecuted: clergy were being turned out of their rectories and presbyteries; the Anglican cathedral at Maciene had been 'nationalised'; theological students were being taken away from their studies to undertake government duties; and nuns were being ordered to nurse in State hospitals. Selected pupils in secondary education were being sent to Cuba and Eastern Europe to be 'educated', without being allowed any choice as to whether or not they went.

It was a grim, horrifying story, and during my visit I checked discreetly what I had been told. I discovered overwhelming confirmation of its truth, and I saw for myself the political slogans crudely daubed on many buildings, the empty shelves in the shops, the queues wherever food was on sale, and the neglected condition of the roads. I was glad that I wore my clerical collar throughout my visit. Many people came up to me in the street and shook my hand. 'Pray for us, Father,' was the constant plea, 'we really need it'.

I flew out of Mozambique from Beira to Blantyre in Malawi. There were just four passengers, and we were told to report at least two hours before the flight. The departure procedures were formidable. First every item in my suitcase was removed and carefully examined. Then I was told to re-pack it. A dispute arose over some cashew nuts I had bought. 'You can't take these,' I was told, 'they're the property of the Government.' 'But I bought them from a government store,' I protested. 'You can't take them', I was told again. But as nobody took them away, I put them back in my case, and nothing was said! The hand luggage search was equally thorough; and the body search left nothing to the imagination! As required, I handed over what was left of my Mozambique currency and was then free to proceed to the departure lounge. There was a wonderfully stocked bar there. It was very hot and sticky, and the prospect of a cold beer was suddenly very attractive. So I went to the bar and asked for one. 'Have you got Mozambique money?' the barman asked. 'No', I replied, 'I've handed it all over.' 'No Mozambique money, no beer' he said. My self-control deserted me for a moment, and I expressed my frustration succinctly.

I was not sorry to board the aircraft. I had felt uneasy and vulnerable throughout my brief stay. I had seen at first hand the workings of a militant Communist régime, and I did not like it. But I had also observed the brave witness of some fine Christian people, and I was ashamed of my weak and feeble attitude.

★    ★    ★

In October and November 1978 I visited North America, the Far East, the Indian sub-continent and the Middle East. It was a significant tour for a number of reasons.

After visits to our stations in Eastern Canada and Ontario I went on to New York for the third triennial conference of ICMA (the International Christian Maritime Association). 154 delegates were present from seventeen countries, representing all the major Christian organisations serving seafarers. There were also observers from the International Labour Organisation (ILO), the Inter-Governmental Maritime Consultative Organisation (IMCO), and the United Seamen's Services (USS). The theme of the conference was 'Christ in the Maritime World: Evangelisation and the Pastoral Care of the Seafarer.' Evangelisation, or proclaiming the good news of Jesus Christ, is an area of maritime ministry calling for extreme sensitivity. Many considerations have to be borne in mind, such as respect for the individual seafarer's dignity, background and culture; a recognition and acknowledgement of sincerely-held religious or political beliefs different from our own; and our calling to love people for our Lord's sake. In a paper delivered to the Conference I spelled out my views, including this passage:

> The Gospel is communicated by quality of life. A dedicated Christian life is a most effective instrument of evangelism. Basic moral integrity, a disciplined lifestyle, a healthy outlook on life underpinned by a simple but deep faith, and a respect for others which does not seek to force personal convictions on them, all combine to make a powerful witness to the love of Christ and His Church. A committed Christian is soon recognised for what he or she is.

My memories are of the challenges of the major papers and of the splendid and challenging discussion groups, the warm fellowship which developed, the willingness of everybody to listen as well as to talk, the opportunity to meet people from other countries, the easy relationships with people at every level of Church life, and above all of worshipping together.

I was delighted when a number of chaplains serving in the Episcopal Church of the U.S.A. (ECUSA) asked if they could be appointed Honorary Chaplains of The Missions to Seamen as the Anglican Church ministering to seafarers. We welcomed them with open arms. When the Presiding Bishop of ECUSA, John Allin, visited the conference, Bruce Evans, our Liaison Bishop in South Africa, advised him of the request. Bishop Allin was delighted with the arrangement and promised to inform the Bishops of ECUSA. It marked the beginning of a new and fruitful partnership between the chaplains and bishops of ECUSA and The Missions to Seamen. The Missions to Seamen was now truly becoming the Anglican Church ministering to the seafarers of the world and ceasing to be a British missionary society working in many parts of the world.

After the ICMA conference we had a one-day conference of the chaplains of The Missions to Seamen serving in Canada. It was the first time most of them had met each other and it brought us all much closer together. We agreed that we should ask the Canadian House of Bishops to appoint a Liaison Bishop, and also to try to establish a North American and Caribbean Region of The Missions to Seamen. After the conference I went on to Vancouver, where Archbishop David Somerville was enthusiastic about the request for a Liaison Bishop for Canada and promised to refer it to the House of Bishops.

From Vancouver I flew on to Tokyo and Yokohama. The flight took us north from Vancouver along the West coast of Canada and the U.S.A. in broad daylight and bright sunshine. The views along the coast were spectacular, and it was an eerie experience to cross the dateline and arrive in Japan a day later with no night intervening.

I made a first visit to Chittagong in Bangladesh. Our Honorary Chaplain there, Bill Bromley, had asked me to come and advise as to whether it might be possible to establish a much-needed seafarers' centre there. I received a warm welcome from Bill, his church members and all the port officials I met, and I produced a comprehensive report which I sent to the Government of Bangladesh for their consideration. They took a long time to consider it and laid down conditions we could not meet.

In Singapore I attended the Far East Chaplains' Conference, which once again was a time of happy fellowship with fellow Christians of other denominations and of growing together. It also became clear there that The Missions to Seamen in Singapore might have to decide its future on its own, since the projected Roman Catholic interconfessional centre was probably not now going to materialise. The situation was becoming urgent for us and I was glad to be on the spot to monitor developments.

At the end of this tour, in Dubai and Port Said, I completed the round of first-time visits to all our stations. I now had a working knowledge of most of our work that I could build on steadily in the future.

Exciting opportunities beckoned. The setting up of the Australian Council of The Missions to Seamen; the prospect of appointing a Liaison Bishop in Canada; a closer link with the seafarers' chaplains of the Episcopal Church of the U.S.A.; the success of interconfessional chaplains' conferences, and the consequent breaking down of denominational barriers; the formation of a Southern Africa regional group of the International Christian Maritime Association; the opening of the centres in Dubai and Port Said; the progress towards establishing new centres or ministries in Jakarta, Dampier, Khorramshar and Chittagong; and growing trust and co-operation at the highest level of interconfessional collaboration – all these combined to make my life challenging and exciting. I was enjoying robust health, which lightened considerably the burden of frequent air travel. Apart from occasional bouts of 'Delhi Belly', the 'Jakarta Quickstep' and 'Rashid's Revenge' (in Dubai), I kept very fit. Only once, in fact, in fifteen years of extensive travel did I need brief hospital treatment.

CHAPTER TWELVE

# London 1975-1990:
# General Secretary 1976-1990
# Fruitful Years 1979-1990

THERE WERE TWO main reasons why I was able to travel extensively and be available to the people involved in the work of The Missions to Seamen throughout the world: the first was the excellence of the staff at Central Office, to whom I could delegate responsibility with confidence; the second was the encouragement, support and wise advice I received from the chairmen and members of our major committees in London.

**The Society's Leaders**

The Society's President and Chairman of Council, when I became General Secretary, was Viscount Leathers of Purfleet. A shipowner with a wide range of interests in the maritime world, Fred, as he liked us all to call him, was a tower of strength to us all. He listened carefully to everybody, and asked many questions in order to be sure that he had grasped every aspect of a problem. He gave generously of his time, experience, knowledge and wisdom. An unassuming man, he handled major public occasions dexterously and unobtrusively. He was a good man to have with you in a crisis, and he did not lack courage. He was forthright and kind, and calm in a storm. He worked for consensus, and we all held him in high esteem and affection.

In 1981 the Society celebrated its 125th anniversary with a service in Westminster Abbey attended by Her Royal Highness The Princess Anne. At the end of the service I asked her if she remembered visiting the new Flying Angel Club in Hull in 1969 with The Queen and The Duke of Edinburgh. 'Very vividly!' she replied. She recalled that she had been wearing a yellow outfit on the day, which had become generously covered by greenfly on the journey in an open-topped vehicle, and that she had been acutely embarrassed by this. I did not meet her again until 1983, when she attended a Dinner Dance in Birmingham to mark the 60th anniversary of the Society's Birmingham Association. I sat next to her throughout the meal and we had a long and wide-ranging conversation, in the course of which we talked about the Society's work and our experiences of international travel. She mentioned that she would be visiting Australia later in the year, and this set me thinking. Our new centre in Singapore was due to open in the autumn. It was an old

Chinese house which was being beautifully and imaginatively restored, refurbished and adapted for use as a seafarers' centre under the direction of a Chinese architect, who was donating his services. I wondered whether the Princess would be prepared to open it. Next day I rang her Private Secretary, Lt. Col. Peter Gibbs, to enquire about the possibility of the Princess stopping over on her outward or return journey to Australia to perform the ceremony. He said that he would certainly ask, and I was delighted when he rang back shortly afterwards to say that the Princess would be happy to do so if the necessary arrangements could be made; it would be several weeks before we could expect a firm decision. It was a great joy when we heard that she would indeed open the centre and spend an hour and a quarter there.

The occasion was memorable. Lord Leathers and I represented The Missions to Seamen's Central Office, and the chairman, John Evans, and the members of the Singapore station's Committee of Management were all present. A number of seafarers from different countries were there, together with representatives of the Diplomatic Corps. The time flew by, and when the Princess departed she left behind a party of people who felt greatly honoured by her visit and who had been made to feel that their work was important.

On my return to London at the end of a six-week tour which took me around the world, I had a long talk with two key figures: Lord Leathers and Captain Ray Hart, who had succeeded Admiral Sir Andrew Lewis as Chairman of the Society's General Committee in 1978. We agreed that we should invite Her Royal Highness to become the Society's President. If she accepted, Lord Leathers would retire as President, but continue as Chairman of the Council. Everybody was delighted when the Princess accepted the invitation for a period of five years, and a splendid Installation Service was held at St. Michael Paternoster Royal in May 1984. At the time of writing, her Presidency has extended to almost twenty years, for which the Society is immensely grateful. During these years she has visited more than half of the Society's stations throughout the world, some of them a number of times, and she has given great encouragement to us all.

Ray Hart, Chairman of The General Committee, had had a very distinguished career in the Royal Navy, being decorated for gallantry three times in the Second World War. After he retired from the Navy, he joined The British and Commonwealth Shipping Company, first as Nautical Advisor and later as Fleet Manager, and became a member of the Society's General Committee. He was an admirable chairman. A man of great integrity, he listened carefully, spoke plainly but kindly, and could ask penetrating questions without giving offence. He took care to inform himself fully, gave a clear lead, and supported the staff in what we were doing. He was a man whose yes meant yes, and whose no meant no, and he was a true and loyal friend. He was highly respected and loved.

The Chairman of the Finance Committee was The Hon. Antony Cayzer, a member of the shipping family who owned the Union Castle Line and The British and Commonwealth Shipping Company. He took a keen interest in the Society's work, as well as overseeing our finances. A devout Christian, a member of the congregation at St. Albans Abbey and Cathedral, he spoke quietly and thoughtfully. He was not afraid to speak out when he felt it necessary. On one occasion, when Sir Andrew Lewis was painting a worst-case scenario of the Society's possible future, he gently intervened to say: 'Chairman, there is someone called God involved in all of this.' He watched our finances closely and was always ready to listen if we wanted to undertake new work. But we knew that we would have to make a good case to convince him. When he retired as Chairman of The Finance Committee, he was succeeded by Ian Campbell, another fine Christian and Senior Partner of Binder Hamlyn, a leading firm of accountants in the City of London. Ian continued this demanding task unobtrusively but very efficiently; our finances were in very capable hands. He was also Churchwarden at our parish church of St. John's, Stanmore.

When Ray Hart retired after 10 years as Chairman of the General Committee, he was succeeded by David Newbigging. David had been Chairman of the Committee of Management of the Mariners Clubs in Hong Kong, the one in Kowloon being one of the biggest seafarers' centres in the world. He had also been Chairman and Managing Director of Jardine Matheson, one of the largest companies in Asia. He saw the role of committees of The Missions to Seamen as being to ensure that the chaplains had the resources they needed to exercise their ministry without undue financial worries. He worked tirelessly to achieve this, and I was deeply grateful for his knowledge, experience and brilliant financial thinking and planning. We had always got on well when he was chairman in Hong Kong, and we remain firm friends.

There were several important changes among the senior staff at Central Office during these years. When Jimmy Wilson-Hughes retired as Assistant General Secretary with Responsibility for Ministry in 1979, we appointed Ken Good, formerly Chaplain in Antwerp and then Chaplain in Kobe, to replace him. It was an inspired appointment. Aged 38, and with an impressive record of collaboration with chaplains of other denominations, Ken brought a first-class trained theological mind to his task. He had a clear vision of The Missions to Seamen becoming the Anglican Church ministering to the seafarers of the world and leaving behind its image of a British missionary society working overseas. He worked out how this could happen and expressed his views succinctly and comprehensibly. He related easily to people, and it was he who in 1981 brought the chaplains serving in the Episcopal Church of the United States of America (ECUSA) voluntarily and officially into the fold of The Missions to Seamen. The appointment of Liaison Bishops for the Society in the U.S.A. followed soon afterwards. Ken also had a vision of the Society becoming much more closely integrated into the life of the Anglican Church. He realised that the Society had to continue to adapt to changes in the shipping world and in the Church, and the training conferences for chaplains and lay staff which he organised stretched people's minds and challenged their long held beliefs. He and I worked happily together, and I was deeply indebted to him for the way in which he advanced the Society's thinking. I was very sad when he felt that his work was done and moved on to a parish in the North East. His talents were recognised there, too, and his next appointment was as Archdeacon of Richmond in Yorkshire.

In 1981 Neville Barwick retired as Assistant General Secretary with Responsibility for Administration, and was succeeded by Jock Miller. Jock was a wonderful man. At the early age of 45 he had been promoted to Rear Admiral in the Royal Navy, but the pressures and demands of his new duties temporarily overwhelmed him. Before he was 47 he was invalided out of the Navy with an alcohol problem. With the devoted support of his wife Rosanne, he came to terms with his problem and resumed his life. After two years of employment with a finance company, he applied to join the staff of The Missions to Seamen as Regional Director for London and the South East of England. I was one of the panel of four who conducted the final interview, and Jock really impressed me. He spoke honestly and freely about why he had left the Navy and why he wanted to join the Society. We appointed him and he did a superb job. In 1981 we appointed him Assistant General Secretary (Administration). Before he accepted the appointment, he asked to talk to me. He told me that it was too much responsibility too soon which had caused his problems before, and he did not want to repeat the situation. I told him that neither he nor I carried the burdens of the Society on our own shoulders alone, and that in any case God was always there to guide and assist us. He accepted the job, and for $5^1/2$ years did it brilliantly. His strong Christian faith enabled him to keep his alcohol problem completely under control, and it was a devastating blow when he suddenly collapsed and died while addressing the Society's Annual General Meeting in 1986. He had won the hearts and respect of us all.

Also in 1981 Bobbie Newman, my Personal Assistant, retired. She had continued beyond retirement age, and had been invaluable to me. I knew that she would be very hard to replace, and I dreaded the prospect; but it had to be done. I realised how vital it was to make the right appointment, and I prepared thoroughly. I wanted a person with proven ability, discretion and loyalty, but also someone who would not be afraid to express a contrary opinion if it was called for. I prepared a list of some important questions to which I would want satisfactory answers. The position was widely advertised, and from a total of 25 applicants I selected a shortlist of seven. I interviewed them all on one day, and one candidate, Rhos Charles, stood out from the rest and I appointed her. Rhos was a former History teacher at Benenden School, who in her late thirties had exchanged teaching for secretarial work. Rhos threw herself enthusiastically into the life and work of The Missions to Seamen. Highly intelligent, passionate, thoughtful, loyal, efficient, and with a splendid sense of humour, she came to be able to draft letters and articles in my style and thereby saved me a lot of time and effort. She mastered the complexities of the computer and word processor, and I relied on her more and more as the years passed. She typed my first book, *On Course Together* (a volume dealing with the Churches working together in the maritime world), and made a marvellous job of it.

**Formulating Policies**
When I became General Secretary, I knew that I must continue and develop the policy of transferring responsibility for the Society's worldwide work from 'Headquarters' to the Church locally.

I thought it would be wise to move forward with this first in Australia, where I had a good knowledge of the chaplaincy staff and of the local situation. Chapter Eleven contains a description of how we set about this, and it was only after the Australian Council of The Missions to Seamen had been established in 1977 that I came to see that this was only a beginning. Much remained to be done, including asking the Australian House of Bishops to appoint a Liaison Bishop, arranging initial finance for the Council, monitoring progress, and dealing with queries as they arose.

In 1978 we initiated the process in Canada, and in 1981 in the United States. It was not something that could be hurried, because it was vital that we carried everybody with us, and in Canada it was three years before a Liaison Bishop was appointed; but we had the satisfaction of knowing that all the proper procedures had been followed. By 1987 we had Liaison Bishops in Australia, New Zealand, Southern Africa, Canada, the U.S.A., Japan, Jerusalem and the East, the West Indies, Europe, England, Scotland, Wales and Ireland, and the network was growing steadily. This was remarkable recognition of what had been achieved.

★    ★    ★

At the same time as we were devolving responsibility for the ministry to seafarers from Central Office to the Anglican Church locally, we set out to promote a spirit of mutual responsibility and interdependence between the individual stations. Stations with significant financial assets were encouraged to assist stations where there was a vital need for ministry, but difficulty in achieving economic viability. The policy worked well and the spirit of partnership thus fostered was invaluable. Contributions ranged from substantial to small and they made a great difference to what could be achieved.

★    ★    ★

Alongside these policies we were totally committed to a policy of ecumenical collaboration. Wherever possible we worked in partnership with Christian organisations of other denominations. Ownership of buildings was not a problem: if one organisation invited others to work from its premises, the principle we followed was that the newly-joining organisations became full partners in the ministry and guests in the building. If a new building was being planned in a port where there was currently no seafarers' centre, it became common practice for one organisation to take the lead and invite the others to support and participate in the project. An outstanding instance of this was the port of Tomakomai in Japan.

Tomakomai is a busy port on the East coast of Hokkaido, the northernmost island of Japan. Early in 1986 I conducted a training course for honorary chaplains and lay workers of The Missions to Seamen on the island in Hakodate, a small port. One of the participants was Iwao 'Joe' Machida, a layman who was keen to establish a ministry to seafarers in his home port of Tomakomai. Joe was in his early forties, and his enthusiasm was infectious. He questioned me at length about what he needed to do to set up a ministry to seafarers, and I promised to visit Tomakomai the following year. When I arrived I found that Joe had been extremely busy. He had visited the clergy of the five Christian churches in the city, and recruited them all as ship visitors and honorary chaplains. He had persuaded the Roman Catholic priest to make available a building as a temporary seafarers' centre, had named it 'The Stella Maris Flying Angel Club', and had opened it on two nights a week. A year later it was open four nights a week, and had no fewer than 60 voluntary helpers – in a country where voluntary service is almost unheard of! In 1989, when I made a further visit, the centre was open four nights a week; the International Transport Workers Federation had donated a 26-seat bus to transport seafarers to and from their ships; and plans were in hand for a purpose-built seafarers' centre. It was duly built and paid for, by which time Joe had 200 voluntary workers, all unpaid. In 1990 Joe's work was recognised by The President's Award for services to The Missions to Seamen, it was a fitting and well-deserved reward for his vision, enthusiasm and ability to work with Christians of other denominations.

Another example was the port of Napier in the North Island of New Zealand. An exploratory visit I made to the port in 1977 at the request of our Honorary Chaplain there, Rod Falconer, led to the opening of Hawke's Bay Seafarers' Centre in 1983. The building was financed jointly by the

Apostleship of the Sea, the British Sailors' Society and The Missions to Seamen, with the help of a grant from the International Transport Workers Federation. No fewer than nine clergy persons from a number of denominations volunteered to serve as Honorary Chaplains, a Committee of Management was formed, and a large number of voluntary workers came forward to help. There were no paid staff, and the centre was a huge success from the outset. In the first year 5,000 seafarers visited it, and there were no financial problems. Relations between the people involved with the running of the centre remained excellent; the whole operation was a triumph of ecumenical collaboration.

★   ★   ★

In the 1970's a worrying trend emerged of seafarers not being paid their wages on time. Sometimes the delay lasted several months, and the seafarers became desperate because their families had no money to live on. My first direct experience of this happened in 1974 in Fremantle, when a West Indian crew came to the Flying Angel Club seeking assistance; they had not been paid for several months. I contacted the representative of the Seamen's Union of Australia, who responded immediately. The wages were soon paid, but we learned afterwards that in similar circumstances protesting crew members were often dismissed and/or blacklisted for future employment when their ships arrived in another country. This happened for the most part with flag of convenience* ships, which were beginning to pose many problems. They often recruited seafarers from developing countries, because they cost less to employ than those from developed countries, and because, in their desperation for work, they were prepared to sign less demanding contracts. Furthermore, these were sometimes drawn up in a language they did not understand.

In 1981 The Mission to Seamen appointed The Revd. Glyn Jones, Senior Chaplain of the Port of London team, as Auxiliary Ministries Secretary, and many cases of unjust treatment of seafarers were referred to him by our Honorary Chaplains. In the same year the Seamen's Church Institute of New York and New Jersey established its Center for Seafarers' Rights, and this rapidly became a force to be reckoned with. In 1985 The Missions to Seamen appointed The Revd. Chris Collison to deal with cases of justice (or injustice) and welfare. We were very conscious of the fact that the vast majority of shipowners treated their crews well, but the problems with rogue owners were serious, increasing, and could not be ignored.

---

*By the term 'flag of convenience' is understood the practice of registering a ship in a country other than the one in which it is owned. This is often done to obtain more favourable tax concessions, or to avoid the stringent safety standards of the country of ownership, or to escape the attentions of trade unions over conditions of employment.

## Port developments – Europe and the United Kingdom

Throughout the late 1970's and 1980's The Missions to Seamen reviewed and rationalised its ministry to seafarers. In Europe and the United Kingdom there were many excellent seafarers' centres which had been built before, or not long after, the Second World War. With the advent of container ships, the reduction in size of crews, and the significant lessening of the time ships spent in port, some of these centres had become too big and too expensive to run. Since the changes on the shipping scene were plainly irreversible, the Society needed to act decisively.

The centre at South Shields was drastically reduced in size and imaginatively modernised. The lovely chapel, with its many memorials to past seafarers, was retained unchanged. On Teeside continuing changes in the pattern of shipping led to the return of the 1960's seafarers' centre at Wilton to the landlords, ICI, and the establishment of a small relocatable centre within the dock complex. Athlone House at Tilbury, built in 1956, was sold when the Society joined forces with the Apostleship of the Sea there. In Southampton we moved into smaller, purpose-designed facilities. At Avonmouth the Apostleship of the Sea, the British Sailors' Society and The Missions to Seamen established an excellent working relationship and took over the former Merchant Navy Club from the Merchant Navy Welfare Board, each disposing of its own former premises. At Cardiff a new, compact, purpose-built centre replaced large, under-used premises. In Glasgow the ministry of The Missions to Seamen was combined with a dockland parish, and the former centre sold. New centres were established at Seaham, Fowey and Boston. The new centre at Felixstowe, a partnership between the German Seamen's Mission, the Apostleship of the Sea, the British Sailors' Society and The Missions to Seamen, was an immediate success, and went from strength to strength.

In continental Europe, the port of Rotterdam was continually expanding. Already the biggest port in the world, it had ample space for expansion. In Europort the Dutch government established the magnificent De Beer International Seamen's Centre, and The Missions to Seamen closed its little club nearby in a converted barge, the *Pelican*. For sentimental reasons this was a hard decision to make, because the centre had a wonderful atmosphere, but in the cold light of day it was a decision that had to be made. Other changes in the port led to a reduction of the extent of our ministry in central Rotterdam and the redevelopment of our work in Schiedam.

A development which gave me enormous satisfaction was the establishment of an ecumenical ministry to seafarers in Fos, part of the port of Marseille. In 1974 I had sailed into Fos on the 28,000 deadweight ton container ship *Discovery Bay* on my way back from Australia to England, and I had been struck by its remoteness and by the lack of basic services and amenities for seafarers. Because of the distances between the three main areas of the port, and the absence of any major centre of population in the immediate vicinity, it was difficult to determine where any operation might be located. In 1981 Cardinal Roger Etchegaray, the Roman Catholic Archbishop of Marseille, wrote a paper expressing his concern at the lack of facilities for seafarers throughout the port, and calling for action. In 1984 the initial meeting of the Mediterranean Region of the International Christian Maritime Association was held in Marseille, and the delegates visited Fos. They requested that a feasibility study should be undertaken to determine what sort of ministry would be appropriate, and where it should be located.

In 1986 the Roman Catholic organisation, La Mission de la Mer, and a secular organisation, Les Amis des Marins (with whom The Missions to Seamen worked in partnership in Dunkerque), rented a house at Port de Bouc near Fos, with the intention of adapting it for use as a seafarers' centre. The dioceses of Marseille and Aix-en-Provence accepted responsibility for the salary of the chaplain and leader of the project, Father Philippe Plantevin of La Mission de France, an order of worker priests. The Missions to Seamen welcomed, and happily accepted, an invitation to become partners in the project, and together the societies approached the International Transport Workers Federation for help with the cost of purchasing the building. A substantial grant was forthcoming, together with another for the purchase of a minibus to transport the seafarers, and the work of reconstruction was begun. The centre was opened officially on November 27th 1986, almost twelve years after my first visit.

It has proved to be a godsend. The minibus revolutionised the outlook for seafarers visiting the port. Now they could get to the centre from the outlying berths without difficulty or crippling expense. They could phone home in comfort. There was a small but well equipped and well stocked shop, bar and canteen, and a simple, dignified chapel. All the helpers except Father Philippe were volunteers, and there was a wonderful atmosphere. It was a great moment for all when Her Royal Highness The Princess Royal visited the centre in 1987; she spoke French throughout her three-hour visit, and impressed everybody.

## Port Developments – Overseas

The late 1970's and 1980's saw exciting developments in maritime ministry all over the world. A number of factors contributed to this. The shipping industry was changing radically and rapidly. The Churches were working happily together in ecumenical partnerships in the maritime world. The International Transport Workers Federation warmly welcomed the collaboration between the Christian Societies serving seafarers, and made substantial grants from its Welfare Fund to jointly-undertaken capital projects.

The transfer of responsibility for its work by the Central Office of The Missions to Seamen to the Anglican Church locally was encouraging local initiatives in many ports, and the Society's policy of mutual responsibility and interdependence offered some of the financially secure stations the opportunity to assist the more needy and newly-established operations.

★  ★  ★

Port Walcott in North West Australia commenced operations as a port in 1972. It was an iron ore exporting terminal, the outlet for ore mined inland at Parraburdoo by Cliffs Robe River Iron Ore Associates (CRRIA), and was situated between Port Hedland to the East and Dampier to the West, 21° South of the Equator, and very hot and humid. It was a remote place, five miles from the small company town of Wickham, which was itself a further seven miles from the township of Roebourne. From the dock gates to the landward end of the jetty where the ships berthed was a two-and-a-half-mile journey through the railway truck-tipping terminal, the ore crushing plant and huge stockpiles of reddish-brown iron ore. A thick haze of iron ore dust often hung over the whole area, and the dust permeated everything. The ships berthed at the seaward end of the jetty, which was 1.6m miles long, 70 feet above the level of the sea, and had a huge conveyor belt running its entire length.

The blazing sunshine and intense heat, the height of the jetty above the sea and the dazzling reflection of the sun's rays from the sea, together with the constantly running machinery, made walking along the jetty potentially hazardous, and the Company wisely decreed that nobody should walk its full length. But this made life very difficult for visiting seafarers, who had often spent several weeks at sea and were looking forward to a trip ashore. The problem was compounded by the distance of the landward end of the jetty from the dock gates, and from the dock gates to Wickham, where the only social centre was the Company's Social Club. Unless a port worker offered to drive the seafarers ashore and bring them back again later, there was no alternative to remaining on board. The plight of the seafarers caused great concern to the Harbour Master, Captain Bob Hudson, and to some of the port workers, notably 'Snowy' Goldstraw. They asked for advice and help from The Revd. Ted Cosens, Chaplain of The Missions to Seamen in Dampier, who in turn kept us in Central Office fully informed. We were very aware of the need for a ministry to seafarers there.

By 1980 approximately 100 large ore carriers were calling at Port Walcott each year, exporting 14 million tonnes of ore, and the port's trade was still expanding. I visited the port that year and listened to the plans of the small committee which had been formed to provide a ministry to seafarers. They proposed to buy a minibus to transport seafarers wanting to go ashore from their ships to the Social Club at Wickham, which the Company had generously agreed they could use. They would drive them back to their ships at the end of their visit. They would also build a small extension to the Social Club to cater specifically for seafarers and to be staffed by volunteers. I promised the full support of The Missions to Seamen and the work went ahead. A minibus was purchased with a very generous grant from the Company, and volunteers built the extension to the Social Club. All the necessary finance was raised locally. In the first year of operation volunteers drove more than 1000 seafarers to and from the centre and their ships, and a vital service was provided. It was a great honour for me to be invited to perform the opening ceremony in 1982.

★　　★　　★

On the East coast of Australia, at Gladstone in Queensland, a splendid ministry to seafarers was developed by a retired priest from England, Peter Calaminus, who arrived there in 1980. Gladstone was growing fast as a port; it exported coal and alumina and brought in bauxite. In 1977, when I had made my first visit, it was handling 15 million tones of cargo annually; by 1983 this had grown to more than 23 million tonnes, carried in 510 ships. Its growth had coincided with the rapid development of Port Hedland on the North-West coast at the end of the 1960's, and The Missions to Seamen had had to make the very difficult decision as to where it should allocate very limited resources. In the event Port Hedland took precedence over Gladstone. In the early 1970's a seafarers' centre was established in Gladstone by a group of volunteers, and with a constitution supplied by The Missions to Seamen. But the need for the centre to be financially self-sufficient led to its becoming more of a social centre for local people than a genuine seafarers' centre.

Both the Anglican and Roman Catholic Churches felt that there was a need for a centre specifically for seafarers, and in 1983 The Flying Angel Stella Maris Seafarers' Centre was opened. By now the policy of mutual responsibility and interdependence had been thoroughly accepted within The Missions to Seamen, and donations towards the cost of equipping the new centre, which was very generously made available by the Gladstone Port Authority, were received from the Society's stations in Brisbane, Port Pirie, Newcastle, Sydney and Hobart, and from the Victoria Council; they also came from the Anglican Diocese of Rockhampton, the Bishop of Willochra, the Apostleship of the Sea in Gladstone and the Roman Catholic Bishop.

Peter Calaminus served tirelessly as Honorary Chaplain of The Missions to Seamen in Gladstone for eight years, by which time he was well into his 70's. He saw the centre well established and flourishing. Blessed with an eirenic nature, high intelligence, great ability, much commonsense, and a happy knack of relating easily to people from all walks of life, he made a great impact on the port, on the city and on the Church in Gladstone. He and his wife Betty were a godsend to the Society.

★　　★　　★

In 1988, during a routine tour of the Australian stations, I was taken by our Honorary Chaplain in Hobart, Fred Harland, to the new development at Bell Bay in the port of Launceston, Tasmania. We were accompanied by the local parish priest, who was keen to start a ministry to seafarers there. There were five berths already in use, and ships of up to 44,000 deadweight tonnes were using the harbour, which was handling timber and containers. There was a total absence of amenities for seafarers in this remote place, and I made a note that action to meet the need should be taken as soon as possible.

Next morning, as we drove through Launceston, I asked Fred to stop at the Port Authority office so that I could pick up a copy of their Annual Report, with all its information about the port. At the reception desk I introduced myself and asked for an annual report. One of the Personal Assistants brought out the report and then questioned me. 'You're from The Missions to Seamen?' she asked. 'Yes,' I replied, 'from The Missions to Seamen in London.' She then told me that the Port Authority was holding a significant amount of money in a trust fund for the use of The Missions to Seamen in the port, and that they did not know how to apply it. It emerged that the money was a bequest of some £700 dating back to the Second World War; with accumulated interest it had swelled to $A 50,000 (£23,500 sterling)! In due course it provided the basis for establishing a ministry at Bell Bay, and the Australian Council of The Missions to Seamen was very glad that I had called on the Port Authority!

★　　★　　★

There were many other significant developments in ports around the world.

In Australia the carefully planned seafarers' centre in Dampier opened in 1979. On the East Coast a second centre was opened at Fisherman Islands in the port of Brisbane. Situated on the south bank of the Brisbane River, 10 miles from the nearest centre of population, the centre was built and paid for by the Brisbane Port Authority, maintaining close consultation with The Missions to Seamen and the Apostleship of the Sea, who were already working together in partnership; the Port Authority wanted the two Societies to run the new centre. In 1985 a new centre replaced the out-dated premises at Geelong in Victoria. Another new centre replacing an old one was opened at Townsville in Queensland. In Sydney the ministry to seafarers was relocated in more compact premises.

In New Zealand, in 1980, a new centre was opened in Nelson, a busy small port in the South Island. In 1981 Paul Rendle, a retired Master Mariner and former college teacher, was asked by the curate of the parish of Nelson to consider whether he was prepared to run the centre on a voluntary basis. Paul replied that he had just retired and was not keen to take on a new commitment. It was Paul himself who told me, with a broad grin, that the curate had then said that that was fine, but had he thought about what he would say about it to the Almighty on the Day of Judgement? Paul and his wife Vivienne threw themselves wholeheartedly into the work, and made a huge success of it. They became known, trusted and loved by thousands of seafarers, as this letter from a mainland Chinese crew testified. It is reproduced exactly as it was written.

> Dear Mrs Vivienne, Dear Mr Paul,
>     We Chinese seamen 19 persons come to Port of Nelson in Newzealand first time. Here, we are happy to know you. We are accorded a enthusiasm reception. Your spirit of warm-hearted service to the seaman will remember in our heart forever. We shall leave Nelson for China tomorrow evening. We wish to avail ourselves of this opportunity to extend to you our heartfelt thanks. We wish you good healthy and long life. Next time we shall give ourselves the pleasure of calling on you again. MV Maritime Victory crew 19 Chinese seamen.

In Asia a new centre was opened at Pusan in Korea in 1987, and another in the same year at Kobe in Japan. Here a truly magnificent centre replaced the existing building, which, because of radical port redevelopment, was now in the wrong place. In 1984 the new Jakarta International Seafarers' Centre finally opened. The frustrations encountered in building and opening this superb centre were truly horrendous, and only sheer determination and cussedness stopped us from giving up several times; I had not fully appreciated before the lengths to which bureaucratic red tape can extend! Eventually a happy solution was found, as the participating Societies transferred the ownership of the building to the Indonesian Council of Churches, but provided chaplains to assist with its operation. From the start of the project to the moment when it was truly up and running took 11 long years.

In the Gulf new centres were opened in Bahrain and Jebel Ali, thanks to the great generosity of the respective Port Authorities. The Dubai International Seafarers' Centre flourished and extended both its buildings and the services it provided.

In Egypt The Missions to Seamen reopened its centre at Port Said in 1978. In South Africa an ecumenically-operated centre was opened in the Bay Head area of the port of Durban in 1981. In 1985/86 a small centre was opened at Saldanha Bay, 90 miles north of Cape Town on the Atlantic coast. This natural deep water port handled huge tankers and bulk carriers, but the town was small and a long way from the jetties, and the seafarers' centre was greatly appreciated.

On the west coast of Canada a new centre was established in 1985 in the rapidly growing port of Prince Rupert in British Columbia. In the Great Lakes a mobile centre was introduced at Sarnia in 1982 to provide a service to seafarers whose ships berthed briefly at out-of-the-way jetties along the 19 mile length of the St. Clair River, which links Lake Huron with Lake Erie. 90 ships a week stopped for between 2 and 14 hours at these jetties and there was almost no opportunity for seafarers to go ashore. Altogether 15,000 ships a year passed through the St. Clair River, which is a key waterway in the Great Lakes. The mobile centre was 35 feet long and superbly equipped with a small kitchen, shower room, lounge, TV area and book exchange facility. A huge Flying Angel logo was painted on the roof, to assist identification from the height of a ship's deck, and inevitably the vehicle became known as 'Angie'. The ministry thus provided was much appreciated, and one seafarer, who was greatly helped by the chaplain, sent a cheque for $1,500 as a thank offering. In 1984 a splendid new North Ontario cottage-style centre was opened in Toronto to supplement the basic amenities provided hitherto in a battered former streetcar and a wooden hut. In 1988, in Halifax, Nova Scotia, a purpose-built mobile telephone centre was presented to The Missions to Seamen by a major telecommunications company so as to facilitate the huge number of international telephone calls being made by seafarers from the seafarers' centre. Some of the berths in the port of Halifax are a long way from the city and difficult to get to by public transport, and the mobile centre proved invaluable. The telecommunications company made a substantial annual contribution towards the running costs. New centres were also opened in Quebec and St. John's, Newfoundland.

## Crises

In any large worldwide organisation major crises of various kinds can occur suddenly and unexpectedly, and in The Missions to Seamen we had our share of these.

In 1983 the Port Hedland Seafarers' Centre experienced a severe financial problem. The Apostleship of the Sea, the British Sailors' Society and The Missions to Seamen, who had been equal partners in the establishment of the centre, took turns in appointing the chaplain and/or club manager. When the Club Manager appointed by the British Sailors' Society reported that the centre was on the verge of bankruptcy, and that the prospects for future financial viability were poor, the British Sailors' Society proposed that the centre should close. The Apostleship of the Sea and The Missions to Seamen strongly disagreed, stressing the needs of the thousands of seafarers who visited the centre each year; there was a strong case for keeping it open. The British Sailors' Society withdrew from the operation and The Missions to

Seamen, with the full agreement of The Apostleship of the Sea, appointed Brother Aidan, a Franciscan monk, as chaplain.

It was an inspired choice. Aidan had wide experience of chaplaincy among seafarers, having served with The Missions to Seamen in Dar es Salaam and Pusan, and he threw himself wholeheartedly into the task of saving the centre. He was a dynamic man, blessed with an exceptional ability to relate to people from all backgrounds. He had a great sense of humour, was a wonderful story teller, and his love for people shone through all he did. He worked long hours and gathered round himself a number of excellent volunteer helpers. Within a year he had turned the situation around. The overdraft at the Bank was paid off, the centre was humming with activity and Aidan himself was nominated Port Hedland's Citizen of the Year by the Rotary Club. I was delighted and relieved by the success of his efforts, because I was sure that if we had closed the centre, it would never have reopened. It has continued to meet a vital need, and it was good to welcome back the British Sailors' Society a little later.

In 1980 we appointed The Revd. Joe Humble, a bachelor priest in his early 50's, to the chaplaincy of The Missions to Seamen in Buenos Aires, after an initial training period in Hong Kong. A succession of domestic mishaps soon after his arrival led Joe to telephone me after six weeks to ask to be relieved of his appointment immediately. After a few minutes conversation I asked him not to make any decision about leaving until the following week. I would fly out to Buenos Aires, and spend four days with him; we could then see if we could resolve his problems. He agreed, and I flew to Buenos Aires at the beginning of the following week. In the days that followed we ironed out his difficulties, and he expressed a strong desire to carry on. His ministry there proved to be very effective, and when the Falklands War started in 1982, Joe stayed on in Argentina, declining our offer of immediate repatriation.

During the Falklands War of 1982 The Missions to Seamen played an important role in ministering to the families of seafarers involved in the war. When the container ship *Atlantic Conveyor* was sunk, Cunard, the owners, asked The Missions to Seamen to arrange immediate visits to the families of every member of the ship's company. We had been asked previously to be prepared for such an eventuality, and within two hours members of the Society's staff and honorary chaplains had visited every family. Their ministry was greatly appreciated.

In the Iran-Iraq conflict in the mid-1980's The Revd. Ernie Arnold, the Society's chaplain in Dubai, spent hundreds of hours ministering to traumatised seafarers. Many of the merchant vessels damaged in the war were brought to Dubai for drydocking and repair, and many injured seafarers were hospitalised there. The damage to some of the ships was horrendous, and the chaplain was frequently involved in the most basic tasks of ensuring a dignified burial for the dead, some of whom had been literally blown to pieces. In Bahrain our Lay Chaplain, David Pellatt, did similar wonderful work.

**Bishops as Chaplains**
In the mid-1980's two Asian bishops joined the full-time chaplaincy staff of The Missions to Seamen.

Bishop William Choi was the first Korean Bishop of Pusan, and after more than 10 years in office he felt called to a ministry among seafarers. He had watched the blossoming of the work of The Missions to Seamen in his own diocese, and he enquired whether there might be an opportunity for him to serve within the Society's fellowship somewhere in the world. He was in his early 50's, spoke excellent English and was a humble and loving man of God. We welcomed him into our fold, and in 1987 he went to New York and Houston for training, before being appointed Chaplain of The Seamen's Church Institute of Los Angeles.

In 1986 Bishop John Watanabe, Presiding Bishop of the Nippon Sei Ko Kai (the Episcopal Church of Japan) asked if he might join our chaplaincy staff. He was 58 years old and had been Bishop of Hokkaido for 14 years. 41 years previously he had been the Senior Cadet at the Japanese Naval Base at Hiroshima, and was being trained for a midget submarine suicide attack. He was there when the atomic bomb was dropped on Hiroshima. The appalling devastation, horrific injuries and heavy loss of life made an indelible impression on him. When the War ended a few days later, he returned to his home on the northernmost island of Hokkaido, where he and his sister nursed their mother in her last illness. Their father never returned from a Russian prisoner-of-war camp. When their mother died, there was no money to pay for the funeral, and the Christian doctor who had treated her met the funeral expenses himself. He gave John and his sister a New Testament, with the words, 'I hope that this comes to mean as much to you as it does to me.' He visited them regularly, and a year later they were both baptized. Two years later John went forward to the ordained ministry of the Church, and at the age of forty-four he was consecrated Bishop of Hokkaido. In his mid-fifties he was elected Presiding Bishop. He began to feel strongly that he should spend the closing years of his full-time ministry among seafarers, and when he asked if he might become a chaplain with The Missions to Seamen, we welcomed him gladly. We posted him to Dar es Salaam in Tanzania.

He took to his new ministry like a duck to water. Every day in the stifling heat and high humidity he walked from one end of the docks to the other, visiting every ship. He soon became well known, trusted and loved, and the seafarers' centre was well used. He learned to speak Swahili, and when the Bishop of Dar es Salaam was seriously ill for many months, and eventually died, John carried out the episcopal duties of the diocese. His excellent command of English and Swahili was invaluable. He was deeply content with his ministry there, and when I asked him if he planned to attend the 1988 World Conference of The Missions to Seamen, he replied, with a seraphic smile, 'No, Father, I don't. I've attended the last conference I'm ever going to!'

### The International Christian Maritime Association

One of the most important and rewarding elements of my ministry as General Secretary of The Missions to Seamen was my membership of the Standing Committee of The International Christian Maritime Association (ICMA). The Standing Committee comprised the General Secretaries of The Missions to Seamen, the British Sailors' Society, the German Seamen's Mission and the Dutch Seamen's Mission; the President of the International Council of Seamen's Agencies (later re-named The North American Maritime Ministries Association); a representative of the Nordic Seamen's Missions, and a representative of The Apostleship of the Sea; and the General Secretary of ICMA. The Chairman was elected by the members of the committee; he/she served for three or four years, and presided over one plenary conference. Care was taken to ensure that each organisation represented on the committee took its turn to provide the chairman.

The aim of ICMA was to promote ecumenical collaboration and to enable it to happen, and I was privileged to be in office as the association developed and flourished. All over the world there was increasing understanding and co-operation between the personnel of all the member Churches and Christian agencies ministering to seafarers. There was a perceptible desire to draw closer to each other and to understand each other better. Triennial plenary conferences assisted this process, but it became apparent that regular, more frequent, and smaller gatherings were necessary. A number of regional branches of ICMA were accordingly constituted in the 1970's and 1980's, and the collaboration which ensued was reflected in the establishment of a number of new, ecumenically-operated seafarers' centres. Competition between the various Christian agencies had given way to willing co-operation. There were occasional clashes, which were discussed and amicably resolved, and we were undeniably drawing closer together.

Plenary conferences were held at Elsinore in Denmark in 1975, New York in 1978, Berlin in 1981, Baguio City in the Philippines in 1985, and Athens in 1989. I was Chairman of the Standing Committee between 1982 and 1986, and presided over the conference in the Philippines. A feature of that conference was the public attention we focussed on the unjust treatment of many Filipino seafarers by their own authorities; our concerns were expressed directly to the Government by Cardinal Sin, Head of the Roman Catholic Church in the Philippines. A treasured memory is of the Cardinal's greeting

*ICMA Meeting in The Philippines, with Jim Whittemore, Archbishop Clarizio, Bernard Krug (ICMA) and Bishop Reyes, 1985.*

to the assembled delegates at a reception at his home: 'Welcome to the house of Sin!', he began.

The plenary conferences were notable for the excellence of the main speakers, the joyful fellowship, the willing sharing of knowledge and experience, the careful preparation, the generous hospitality, and a universal desire to present a visible unity to the seafarers of the world. We were on course together.

## Miscellaneous Matters

One aspect of my daily work at Central Office which gave me particular joy was reading the monthly reports sent in by our chaplains. I could picture clearly the ports where they were serving, and also the people who wrote them (unless they had only recently joined our staff). From many memorable reports I have selected just one.

Bernard Dalton was our chaplain at Walvis Bay in South West Africa (later Namibia) from 1976. He was a remarkable man: dynamic, enthusiastic, compassionate, opinionated, extremely competent, and with a wonderful sense of humour. He had served as a Customs Officer for 37 years, and rose to be Senior Customs Officer for South West Africa. He retired at the age of 53 to train for the ordained ministry of the Church, and before ordination was appointed Reader-in-charge of The Missions to Seamen in Walvis Bay. His knowledge and experience of the shipping world, and his ability to relate easily to people of any background, were great assets, and his boundless energy, artistic ability and administrative skills enabled him to make his seafarers' centre very attractive. He understood seafarers, and they opened their hearts to him. This report from him, as written by a Romanian seafarer who had talked to him, was lonely, and acutely aware of his poverty, makes moving reading. This is what Bernard wrote:-

> I attended chapel at the The Mission this morning. I joined the chaplain and his little band at their morning prayers. I could not understand all the words, but I felt the peace of the place, and left feeing very good as I walked the short distance into town. It was a lovely day, and all was well, at least on the face of things. I have many worries. The situation in my country worries me. Being so far away from my family worries me. My wife isn't well, and medicine is difficult to get. So are many other things. Worst of all, I'm thousands of miles from those I love, and I can do nothing about it. But for the moment I'm happy. I'm alive. I have 51 cents in my pocket, so I'll spend the rest of the morning shopping. I can't buy much, but I can look at and touch many things – things taken for granted here, but pure luxury at home.
>
> I look at a young mother with her small son walking slowly along the pavement. I remembered my own small son, and crossed the street. I patted his head with what I thought was a pleasant smile. The mother gave a gasp of alarm, picked up the child, and hurried on. I felt the sun go down. I had meant no harm. I went into a supermarket; the security officer kept her eye on me – twice I found her following me between the aisles. My 51 cents were not enough for a beer, not enough it seems for anything.
>
> I'll go back to my ship. I remember the smell of the fishing vessel: the cabbage soup for lunch; the lack of privacy, where a man can't even cry in private, not even in the toilet, where there's only a strip of a door.
>
> I pass The Missions to Seamen centre. I'll go in there. The Padre welcomed me. 'Well, did you have a good morning in town?' he asked brightly. 'Yes, thank you,' I replied, looking down. How is it that the Padre seemed to know that things were not right? 'Come and have some tea,' he said. I sat down with the Padre, and he asked me about my family, my life, my town. I talked and talked and talked. How he understood my halting English I don't know...The sun comes out again. I feel better. I'll be back this evening, and my 51 cents is going into the little Flying Angel collecting box, every cent on it. I could not buy anything in town, but here at the Mission I get for free what money can't buy – caring human love.

★   ★   ★

Most of our centres had supplies of Bibles in different languages for seafarers to take away with them, and it always encouraged me to see seafarers taking advantage of this service.

In 1979 I visited the Houston International Seamen's Centre in Texas. One evening I was standing near the Literature table, and watched with interest as a Russian seafarer picked up two Bibles in Russian and slipped them into his pocket. He looked around and saw me standing there in clerical attire. He came up to me and told me that because very few Bibles had been available in Russia in recent years, he was going to take the two Bibles to his church at home. There they would take the Bibles apart, page by page, and insert each page between two sheets of clear plastic. The pages would then be passed round the congregation, and each church member would thus have an opportunity to read the Bible. This incident took place when the Cold War was at its frostiest and I was deeply impressed by the seafarer's faith and courage.

⋆   ⋆   ⋆

During the 1970's and 1980's, Sea Sunday, the second Sunday in July, was increasingly being observed in churches of many denominations all over the world. In the United Kingdom representatives of the Roman Catholic Apostleship of the Sea, the Anglican Missions to Seamen and the inter-denominational British Sailors' Society met each year to produce a set of publicity material to be used by all.

The Roman Catholic Church publicised Sea Sunday all over the world through its official channels, and an informal and unscheduled meeting I had with the Archbishop of Canterbury, Robert Runcie, at Lambeth Palace, led to the regular inclusion of Sea Sunday in the annual Anglican Cycle of Prayer. Sea Sunday is now widely observed in churches all over the world; it has brought a knowledge and understanding of seafaring and seafarers to huge numbers of people.

⋆   ⋆   ⋆

When I joined the chaplaincy staff of The Missions to Seamen in 1963, a World Conference of the Society was held in Oxford every five years. The first one I attended, in 1967, was the last of its kind, and the last for 21 years. A number of elderly members of the Society's committees attended, together with some voluntary workers, staff from Headquarters, and a selection of chaplains serving in different parts of the world. I was one of a small number of younger chaplains present. It was a dignified conference, moving at a gentle pace, and I was disappointed by it. It seemed that this was also the view of the incoming General Secretary, Tom Kerfoot; the conference was discontinued as being too costly and not meeting current needs. It was a wise decision at the time, which was further vindicated when the International Christian Maritime Association came into being in 1969, and held triennial world conferences, the first of which took place in London in 1972.

In the late 1970's and 1980's The Missions to Seamen progressively devolved responsibility for its work around the world to Provincial or National Councils presided over by a Liaison Bishop, and including lay representatives as well as chaplains. The increasing incorporation of the Society within the Anglican Communion led Joe Parker, the senior chaplain in Vancouver and a participant in the 1967 World Conference, to propose that the time had come to plan a new-style World Conference to be held in the week preceding the 1988 Lambeth Conference of the Bishops of the Anglican Communion; this would enable our Liaison Bishops to be present, since they would all be in the United Kingdom at that time. He had thought it all through, and first mentioned it to me in 1985. The more we thought about it at Central Office, the more compelling became the reasons for proceeding. The Society's General Committee and Council approved the proposal, and I wrote to all the Liaison Bishops two years before the Lambeth Conference to let them know what was being planned.

The Conference was held at Churchill College, Cambridge, between July 11th and 15th 1988. 10 Liaison Bishops were present throughout, and in all some 150 delegates from all over the world attended. The Society's President, H.R.H. The Princess Royal, spent part of one day with us, and the whole conference was a phenomenal success. At the ensuing Lambeth Conference our Liaison Bishops tabled a motion, which was unanimously approved by the Bishops, recognising The Missions to Seamen as the outreach of the Anglican Communion to the seafarers of the world. It read as follows:-

> This Conference thanks God for the world-wide Missions to Seamen which began its work in 1856. It supports and endorses the remarkable way in which the Society has adapted its ministry to changed circumstances, acknowledging the fact that there is no part of the Church which has greater ecumenical involvement and experience; that it is deeply involved in dialogue with people of other faiths every day; and that through the Center for Seafarers' Rights and through almost every member of staff, it is daily involved in issues of social justice. The Conference, encouraged by the appointment of Liaison Bishops throughout the Anglican Communion, accepts the Ministry and Mission of the Society as the Mission of the Church to all seafarers, regardless of creed, class or colour.

This was a remarkable affirmation of the Society's work, and the World Conference of The Missions to Seamen in 1988 set a new pattern for the Society's work.

### Personal

During the 15 years I served first as Deputy General Secretary and then as General Secretary of The Missions to Seamen, I travelled more than two million miles by air, visiting every continent except Antarctica, drove many miles by road (including 15,000 miles a year in my own vehicle), and spent

120 days and nights a year away from home. Throughout these years I was blessed with excellent health.

The sole exception to this happy state of affairs occurred in 1989 in the course of a tour of our stations in South East Asia. I had spent time in Bombay and Calcutta before flying on to Korea via Bangkok, where I stopped over for a night. Somewhere along the route I picked up a vicious germ, which began to manifest itself on the flight from Bangkok to Seoul and Pusan. When I arrived in Pusan I struggled on for nearly 24 hours, with a rising temperature and frequent bouts of diarrhoea. I retired to bed, and early next morning fainted in the bathroom, falling off the toilet seat in the process! I was taken to the Baptist Hospital, where I was diagnosed as suffering from dysentery. I was put on an intravenous drip and felt very sorry for myself for 24 hours. Our chaplain in Pusan, Colin Harrison, and his assistant, Miss Mi-Kyung 'Miki' Kwon, were kindness itself; they spent hours sitting with me and translating for the excellent nurses, and I was discharged from hospital after 36 hours. I spent the next three days recuperating, but it was a long time before my internal workings resumed completely normal functioning.

The enforced rest in Pusan was not without a brighter side. I came to appreciate the sterling qualities of Colin Harrison and Miki Kwon, and I kept in touch with them after I left The Missions to Seamen in 1990 to become Bishop of Bermuda. Colin visited me in Bermuda, and in April 2000 I conducted Miki's marriage service at Palmerston North in New Zealand. We had written to each other at intervals, but I had not seen her for 10 years when she telephoned at 7:30 a.m. on New Year's Day 2000 to tell me that she was getting married, and to invite me to conduct the ceremony. I was delighted for her, and accepted joyfully; and towards the end of March 2000 I flew to New Zealand for the happy occasion. I spent a memorable week there, and the break from a particularly busy period of diocesan duties was very welcome.

★   ★   ★

In 1985 I was appointed an Honorary Canon of the Cathedral of the Holy Trinity, Gibraltar, in the Diocese of Europe. It was a great honour and I was thrilled by it. I felt that it reflected well upon the great contribution to the life of the Church over many years made by The Missions to Seamen, and I flew to Milan to be licensed by the Bishop, John Satterthwaite. Sally and I later went to Gibraltar for me to be installed in the Cathedral by the Dean, John Rowlands, formerly Personnel Secretary to The Missions to Seamen, and we spent a most enjoyable weekend with him and his wife Jean.

In 1987 I was appointed an Honorary Canon of St. Michael's Cathedral, Kobe, in Japan. The Nippon Sei Ko Kai, the Episcopal Church of Japan, gave great support to The Missions to Seamen. In every port, however small, the Church had appointed an Honorary Chaplain to minister to seafarers, and on

*General Secretary in a quiet moment in New Zealand, 1988.*

Sea Sunday all Church collections in Japan were given to the Society. The Bishop of Kobe, Paul Yashiro, was the first Liaison Bishop for The Missions to Seamen in the Nippon Sei Ko Kai and it was he who appointed me an Honorary Canon.

In 1989 I was delighted when the Master of the Honourable Company of Master Mariners announced at a Reception on the Company's Headquarters Ship *Wellington*, on the occasion of the launching of my book *On Course Together*, that I was to be offered honorary membership of the Company for the length of my service as General Secretary of The Missions to Seamen, and that the same offer would be made to succeeding General Secretaries. It was an honour I prized.

★ ★ ★

In 1987 I was granted sabbatical leave from Christmas 1987 until Easter 1988 in order to start writing a book about the Churches working together in the maritime world.

It was a book I had wanted to write for a number of reasons. The first was that the quarter of a century in which I had served with The Missions to Seamen had been a time of revolutionary change, both on the shipping scene and in maritime ministry, and I felt that someone should record this. The second was that in these years ecumenical collaboration in maritime ministry had grown from a small shoot into a flourishing tree, and I felt that what had been achieved was of enormous value to the Churches individually and to the Church as a whole. I had been intimately involved in the process of change, both as a chaplain in several ports and also, more recently, in the joint decision-making of ecclesiastical partnerships, and I knew at first hand what had happened. The third was that the two people best qualified to write the book, Prebendary Tom Kerfoot (my predecessor as General Secretary of The Missions to Seamen and the first General Secretary of the International Christian Maritime Association) and Monsignor Francis Frayne (of The Pontifical Commission for Migrants and People on the Move, and a moving force in the establishment of ICMA), had both died. There was nobody in a better position to write the history than myself.

After 25 years of active and full ministry in the Church, it was good to have the opportunity to stop and assess unhurriedly all that had happened. I worked on the book from 7:00 a.m. until noon every day, and took a long walk in the afternoon before picking up Tim, our younger son, from school. In the evenings I wrote up anything that I had drafted in the morning and spent time with the family. After resuming my duties at Easter, I spent a full day each week for six months completing the book.

Writing the book was a fulfilling experience. I had the time and the opportunity to read and research around my subject, and putting my knowledge and experience into words deepened my understanding of my ministry. It was a great delight, too, to be at home with Sally during the day for much of the time I was writing.

## Family

I was 41 when I began my ministry as General Secretary of The Missions to Seamen on January 1st 1976, and during the 14 years I was in office Sally and I saw our children growing up, moving on to university education, then into their chosen careers, and Andrew and Helen into marriage.

When we returned from Australia in 1974 Sally was pregnant with Tim, our fourth and youngest child. Andrew was 12, Helen 10, and Julia 6. Andrew went into the second year at Watford Grammar School, and after an initial struggle to make up on gaps and differences between the Australian and English curricula, he settled very well and forged ahead. Helen went into the top year at Hartsbourne Primary School, 300 yards from home, and Julia into the Infants department. Because of her Australian accent and background, Helen was known as 'the Aborigine', and Julia as 'the Aborigine's sister'. Julia's teacher delighted in her Australian pronunciation.

For Sally Tim's arrival meant a long postponement of her pursuing wider interests or resuming her teaching career. She was a firm believer in being at home when the children were small, and when they arrived home from school, and with me away from home often for weeks at a time, her life was unavoidably restricted. When Tim started school she undertook a course of further studies, and in 1982 embarked upon an external four-year Diploma of Religious Studies course at London University. She enjoyed the course, which she interrupted for two years while teaching at St. Margaret's School, Bushey, completing it in 1988. In 1989 she began training to become a Licensed Lay Reader in the Diocese of London and completed that course in 1991.

Andrew did well at Watford Grammar School. He particularly enjoyed life in the Sixth Form, delighting in completing *The Times* crossword most days! He became a good Cross Country runner, played chess, achieved considerable skill in setting up the lighting for school dramatic productions, won an inter-schools Maths competition and was awarded a scholarship at Lincoln College, Oxford, to read Maths. He was also a Meccano enthusiast and he put together the most amazing constructions. A committed Christian, he met Frances Stone, an undergraduate reading scientific subjects at Durham University, at a Scripture Union Children's Holiday at which they were both helping, and they married in 1984. Andrew taught for a year at Magdalen College School, Oxford, before entering the fast developing world of Information Technology. Frances also embarked on a teaching career and showed herself to be extremely gifted.

From Hartsbourne Primary School Helen went on to Watford Girls Grammar School. She played a full part in the life of the school, singing in the choir, playing important roles in dramatic productions, representing the school in public speaking competitions and being Head Girl in her final year. She was a Girl Guide, and later a Ranger. Academically she was on the Arts side, and was awarded a place at Downing College, Cambridge, to read English. In her gap year she worked in a general store before spending six months in Israel, where she came to a deeper Christian commitment. Before embarking on a Post Graduate Certificate of Education at Oxford University, she served for a year at a residential school for physically handicapped children and young people, and in holidays she worked as a volunteer in old people's residential homes. In 1988 she married Geoffrey Burn, an Australian research scientist with a doctorate in computer science and who was also a member of the congregation of St. John's Stanmore, where we all worshipped. She embarked on a career as a teacher.

Julia progressed happily through the Infants and Junior Departments of Hartsbourne Primary School. As a little girl she was very shy, but her confidence grew steadily. She learned the piano at home and the cello at school, and showed considerable aptitude with both. She was a Brownie, and later a Girl Guide. She moved on to Watford Girls Grammar School, where she achieved high grades in her General Certificate of Education O Level examinations. It was at this point that a steely determination in her character manifested itself. The school was unable to cope with her desire to study Pure and Applied Mathematics, Latin and Music at A Level, so she quietly but resolutely investigated the local education scene until she found an institution that could accommodate her. To the chagrin of the staff at Watford Girls Grammar School, she announced her intention of transferring to Harrow Weald Sixth Form College in order to pursue her chosen subjects, and she did just that! She enjoyed the life of the College, and did well in her examinations. Her Christian commitment deepened through her involvement with the Crusader movement, and she was always in demand as a musician. In addition to her considerable instrumental accomplishments, she had a fine soprano voice, which she later had trained, and was a member of the choir of St. John's, Stanmore, where she and some friends successfully persuaded the organist/choirmaster that girls would be an asset to his existing all-male top line! She went on to Manchester University to read Maths and Philosophy; a career in Occupational Therapy beckoned.

Tim, our youngest child, was born in 1975 and spent the first 16 years of his life in our home in Bushey Heath. He thus escaped the upheavals the others had experienced early in their lives, when we moved from one posting to another. Being nearly seven years younger than Julia, eleven than Helen, and thirteen than Andrew, he received plenty of attention from all of them and from their friends. He made his own friends at nursery school and later at Hartsbourne Primary School. Our house was situated very close to a Royal Air Force officers' housing estate, and he had many friends there. At school he showed a real aptitude for Maths, and it was apparent that he had a very good treble, and later tenor, voice. He sang in the choir at St. John's, Stanmore, and got into the usual boyish scrapes. He was very keen on football. He played in a local junior team, and supported Watford's Football League team. He loved going to watch their matches, and his support for them has not wavered over the years. He went on to Watford Grammar School, where some of the teaching staff occasionally confused him with his older brother Andrew!

## St. John's Church, Stanmore

St. John's Church in Stanmore came to mean a great deal to us as a family. We all worshipped there throughout the years I was based in London, and Michael Bowles, the Rector, was a true friend and pastor to us. We all played our individual parts in the life of the church: Andrew was always there, helping cheerfully; Helen assisted at Junior Church; Julia and Tim sang in the choir; Sally led Ten Plus, a mixed pre-Confirmation group of young people, and later trained as a Lay Reader; and I preached around 15 sermons a year at the Sunday Services. We made many lifelong friends, and the welcoming atmosphere of the church was a tribute to the leadership of Michael Bowles. The standard of the ministry to the children was extremely high: one good

*London, Chaplain Worshipful Company of Carmen.*

leader followed another, and for the last 25 years Phyllis O'Leary has supervised Junior Church outstandingly.

### A Fresh Challenge

In the summer of 1989 I was telephoned by Hector McLean, the Archbishop of Canterbury's Senior Appointments Advisor, to ask if I was prepared to be considered for appointment as Bishop of Bermuda. He explained that if I agreed, I would be one of several people on a very short list. I asked for time to talk this over with Sally, because Tim's education was at a vital stage and there were other family factors to consider.

Tim was a particular concern. He was just about to begin his two-year General Certificate of Secondary Education course, and we would not want to move him before he completed it. My parents were becoming frail, and Sally's mother had been widowed and was in indifferent health. We agonised over the decision for a long time. We made enquiries in Bermuda as to whether Tim would be able to take English A Level examinations on the island, but the enquires had to be very discreet because of the confidential nature of the appointments system. We were advised that he would indeed be able to take his A Levels there, but in the event the information proved to be incorrect. Sally said that if I were appointed, she would stay on in Bushey Heath with Tim until be completed his GCSE course.

Eventually I rang Hector McLean to advise him that I was prepared to let my name go forward. I had a long interview with the Archbishop of Canterbury, Robert Runcie, who left me in no doubt about the particular difficulties of the appointment, and in due course I was appointed. I would be consecrated Bishop in St. Albans Abbey on January 25 1990, on the Festival of The Conversion of St. Paul.

Sally and I were very moved by the huge number of letters and other expressions of good wishes which we received, and she dealt with them all wonderfully when I left for a long-arranged tour of Southern Africa a few days after my appointment was announced. We both had mixed feelings about the appointment for the reasons already set out, but I was excited by the prospect and ready for a fresh challenge. After 14 years as General Secretary of The Missions to Seamen, it was time to move on.

# CHAPTER THIRTEEN

# Consecration as Bishop:
# January 1990

MY APPOINTMENT as Bishop of Bermuda was announced in a Press Release from the Archbishop of Canterbury's office on October 20th 1989. It was the culmination of a long process rendered necessary by the particular circumstances of the Anglican Church of Bermuda.

The Anglican Church of Bermuda is an extra-provincial diocese of the Anglican Communion. It does not form part of any ecclesiastical Province and is under the metropolitical jurisdiction of the Archbishop of Canterbury. It is one of a very small number of such Churches or Dioceses, which includes the Church of Ceylon (Sri Lanka), the Falkland Islands, the Lusitanian Church (Portuguese Episcopal Church) and the Spanish Episcopal Reformed Church. Bermuda does not fit naturally into the ecclesiastical groupings of the Church of the Province of the West Indies, the Episcopal Church of the U.S.A. or the Anglican Church of Canada. It became independent from the Anglican Church of Canada in 1925, when it was constituted as a diocese in its own right.

From 1925 onwards the nine Bishops of Bermuda had been drawn from the United Kingdom or Ireland and were appointed by the Archbishop of Canterbury. Many of the parochial clergy came likewise from the United Kingdom. In the 1970's the first black Bermudian clergy were appointed as Rectors of parishes, and the Constitution of the diocese was amended to provide the opportunity for the Synod to elect its own Bishop. But on two separate occasions no candidate for election as Bishop commanded sufficient support, and the appointment of the next Bishop reverted to the Archbishop of Canterbury.

When Bishop Christopher Luxmoore returned to the United Kingdom early in 1989, the Synod again failed to elect a Bishop and the Archbishop of Canterbury was called upon to make the appointment. The Archbishop, after consultation with his Senior Appointments Advisor Hector McLean, considered a number of names and finally came up with mine. He called me into Lambeth Palace, and spelled out in detail the difficulties of the bishopric; I should need to have much love in my heart, he said. He asked me to go away and think about it, and to let him know if I was prepared to accept the appointment. Sally and I had long heart-searching discussions about it, because of the implications for our family and for our surviving parents, and eventually I accepted. A careful legal process followed before the appointment could be formally announced, and it was finally made public five days before I flew to South Africa for a previously arranged tour of the stations of The Missions to Seamen there. I was to be consecrated Bishop by the Archbishop of Canterbury, Robert Runcie, in St Albans Abbey on January 25th 1990.

The period leading up to the formal announcement of my appointment was very difficult for me. There were major family implications, such as Tim's continuing General Certificate of Secondary Education course work; leaving behind Sally's recently widowed mother, who was also in poor health; and concerns about the health and welfare of both my parents. There was also the burden of maintaining confidentiality. I was very aware of my shortcomings, and I appreciated the importance of the appointment. Sally was a great support and I leaned on her heavily. But for three weeks before the appointment was announced, I was away on a tour of some of our Asian stations, and the strain of not being able to talk to anybody about it was considerable. When I got to Manila I visited Cardinal Sin, leader of the Roman Catholic Church in the Philippines. Four years previously I had spent a long and happy evening in his company, and I had met him on other occasions; I had great respect for him. When I called on him, I shared with him all my concerns. I told him about the impending appointment, of my eagerness to prove worthy of the task, of my strong feelings of inadequacy, and of recurring memories of the many stupid mistakes I had made in the past. He was silent for a while, and then he told me a story:

> Some years previously he had met a woman who told him that Jesus spoke to her and told her things. He had been a bit sceptical, so he had said to her that when she next met Jesus she should ask him to tell her about the sins he had committed since boyhood. She was to come back and tell him what Jesus had said. A few days later she returned. He asked her if Jesus had told her about his sins. 'No, Father, He didn't,' she replied with a seraphic smile; 'He said that what He had forgiven He had forgotten.'

His words made a huge impact on me: I felt that God had spoken to me through him.

The days and weeks leading up to the Consecration service passed very quickly. There was much to do, such as preparing to hand over responsibility for the work of The Missions to Seamen to my successor; being involved in the details of the Consecration service and the Reception which would follow it; being measured for new robes; replying to letters from friends; farewell parties; making contact with the Archdeacon in Bermuda; and celebrating Christmas. I was grateful for the three-month gap between the announcement of my appointment and the Consecration service, as it gave me time to begin to come to terms with what lay ahead. I was grateful for wise advice from

*St. Albans Abbey, Consecration as Bishop, 1990.*

Bishop Hawker, chairman of the Pastoral Committee of The Missions to Seamen: 'Do your best,' he said, 'and leave the worrying to God.'

### The Service of Consecration
The Service of Consecration was preceded by a marvellous dinner at Lambeth Palace on the previous evening. A fellow former Ridley Hall student, Robin Smith, was being consecrated with me as Bishop of Hertford, and he and I, with our wives and children, were invited to dine with Archbishop and Mrs. Runcie. It was a fabulous evening, an excellent meal being accompanied by much laughter and happiness.

January 25th., the Festival of the Conversion of St. Paul, began cool and cloudy. As the morning advanced a storm arose. By the time the service started at 11 a.m. a full gale was blowing and increasing in intensity. In the Abbey itself there were fears that one of the great windows might blow in.

The service proceeded majestically. It began with the entry into the Abbey of the processions of Choristers, Lay Clerks, Lay Readers, Cathedral Wardens, Cathedral clergy, Lay Canons, Honorary Canons, the Bishops Designate, the Bishops Assistant, the Presenting Bishops, the Dean and the Archbishop of Canterbury. The Epistle was read by the Bishop of St. Albans and the Gospel by the Bishop of Winchester. The sermon was preached by Cyril Bowles, formerly Bishop of Derby and Principal of Ridley Hall when Robin and I were students there. Cyril spoke about the very different ministries in which Robin and I had been engaged. He made it clear that serving in a diocese which was tiny geographically would be very different from my previous worldwide ministry. He spoke of the wider dimensions of Robin's new appointment. He stressed the need for humility, patience, prayerfulness, courage and a willingness to launch out into the deep in faith. Then, after everybody had affirmed their faith in the words of the Nicene Creed, Robin and I were commended to the Archbishop and the congregation by our Presenting Bishops; in my case these were Dennis Hawker, formerly Bishop of Grantham and Chairman of The Pastoral Committee of The Missions to Seamen, and John Satterthwaite, Bishop of Gibraltar in Europe. The congregation was invited to express its approval of the choice of the new Bishops, and the Archbishop read the solemn charge to new bishops. There followed his formal searching questioning of us and our formal replies. Formal though this was, it was profoundly challenging. After being vested with our episcopal robes, the traditional Veni Creator Spiritus was sung, the Litany said, and then the Archbishop, flanked by the Bishops Assistant, ordained us to the episcopate, all the Bishops present laying their hands on our heads.

It was a truly awe-inspiring moment.

We were then presented with a Bible and our Pastoral Staff, the symbols of our calling. A moving celebration of Holy Communion followed, and then Robin and I were led out by the Archbishop to greet the members of the congregation at the West Door. The storm was at its peak, and the devastation it was causing was apparent. Nearby trees had been uprooted, power lines had been brought down, and we learned that roads were blocked with debris and railway services suspended.

It was lovely to be greeted by many friends and well-wishers, and the Reception and Lunch which followed was a very happy occasion. It was particularly good to meet Canon Thomas Nisbett, representing the Diocese of Bermuda; Lawson Mapp, Warden of Bermuda Cathedral; The Revd. Billy Hayward, a deacon from Bermuda studying at Chichester Theological College; and a number of other people from Bermuda or with strong Bermuda connections. A family meal in the evening, in the calm which followed the storm, brought a memorable day to a happy ending.

Afterwards we recalled with amusement a lighter moment of the service. A formal document, signed by The Queen and commending 'the purity of my manners,' was solemnly read publicly. It appealed to the sense of humour of many members of my family!

# CHAPTER FOURTEEN

# Bishop of Bermuda 1990-1995: A New Challenge

## Introduction to Bermuda

WHEN I WAS INVITED to consider the possibility of appointment as Bishop of Bermuda, I was distinctly hazy as to its exact location. I knew that it was in mid-Atlantic, but the Atlantic Ocean is huge and Bermuda is tiny. Behind my desk in the Central Office of The Missions to Seamen there was a large map of the world, and I studied it carefully until I found Bermuda. It was 32° North of the Equator, 750 miles from the Eastern seaboard of North America, 3,200 miles from the United Kingdom and 1000 miles from the West Indies. It has a population of 60,000 on a group of inter-linked islands covering a total of 21 square miles. I set about learning more.

As soon as my appointment was announced, I received a very comprehensive application form from the Government of Bermuda for a residency and work permit. I was impressed, and somewhat daunted, by the amount of detail required, and spent many hours gathering all the information. I posted it all to Bermuda, and received a prompt reply welcoming me to Bermuda.

## Arrival

I flew to Bermuda on March 1st 1990, a month after my consecration as Bishop and three weeks before my Enthronement in the Cathedral. At the airport I was greeted by the Archdeacon, Tom Dyson, the Canon Residentiary of the Cathedral, James Francis, and the Diocesan Public Relations Officer, Charles Webbe. They were kindness itself to me. Immigration formalities were swiftly dealt with, and I was handed my Work Permit, which I put in my briefcase to study later. I was driven to the home of Captain Sir David Tibbitts and his wife Mary, with whom I was to spend a few days before moving into Bishop's Lodge. I was going to be living on my own for 18 months, with Sally staying in England to look after our son Tim, who had already embarked on his two-year General Certificate of Secondary Education course, so I was deeply grateful to David and Mary for making my baptism into Bermuda life both enjoyable and valuable. They were the parents of our Public Relations Officer at The Missions to Seamen, Gillian Ennis, and I had met them previously in London.

In those early days, and before I became involved with official duties, David drove me round Bermuda. As yet I had neither a Bermuda driving

*Wearing Cope of Diocese of Bermuda, presented by*
*The Worshipful Company of Carmen, 1990.*

licence nor a car to drive, and since all drivers must be in possession of a valid Bermudian licence, I was accordingly enrolled under the direction of a driving instructor. Despite having driven more than half a million miles over the past 30 years, I had a short series of driving lessons, and in due course passed the written and road tests, becoming the proud possessor not only of a Bermudian driving licence but also of a splendid trophy from my instructor! I then took delivery of a new Hyundai hatchback, complete with air-conditioning, a welcome and important feature in Bermuda's hot and humid climate. Travelling around the island with David before I had the car was a great bonus. I could look round freely as he pointed out places and items of interest; I had time to admire the magnificent scenery and I could ask questions and concentrate on the answers. He introduced me to many people, and when the time came for me to move into Bishop's Lodge, he came every day at the beginning to lend a hand.

He and Mary had also looked ahead to my longer-term needs and had asked a widowed friend of theirs in her seventies, Audrey Seymour, if she would be prepared to keep house for me until Sally came to Bermuda. Audrey and I got along very well together; she ran Bishop's Lodge admirably, and we laughed a lot. Between us we got Bishop's Lodge functioning very efficiently, and I came to rely on her absolutely.

## My Work Permit

As soon as I had a quiet moment I took a look at my Work Permit, and was taken aback to see that it was for one year only. I had already been made aware of the difficulties some expatriates experienced with the renewal of these permits, and I could not understand why mine was for so short a period. It is not normal to appoint Anglican Bishops for a specific period of time, and I could see no good reason why Bermuda should be an exception. I sought advice from our Church lawyers, and also from the Chairman of the Bermuda Church Society, which financed the administration of the diocese, and was told not to make an issue of this immediately. I was partially reassured, but still disturbed that I had moved from a long-term appointment with worldwide responsibilities, which I had loved and was enjoying, to one with so little apparent security of tenure. Nor had I been led to expect this. So on the first occasion when I had a meeting with the Minister for Immigration, I asked him privately why he had issued me with such a short-term Work Permit. He replied that there was nothing to prevent my seeking an extension when the time came, but said no more. I was not happy with the situation, but resolved to put it out of my mind until I had to deal with it in a few months' time.

## The Enthronement

Before my Enthronement in the Cathedral, Archdeacon Tom Dyson and his wife Lucette hosted a welcome party for me at their home, St. Mary's Rectory in Warwick. All the clergy were present, and it was a happy and joyful occasion: it was good to meet them all informally.

Sally came for the Enthronement, and it was lovely to be together again for a short period. We were very moved at that time to receive a letter from a solicitor, Philip Byam-Cook, who was a staunch supporter of The Missions to Seamen; he told us that he had arranged for £5000 to be held in trust for us by The Missions to Seamen to provide air fares for the family during the 18 months of our unavoidable separation. It was a godsend, and made family holidays in Bermuda a reality we had not expected.

The Enthronement Service, which was held on Mothering Sunday, the mid-point of the Church's season of Lent, was memorable. The Cathedral was packed to the doors. The Governor, the Premier, Government ministers and members of Parliament, the diocesan clergy, representatives of the Anglican Church of Canada and of the Episcopal Church of The United States, the Roman Catholic Bishop of Hamilton in Bermuda and leaders of other denominations attended. The service was solemn, dignified and joyful. My sermon was based on the words of Jesus to His disciples, 'I am among you as one who serves.' I ended with these words:-

> I have come to serve – to serve God, to serve His Church, to serve you all, and to serve Bermuda. I shall surely make mistakes – we all do. But I trust that in His providence God will use us all to His glory.

> It was time to get on with the job.

### Getting on with the job

The three weeks I spent in Bermuda before the Enthronement service were invaluable. I was able to observe everything in an unhurried way, and also to write a sermon for the occasion which took account of the local scene.

Each Sunday I worshipped in the Cathedral, of which I was to be the Dean in addition to episcopal duties. I met the Wardens, the Organist and members of the Choir, the members of the Vestry (the equivalent of the Parochial Church Council in the Church of England), and the congregation. It was 27 years since I had served in a parish in a full-time capacity, and now I had to learn about the particular role and function of a Cathedral. I was grateful for much practical help and patient friendly advice from Jim Francis, the Canon Residentiary. Jim was a Bermudian by birth, and had served for many years in the Episcopal Church of the United States (ECUSA) in Chicago before returning to Bermuda to become the Canon Residentiary of the Cathedral. As Chairman of the Human Rights Commission, he played a leading role in community affairs. He and I said Morning Prayer together daily throughout my time in Bermuda; it was a good way to start the day and provided an excellent opportunity to share information.

The only immediate change I wanted to introduce at the Cathedral was a punctual start to our worship. Bermuda is noted for its relaxed attitude to time-keeping, but with many overseas visitors attending our Sunday services, I did my best to ensure that the services started on time. So on the first Sunday morning after my Enthronement I spoke to the members of the choir two minutes before the scheduled time of the service. After greeting them cheerfully I announced that the timing of our services would follow Royal

Navy practice. 'Royal Navy time is like God's time,' I concluded, 'It's on time!' Everybody laughed, and my insistence on a punctual start was a regular source of amusement to the choir throughout my stay in Bermuda.

I soon became aware of the great opportunities, challenges and importance of the ministry of the Cathedral in Bermuda. State occasions took place there. The 11 a.m. service of Choral Matins was broadcast live on the radio every Sunday. Marriages, funerals and baptisms were a regular feature of our programme. Sermons can have a powerful impact on public opinion, and I took great care preparing and writing them out in full. Large numbers of tourists visited the Cathedral most days, and few days passed without my having informal conversations with some of them. Sometimes there would be a request for a short service of renewal of marriage vows; sometimes it might be a request to say a prayer with them; sometimes it was the sharing of a heart-breaking problem. My understanding of the role of a Cathedral Dean broadened and deepened rapidly.

With the Enthronement and the concentrated programme of Lent, Holy Week and Easter services behind me, I could concentrate on expanding and implementing the vision I had spelled out. Among my priorities were getting to know the clergy and lay people of the Anglican Church of Bermuda; establishing good working relationships with Christians of other denominations; getting to know more about the history and life of Bermuda; establishing good relations with the leaders of the community, such as the Governor, the Premier, Government ministers, civil servants and local government officers; and being available to people.

I determined to pursue all these aims simultaneously, and review my thinking as I became more familiar with the island and its life.

## Living in Bermuda

Living in a small community on a tiny sub-tropical island of exceptional beauty, 750 miles from the nearest landfall and with its own particular history and way of life, is a unique experience.

My first, overwhelming, and abiding impression of Bermuda was of the magnificence of the scenery. As our incoming aircraft circled before landing I could clearly see the vivid blue of the sea, the rugged coastline, the lighter blue water covering the reefs which surround Bermuda, the superb beaches, the host of small islets dotted around the seven inter-connected islands which form the main chain, and the lush green of the trees and vegetation. Closer acquaintance reinforced and enhanced this impression.

As I settled into life in Bermuda, I soon became aware of the incredibly complex nature of the community and of the many inter-linked historical events and factors which have made Bermuda what is it today. Whole books have been written on this subject, and historians and social commentators continue to disagree over their conclusions. An outline of some of the significant features of Bermuda's history may be helpful here.

⋆　　⋆　　⋆

Bermuda has been a British colony since 1612, and is now the oldest. Before 1609, when an English ship, the *Sea Venture*, was wrecked on the reefs surrounding the islands by a hurricane while sailing from Plymouth to Virginia, the islands had been inhabited for limited periods of time by seafarers whose ships had been wrecked on the reefs. The *Sea Venture* was the flagship of a convoy of seven ships and two pinnaces of The Virginia Company of London, and was under the command of Admiral Sir George Somers. It was carrying 150 passengers and crew, including the new Governor of Virginia, Sir Thomas Gates. All on board the ship managed to scramble ashore to safety when the vessel was wrecked, and they stayed there for nearly a year while two ships, the *Patience* and the *Deliverance*, were built to carry them on to Virginia. They found the islands very pleasant: the climate was agreeable; there was an abundance of wholesome food readily available, including fish of many kinds, sea turtles, prickly pears, wild olives, and even wild pigs, descendants of some which had been brought ashore in the 16th century by Spanish sailors wrecked on the rocky shores; there were no venomous reptiles; and there were no hostile inhabitants.

When the survivors reached Jamestown in Virginia in the two little vessels they had built, they found the colony in poor shape. Many of the original settlers had died of disease or starvation, and others had been killed by hostile Indians. By contrast Bermuda seemed very attractive. Sir George Somers returned to Bermuda immediately to organise a relief expedition from there, but his health deteriorated and he died in Bermuda in November 1610. His body was shipped back to England for burial, but his heart was removed and buried in Bermuda at St. George's.

Accounts of Bermuda's beauty and natural assets persuaded the Virginia Company to apply to King James the First to extend their charter to include Bermuda, and in 1612 Bermuda became a colony. In 1615 the King granted the islanders the right to have a House of Assembly to administer their affairs, and in the same year the Virginia Company transferred its mandate for Bermuda to the Somers Island Company, which administered the islands for the next 69 years. It was an unsettled and contentious period, however, and in 1684 the Company's charter was forfeited to the Crown. Thereafter Bermuda's Governors were appointed by the Sovereign rather than by the Company.

⋆　　⋆　　⋆

An early and influential factor in the shaping of Bermuda's community life was slavery. In the first two decades of the colony's existence only a small number of slaves were brought in, but in the middle of the 17th century a significant number were introduced. Most were black Africans from the West Indies, although there were also a few North American Indians and some Scottish and Irish soldiers who had been taken prisoner and sold into slavery after the English Civil War. Opinions differ on the treatment of the slaves in Bermuda, with some maintaining that because there were no plantations on the islands, the slaves experienced a less severe regime than in other places. A number were employed in the harvesting of salt on Turk's Island, 1000 miles South of Bermuda, where in the latter part of the 17th century Bermudian seafarers had dug huge salt ponds on the uninhabited island and established a lucrative business. Most of the slaves in Bermuda in the 17th and 18th centuries, however, were employed as servants or seafarers, and at least one contemporary writer claimed that they were better treated than in the West Indies. In 1834 the English Parliament passed legislation abolishing slavery throughout its domains, and this was implemented immediately in Bermuda.

So a thoroughly reprehensible practice came to an end. It was cruel, degrading, inhuman, unjust, immoral, and an abuse of the intrinsic dignity and value of every human being. But legislation does not change attitudes or society overnight. The legacy of slavery is still apparent in Bermuda in a continuing deep-seated resentment of past and present perceived injustices and indignities among some of the black people, and in a perceived arrogance among some of the white people. Many people from all sections of the community have moved on from these attitudes, but the legacy of slavery has not yet been fully worked out of the system.

★   ★   ★

Bermuda has always been dependent upon maritime communications and trade. Because of its remoteness, isolation, and the ever-present dangers of navigation around the islands, Bermudians became accomplished seafarers. Mention has already been made of the construction of two small ships to transport the survivors of the wreck of the *Sea Venture* in 1609 to Virginia, and Bermuda gained a reputation for the excellence of the ships built there. The cedar trees growing in abundance on the islands were ideal for shipbuilding, and a succession of fast and graceful vessels were built. These were required for trading, communication and defence purposes, as became evident during the 18th century war between Britain and the United States, when a small force from an American brig came ashore and seized and held one of the forts for a few days.

A permanent British Army garrison was brought in during the following year, and in 1795 the Royal Navy established a permanent base. For the next 200 years Bermuda was an integral part of the Navy's planning and

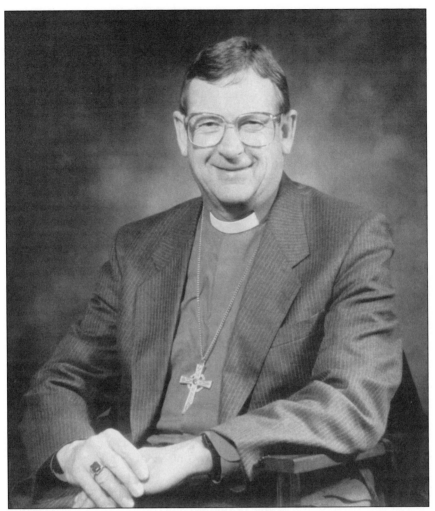

*Bishop of Bermuda, 1990.*

operations: a fully equipped dockyard was set up to build and repair ships; regular service personnel were posted to the islands; high quality communications facilities were introduced; and the base played a key role in the Battle of the Atlantic in the Second World War. During the First World War a small United States Naval Base was established to service American submarines patrolling in Bermuda waters, and in the Second World War a major U.S. base covering 7% of Bermuda's land area was built.

Bermuda's importance as a maritime centre has directly influenced its life and culture. The sea has brought economic prosperity to Bermuda through trade and tourism. Bermuda's merchant shipping register is significant. There is a deep love of the sea among Bermudians, as is evidenced by the large numbers of sailing boats, power boats, yachts and jet skis, as well as by swimmers and wind surfers. The sea is treated with huge respect; hurricanes and Atlantic storms can be truly terrifying.

★   ★   ★

Another major influence in Bermuda's history has been the Christian Church. From its earliest days as a colony, there has been a strong Anglican Church presence in Bermuda, and as the years have passed other Christian Churches have come in and flourished. A population census in the early 1990's revealed that approximately a quarter of the population described themselves as Anglicans, and there are strong Roman Catholic, African Methodist Episcopal, Pentecostal and Seventh Day Adventist Churches. Bermudians are a church-going people; there are more than 150 centres of worship on the islands, serving a total population of 60,000 and a weekly influx of overseas visitors. On Sunday mornings live services are broadcast over the radio from the Cathedral and from an African Methodist Episcopal church, and reports of sermons (and occasionally even full transcripts) in the Press are not uncommon. The Churches have had a considerable influence on Bermudian life and society throughout almost four centuries, and they continue to play a key role.

★   ★   ★

Bermuda has had its own Parliament for nearly 400 years. A legally constituted House of Assembly met for the first time in 1620 in St. Peter's church at St. George's. It passed a number of Bills covering a wide range of activities such as building bridges, protecting wildlife, inspecting tobacco production, and holding Assizes to punish criminals. In 1970 joyful celebrations marked the 350th anniversary of its Parliament, which was the first in the Western World and is younger only than those of the United Kingdom and Iceland in today's world order.

In 1968 a new Constitution was enacted. The Governor, who is appointed by the Crown and holds office for between three and five years, is the Queen's representative and has some executive powers. Parliament has an elected Lower House (the House of Assembly), and an appointed Upper House (the Legislative Assembly). Elections to the House of Assembly are held at four-yearly intervals. There is a permanent Civil Service and a full judicial system.

Bermuda is a lively and well-ordered community, but it was shaken to its foundations in 1973, when the Governor, Sir Richard Sharples, and his ADC were assassinated. Their murders were traced back to unknown killers who had shot dead the Commissioner of Police six months previously. A determined manhunt eventually led to the arrest, trial and conviction of two black activists with links to the Black Beret movement. They were hanged in 1977 amid civil unrest. That was the last occasion when the death penalty was carried out in Bermuda.

There is a strong desire among some Bermudians for independence from Britain, but the financial implications are daunting. In 1995 the Government, led by Sir John Swan, submitted a proposal for independence to a referendum; the proposal was overwhelmingly rejected.

★ ★ ★

When I arrived in Bermuda in 1990 I came to a very small community, yet a nation in microcosm.

It was immediately clear that this was a very prosperous place. It is one of the world's major reinsurance centres. A number of large international companies, including Bacardi, Jardine Matheson, Cable and Wireless and Worldwide Shipping of Hong Kong, maintain offices there. There is a substantial Shipping Register, attracted by favourable taxation rates and high standards. There are excellent legal and accountancy firms with skilled specialist overseas representation. There is no income tax, but high import duty is charged on goods entering the country, since Bermuda is not large enough to produce sufficient resources for its own needs and must therefore import significantly. The standard of living is very high, as are the cost of living and wages and salaries. The Bermuda dollar is maintained at parity with the United States dollar. North American influence is strong: many young people from Bermuda go to the United States or Canada for university education; Bermuda is a popular venue for tourists from North America; and business contacts are strong.

Tourism plays a vital part in the island's life and economy, with up to 15,000 overseas visitors a week entering the country at the height of the season. This is the maximum number that can be accommodated in comfort at any one time. The climate is such that visitors come throughout the year, with the greatest numbers between April and November. Large cruise ships call each week for six months during the summer; they berth alongside the prestigious Front Street in Hamilton (Bermuda's capital city), in historic St. George's, and at the superbly restored Dockyard. There are many luxurious hotels, a wide variety of restaurants, and excellent shops. There are first-class facilities for fishing, sailing, swimming and diving, and there is easy access to historic sites like St. Peter's church in St. George's (which claims to be the oldest church in constant use in the Western hemisphere), the Dockyard, and buildings with particular histories. Luxuriant flowers, shrubs and trees abound. Because of the narrow roads and the stone walls which border them, there is a speed limit of 35 kilometres (22 miles) per hour on all roads, and cars are restricted to residents only and to one car per household. Visitors are encouraged to hire low-powered mopeds, or to make use of the excellent bus and ferry services.

There are no rivers or fresh water lakes in Bermuda, so fresh water is a valuable commodity. Some 60 inches of rain fall throughout the year, and this is channelled down from the roofs into large storage tanks either below or at the side of the houses. The roofs are treated at regular intervals with a limewash solution which keeps the water pure, and as there is no heavy industry within 750 miles, the rain is free from pollutants.

Evidence abounds of Bermuda's historic links with Britain. Police uniforms are similar to British. Red pillarboxes carry the Royal emblem. The Governor represents the Crown. The parliamentary and judicial institutions closely follow British traditions and practices. The Bermuda Regiment is based on British military patterns, although much of its basic training takes place in the United States.

Medical care and facilities are excellent. The King Edward Hospital provides highly skilled medical and surgical treatment, and when individual cases require specialist attention not available in Bermuda, patients are flown in air ambulances to hospitals in the United States or Canada. Most Bermudians have comprehensive private medical insurance cover; it is expensive, but it works well.

The climate is generally benign. Long hours of glorious sunshine are interspersed with spells of heavy rainfall, which occur throughout the year. The months of June to October are hot and at times unpleasantly humid, and there is a risk of hurricanes. The temperature of the sea within the reefs which surround Bermuda ranges from around 63°F (17°C) in March to about 84°F (28°C) at the end of October. There is usually sufficient rain to keep the water tanks supplied, and if there is a shortage of water, it can be purchased and delivered by road tanker. Many of the hotels use desalination plants to cope with demand. One of the first jobs I was asked to undertake after my enthronement was to pray for rain during a drought. All Church leaders were asked to do this, and it was very satisfying when the heavens opened a few days later and the crisis passed. The lowest recorded temperature is 41°F (5°C), and the highest 95°F (35°C).

★    ★    ★

In a small and isolated community with long traditions, where everybody knows everybody, where many are interrelated, and where gossip is the staff of life, strong distinctive characters emerge and play an important role in society. In general Bermudians are outgoing, friendly, kind and generous, but as a black member of the Cathedral choir told me, 'We Bermudians are a funny people. We welcome you with open arms, but we can suddenly turn against you.'

★   ★   ★

Other features of Bermuda life stand out. There is a significant Portuguese community. They came to Bermuda from the Azores after the American Civil War of 1861-1865, and worked as farmers. More arrived after the First World War. They worked hard, settled in well, and have made a real impact on Bermudian society.

There is lively media reporting. There is a powerful and volatile trade union presence. There is a strong emphasis on Human Rights. There is constant friction over Work Permits. There is a powerful and insidious drugs culture. There is a well-defined social hierarchy.

Living in Bermuda as an expatriate is stimulating, enjoyable, challenging, demanding, and daunting – all at the same time!

## A Dark Shadow

As 1990 drew to a close, a dark shadow hung over me. My Work Permit was due to expire on March 25th 1991 and I was acutely aware of the difficulties experienced by many expatriates in seeking renewal of their permits.

In the autumn of 1990 I consulted the Diocesan Registrar, Michael Woods, who advised me that the matter should be handled by the Archdeacon, Tom Dyson, one of whose functions it was to handle all such applications on behalf of the expatriate clergy. Tom duly prepared the application and submitted it to the Minister for Immigration. At the Minister's request, a letter supporting the application was sent by the Secretary of the Diocesan Synod. In December the Archdeacon asked me to leave a regular meeting of the clergy at Bishop's Lodge so that, at the request of the Minister for Immigration, he could ask the clergy to support the application. This they did, and four days later I received a new Work Permit valid for four years.

Although the outcome was satisfactory I was deeply disturbed by the process. Bishops of the Anglican Church are not appointed for specific periods of time, nor is their continuing in office subject to regular confirmation by the clergy or by the Diocesan Synod. I felt that a thoroughly unsatisfactory precedent was being set by referring the continuing of the Bishop's service to the clergy and the Synod. I summarised these concerns in a report I wrote and sent to the Archbishop of Canterbury in February 1991. 'I have to place on record,' I concluded, 'the fact that I found the procedures set out above to be embarrassing, distasteful, distressing and potentially dangerous to the life of the Church and to the proper authority of the Bishop of Bermuda.'

It was clear to me that unless the political climate in Bermuda changed dramatically, there would inevitably be further problems when my Work Permit next became due for renewal. It was also clear that I could not allow the pattern of my ministry to be influenced by such considerations.

# CHAPTER FIFTEEN

# Bishop of Bermuda 1990-1995: Wrestling with the Challenge

## The Anglican Church of Bermuda

As I FAMILIARISED myself with the geography of the islands, I was immediately impressed by the beauty and solidity of our Anglican churches. The hurricanes and severe Atlantic storms which regularly batter Bermuda mean that all buildings need to be soundly and stoutly constructed, and our churches reflected the experience, wisdom and skills gained over the years by the architects and builders.

By the middle of the 17th century there were Anglican churches in each of what became the nine parishes of Bermuda. They were built usually with cedar beams and palmetto thatching, but several were destroyed in a particularly violent hurricane in 1712 and had to be rebuilt. Stone-walled buildings with strong roofing became the norm, but even the strongest buildings were not always able to withstand the force of the elements.

The Cathedral was magnificent. Begun in 1885, the nave was dedicated in 1894, and the church was accorded the status of a Cathedral in the same year. Its dedication was The Cathedral of The Most Holy Trinity, and it was completed and consecrated in 1911. Set imposingly on top of a hill overlooking the city of Hamilton, it was the largest public building in Bermuda. It had a seating capacity of 800, and was the natural setting for great occasions. The High Altar, the great east window, the striking reredos of statues of our Lord and fourteen saints and apostles, and the Bishop's throne, dominate the interior of the building. Beautiful stained glass windows, carved English oak choir stalls, simple side chapels, and a tower rising 143 feet above ground level are other impressive features of the building. The passage of time and the ravages of the humid Bermuda climate were taking their toll on the stonework, windows and organ, and it was apparent that major restoration work would soon need to be undertaken.

A feature of each of our churches was the well-maintained churchyard with its regular rows of whitewashed graves around or alongside the church. There is no crematorium in Bermuda, and the normal practice is to bury the dead in family graves, which are dug deep and re-used after an appropriate lapse of time.

The churches themselves are rich repositories of Bermuda's history. St. Peter's church at St. George's has the Governor's box pew, where the first meeting of the House of Assembly took place in 1620, and also a massive stone font which was brought out from England and is thought to be very ancient. In its churchyard is the grave of Midshipman Richard Dale of the United States Navy; he was severely wounded in the British-American War of 1812 and brought ashore at St. George's, where he was lovingly nursed until he died.

★   ★   ★

The very pleasant welcome party hosted by Archdeacon Tom Dyson and his wife Lucette at St. Mary's Rectory, Warwick, a few days before my Enthronement, had introduced me to the clergy and their wives, and enabled me to begin to get to know them. There were five black Bermudian priests, four of them Rectors of parishes and the other the Canon Residentiary. There were two white Bermudian clergy, one a non-stipendiary priest and the other a deacon completing his training. There were four white priests with Bermudian status: one was the Archdeacon and the others were retired. There were four white expatriate clergy: the Bishop, two Rectors and an Assistant Curate. A white expatriate Rector and a white Assistant Curate with Bermudian status were awaited in the near future.

★   ★   ★

Because of the smallness of the diocese, the roles of Bishop of the diocese and Dean of the Cathedral were combined. James Francis, the Residentiary Canon, was effectively the executive officer of the Cathedral, and our daily early morning meetings at Morning Prayer were invaluable. When I first arrived we shared the services of the Cathedral Secretary, Helena Rawlins, but my work soon expanded to the point where I needed a Personal Assistant of my own.

As the year progressed, I came to realise fully what a demanding task I had. There was at least one sermon to preach on most Sundays, and thorough preparation was essential. There were Confirmation Services in the parish churches, and I loved these because of the infectious enthusiasm of those who were publicly committing themselves to the service of Jesus Christ. There was the Institution of a new Rector and the licensing of a Curate. There was the ordination to the priesthood of the deacon, Billy Hayward. There were special services in the Cathedral (for various occasions and organisations) at which I was expected to preach: these included an annual Civic Service, an Assize Service, Hospital Sunday, Battle of Britain Sunday, Remembrance Day, Police Sunday, Thanksgiving Day, Conservation Sunday, Guild Services, and latterly World AIDS Day: my files of sermons during the Bermuda years are very thick! There were State occasions to which I was invited and asked to say prayers, such as the State Opening of Parliament, Royal Visits and

Remembrance Day. There were also gala occasions such as the celebration of The Queen's Birthday and official visits of naval vessels from various countries.

★    ★    ★

I loved what I was doing and revelled in it, particularly getting to know people from all walks of life, and there were some memorable light-hearted moments. One came at my first Diocesan Synod meeting, when a church-warden got up to make a point and finished by saying, 'Bishop, aren't we putting the horse before the cart?' He joined in the happy laughter when I replied: 'Isn't that where it's supposed to be, Cecil?' Another happened at my first Confirmation service in the Cathedral. I was not yet familiar with the working of a radio microphone, and had just finished the actual Confirmation when one of my lay chaplains approached bearing a small dish of slices of lemon with which I was to cleanse my fingers. 'Bishop,' he whispered, 'we've got too many lemons.' Forgetting that I had not switched off the microphone I whispered back: 'Never mind. They'll do for the gin and tonics afterwards.' For a moment I could not understand why the congregation was helpless with laughter!

My first Remembrance Day was unforgettable. An open air service at the Cenotaph was held annually on November 11th at 11 a.m., and in 1990 November 11th fell on a Sunday. It was a formal and colourful occasion, attended by the Governor in full regalia, the Premier in Morning Dress, Members of Parliament, senior representatives of Bermuda's government services, detachments of the Royal Navy, the Royal Canadian Navy, the United States Navy and the Bermuda Regiment, and members of the public. The excellent Band of the Bermuda Regiment, resplendent in their scarlet uniforms, provided the music, and a small group of robed members of the Bermuda Cathedral choir led the singing.

November 11th 1990 dawned dull, wet and windy. A wet weather programme had been prepared for such an eventuality; if necessary the service would be held in the Cathedral. Since implementing the wet weather programme would require revising the normal pattern of the Cathedral's Sunday morning services, we had agreed with the Governor's office that any decision to implement the wet weather programme would be made at 8 a.m. on the day. When I rang the Governor's ADC at 8 a.m. to receive the decision, I was advised that the Governor wished to postpone the decision for half an hour in the hope that the weather would improve. A decision would be made by 9 o'clock. At 9 o'clock a further delay was announced. I fully sympathised with the desire to hold the service in the open, but I pointed out that with the Cathedral's Sung Eucharist due to start shortly, I really did need a firm decision. A further call to the ADC, reinforced by some quarterdeck language, eventually elicited the decision. The service would go ahead in the open.

The inevitable duly occurred. As 11 o'clock approached the sky grew darker and darker. A heavy squall accompanied by driving wind could be seen approaching rapidly. The wind and the rain arrived together. The main microphone was blown over and short-circuited the sound system. The rain lashed down, soaking everybody to the skin. With admirable discipline the Bermuda Regiment Band played on. The Governor, Major General Sir Desmond Langley, the plumes on his hat drooping forlornly, marched over to me. 'Bishop,' he said, 'how do we foreshorten proceedings?' 'Easily, Your Excellency,' I replied, 'we'll go straight to the Final Blessing.' Gallant to the last, the Band played 2 full verses of the National Anthem before we could all take cover from the elements. A lighter memory of the final moments of the ceremony was of a detachment of Royal Navy personnel forming a close guard round the Senior Naval Officer's wife, whose lovely short black silk dress was visibly shrinking in the downpour.

I retired to the shower in Bishop's Lodge. My robes were soaked, and I was not in the best of tempers. But a gracious phone call from the Governor restored my good humour, and later we enjoyed a good laugh about it.

### Sally's Arrival in Bermuda

In the summer of 1991 our younger son Tim successfully completed his General Certificate of Secondary Education course, and left Watford Grammar School. We had hoped and expected that he would be able to study for his A Level examinations in Bermuda, but sadly the advice we had been given that this would be possible turned out to be misinformed. Our older son Andrew and his wife Frances then invited Tim to live with them in Oxford and attend school there. Both he and we were very grateful for the offer, and he was accepted into the Sixth Form at Magdalen College School, where he settled in very happily. He came out to Bermuda for two holidays a year, and greatly enjoyed exploring the islands on our moped.

With Tim established in Oxford, Sally was now free to take up residence in Bermuda, and she came out in September 1991. It was a great joy to be together again. She had already made three visits to Bermuda and soon became integrated into the community. She joined the Cathedral choir, and also the Bermuda Philharmonic Choir, whose conductor was Graham Garton. He had been a former colleague of hers on the teaching staff at St. Margaret's School, Bushey, and conductor of the Watford Philharmonic Choir, of which she had been a member.

In December 1991 I licensed her as a Lay Reader; she had undertaken and completed the training course in the Diocese of London, and became the first woman Lay Reader in Bermuda. The Cathedral congregation welcomed her joyfully. So did the Canon Residentiary and the Bishop, because we now had a colleague with whom we could share the preaching ministry!

Late in 1991 I dedicated Bermuda's splendid new Reading Clinic, and Sally undertook a course of training there to teach dyslexic students. The training was thorough and the staff were well qualified. Sally enjoyed the one-to-one sessions she had with her students, and spent much time preparing for each one. She continued this work until we left Bermuda, and derived great satisfaction from it.

## Restoration of the Cathedral

Major repair and restoration of the stonework of the Cathedral was urgent when I arrived in Bermuda. This was not because the Cathedral had been neglected; rather it was the unsuitability of the stone with which it had been built that was the problem. It was too soft and too retentive of moisture, and Bermuda's heavy rains, driving winds, high humidity and hot sunshine had wrought havoc with it. Some of it was crumbling badly. The damaged stones would need to be cut out and replaced with hardened reconstituted blocks. A long and expensive task lay ahead.

When we realised that substantial funds would be required to cover the cost of the restoration, we felt that other repair work at the Cathedral should also be undertaken. The stained glass windows were in poor condition due to weathering. The organ required extensive renovation. The tower, which commanded a magnificent view of the whole of Bermuda, needed significant internal repairs. A new and powerful sound amplification system was essential to cope with the poor acoustics. Estimates for the work totalled approximately $3 million, and we knew that we had no alternative to embarking on a major appeal for funds. The Cathedral Vestry decided, therefore, to aim to raise $4 million in order to provide for on-going maintenance work in the years ahead. It was a huge challenge.

I received much excellent advice as to how to set about the task from Walter Maddocks, an English-born solicitor with his own practice. Walter had recently returned to Bermuda after devoting two years of his life to spearheading Rotary International's Polio Plus campaign. He had accepted the challenge of raising $100 million, on an expenses-only basis, in order to vaccinate all the children in the world against polio. Backed by fund-raising consultants Community Counselling Services of New York, he had raised no less than $246 million in a worldwide campaign. He agreed to serve as Chairman of our Cathedral Appeal, to which we gave the name 'The Living Landmark Appeal,' and recommended that we should engage Community Counselling Services as our fund-raising consultants. This we did after due enquiries and consultation.

Walter was then appointed Attorney General of Bermuda and had no option but to resign as Chairman of our Appeal. A distinguished businessman, Kit Astwood, very graciously agreed to replace him, and proved to be a tower of strength. He and I worked very happily together and with our Campaign Director Matt Fitzsimons, and despite problems raised by the Gulf War of 1991, which caused a sharp rise in the value of the pound sterling against the United States dollar at a time when we were buying pounds to pay the English stonework contractors, and also dramatically reduced the number of overseas visitors arriving in Bermuda, we raised the money necessary for the repairs, although we were not able to set up a reserve fund. I personally visited many leading individuals and businesses seeking support; it was challenging, demanding and satisfying, but everybody treated me very graciously.

We engaged an English firm, London Stone, to carry out the building repairs, and their stonemasons spent a full year doing the work. Two of the stonemasons, Terry and Keith, were with us throughout the project. Both came from the East End of London, and they worked hard and with great skill. We became firm friends, and I was thrilled one day when Keith asked me if I would conduct his marriage to his partner Sharon in the Cathedral. I checked with him that there were no legal impediments, and happily agreed.

The wedding was memorable. About 30 family members and friends, mostly Londoners, flew out for the occasion. The couple's two small daughters, Frankie aged four and Charley aged two, were to be bridesmaids, and when they arrived at the Cathedral with their mother they looked delightful. But at that point Charley decided that she didn't want to go through with it. She kept up her protests for a while until her mother, in a stage whisper heard all over the Cathedral, advised her that she had no choice. Her four succinct words left Charley in no doubt! When the bridegroom and the best man arrived they had a distinctly battered appearance: Keith was sporting two black eyes, and the best man's hand was in plaster. After the service I asked Keith what had happened, and in broad Cockney I heard about an altercation with a group of Bermudians in a night club in the early hours of the morning following the Stag Party. 'One of these guys said sumfin' racial to Bert,' Keith told me. 'Well, you don't say fings like that to Bert, 'cos 'e don't like it. So Bert 'it 'im! That started it…'. The whole graphic account remains indelibly imprinted in my memory to this day.

A year after the completion of the repairs, Terry and Keith returned to carry out routine inspection and follow-up work and thoroughly enjoyed their stay. Towards the end of their visit Keith suddenly appeared in my office, ashen-faced. 'Can you come, Bishop?' he asked. 'Terry's fallen off a ladder.' 'How bad is it?' I asked. 'Oh, 'e's not dead nor nuffin. But 'e can't get up.' We rushed around the Cathedral to where Terry had fallen. He was lying on his back on the ground, with a policeman examining his damaged ankle and two overseas visitors shading him from the sun with a wooden board. He greeted me cheerily, and I noticed that he was smoking a cigarette as he waited for the ambulance. Greatly relieved that it was not worse, I told him that I was glad he had not fallen on his head, because if he had there would have been a large hole in the tarmac!

## The Bermuda Church Society

A feature of the Diocese of Bermuda which I had not previously encountered in my service with the Anglican Church in many parts of the world was the absence of a Diocesan Board of Finance. In Bermuda the properties and finances of the diocese were administered by The Bermuda Church Society, and the parishes made no contribution to the central expenses of the diocese.

The Bermuda Church Society financed all the expenses of the bishopric, including the Bishop's salary, expenses of office and the running costs of Bishop's Lodge. It covered the costs of the Diocesan Office at the Cathedral and of the Bishop's Personal Assistant. It owned the 18 feet-long motor launch *Dayspring* which was used to travel to and from Burt Island, an $8^1/2$ acre island assigned to the Anglican Church for Church purposes. It owned a number of commercial and residential properties, and had a substantial income. It paid the medical insurance premiums for the clergy and their families and provided a generous pension scheme for them.

The Chairman was Ted White, a retired General Manager and Chief Executive of the Bermuda-based Bank of N. T. Butterfield and Son Ltd. Ted was a fine man. Several years previously he had suffered serious health problems, and he was on thrice weekly kidney dialysis. I never once heard him complain about his health; he preferred to thank God that he was still alive and able to continue to lead the Church Society. He was highly intelligent, shrewd, forthright and kind. He was a man of unwavering integrity and deep faith, and was highly respected for what was achieved in his years as churchwarden at St. John's, Pembroke. He had a wonderful sense of humour and was a devoted husband, father and grandfather. When he died in 1994, after 45 years of marriage to his beloved Joan, I said in my funeral address that 'they complemented each other magnificently...their family life was a model of attractive no-nonsense Christian living.' We were close friends.

Ted presided over a committee which included an actuary, a senior civil servant, and a Member of the Legislative Assembly (all committed lay members of the Anglican Church), the Archdeacon, two parish clergy and the Bishop. Our meetings were held at Ted's house and were notable for the quality of the discussions, responsible commonsense decisiveness and good fellowship; and they did not drag on!

Some 18 months into my episcopate, it became clear to me that a greater interest in the wider life of the diocese would be encouraged among the

individual parishes if they were to contribute financially to the work of the
diocese. A proposal to this effect was formulated, put forward, discussed fully
and unanimously agreed at the Diocesan Synod. An annual contribution of
$3600 from each parish was introduced in 1993; it was a beginning, a step in
the right direction, the forging of a closer bond between the parishes and The
Bermuda Church Society.

## My Ministry in Bermuda

When Sally took up full-time residence in Bermuda, I had been there for 18
months and was well settled. Many good things had happened. A bookshop
had been opened in the Cathedral Hall. Preparations to launch the $4 million
Appeal to repair and restore the Cathedral were at an advanced stage. The
Synod was busily engaged in producing a strategic plan for the life of the
diocese. An appeal for emergency aid for the people of Bangladesh, stricken
by severe flooding and storm damage, and for Kurdish refugees in Iraq,
resulted in $33,000 (£20,000) being sent from our Anglican churches to the
Red Cross and The Save The Children Fund. The diocesan motor boat
*Dayspring* had been put in good order, and Burt Island brought up to a high
standard of maintenance. St. Peter's Church Hall at St. George's had been
superbly rebuilt and extended, though not without some controversy. I had
visited all the churches and got to know many people. I was quietly satisfied
with progress.

My position as Dean of the Cathedral meant that I was preaching there at
least three times a month, and I took this opportunity very seriously. I
preached on the issues of the day as well as on specifically Biblical subjects,
and published some of these sermons in the monthly Diocesan News. The
published addresses included the following:-

> The Church, AIDS and Condoms: The ordination of women to the priesthood:
> Capital punishment: AIDS: Preparing for a General Election:
> Christian Marriage: Women in the Church: Independence or Interdependence?:
> Racism: Drug abuse: Commemoration of D Day: Commemoration of VJ Day

★   ★   ★

In June 1992 we organised a Diocesan Open Air Eucharist as an act of faith
and witness. All the parishes cancelled their main Sunday morning services,
and we planned to conduct the service on a school playing field at 10 a.m.
Preparations went on over many months. New vestments were made for all
the clergy. Seating and open-sided marquees were hired. A stage was set up
for the altar. Bishop Michael Marshall, one of the Archbishop of Canterbury's
Special Preachers for the Decade of Evangelism, had accepted our invitation
to preach. Everything was ready – except the weather!

It had been a very wet month, and on the day before the Eucharist three inches of rain had fallen. It was still lashing down when I went to bed, and when I woke up at 1 a.m. it was still raining. I tossed and turned in bed, worrying that we would have to implement the Wet Weather programme, which would be far less satisfactory. I prayed fervently that the rain would stop. When I got up at 5 a.m. it had stopped, and a strong wind was blowing. The sun rose, and the wind continued to blow. By 9 a.m. the field was dry, and everything was in place. 1,200 Anglicans marched in procession to the field, the clergy resplendent in their new bright red Vestments. The Eucharist was magnificent: simple, dignified, colourful and inspiring. The sermon lifted our spirits high, and everything proceeded without a hitch. As the service came to a thrilling climax the skies began to cloud over again. Half an hour after we finished the rain returned, but by then everything had been cleared away and the congregation was safely on its way home.

I have often thought about that break in the weather just when it mattered. Was it pure coincidence, or did the Good Lord intervene? I believe that He did.

★   ★   ★

Early in 1993 the Anglican and Roman Catholic Bishops in Bermuda issued a historic joint statement on the subject of homosexuality. This had become a major issue in Bermuda, with many calls for the Government to repeal a law which classified as criminal homosexual acts in private between consenting adult males. No similar law applied to women. Public discussion had become very heated, with many of the predominantly black Pentecostal churches strongly opposed to any changes in the law and Members of Parliament being pressurised by letters, phone calls and even death threats.

Bishop Hennessy, the Roman Catholic Bishop, and I met to discuss the possibility of making a joint statement, and we worked on several drafts before we finally produced a statement to which we could commit ourselves with a clear conscience. We then released it to the media. It read as follows:-

'The Anglican Bishop of Bermuda, The Rt. Revd. William Down, and the Roman Catholic Bishop of Hamilton in Bermuda, The Most Revd. Brian Hennessy, after consultation with their clergy, have prepared the following joint statement:-

We write as Bishops and priests who are deeply concerned about the law concerning homosexual acts. We write also as pastors concerned about God's people. We recognise that human beings are created with strong sexual impulses and that for the vast majority of people these impulses are expressed in heterosexual relationships. We hold firmly to the Biblical teaching that sexual relationships are expressed in lifelong faithful union of a man and a woman in marriage.

We recognise also that a significant minority of people are emotionally and physically attracted to people of their own sex. For some this appears to be the result of the circumstances and environment in which they were brought up as children. For others it appears to be something which has been part of their make-up since birth. Whatever the cause, this is how they are now. As pastors it is our task to minister to all God's people. We hold firmly to the Biblical teaching that we are all made in the image and likeness of God, and that God loves each and every one of us. Each of us is of equal importance to Him. Jesus Christ died for us all. We must beware of casting the first stone.

As pastors it is our task to show and bring the love of God to everybody. It is to help people to find God's strength to cope with themselves, with their sexual orientation, and with life.

Therefore, although we do not condone homosexual acts, we do not believe that to classify them as criminal is appropriate.'

The Statement made a profound impact on the campaign; it caused many people to think again.

★   ★   ★

In 1994 the Synod discussed the desirability and the possibility of establishing partner relationships with dioceses within The Church of the Province of the West Indies, The Anglican Church of Canada and The Episcopal Church of the United States of America (E.C.U.S.A.). I had already had informal discussions with the Archbishop of Canterbury, the Presiding Bishop of ECUSA and the Primate of the Anglican Church of Canada, and I was in the process of arranging a meeting with the Archbishop of the West Indies. In a Charge to the Synod I had said:-

It is very important for the Anglican Church in Bermuda to look outwards as well as inwards. We ARE isolated geographically, but we do not have to be isolated spiritually and ecclesiastically. Our lives as Anglicans will be greatly enhanced if we venture out in faith to make real significant contact with Anglicans from other parts of the world.

I went on to examine in depth what is involved in partner relationships. This was obviously going to be a continuing process, but at least we had made a start.

### The Canadian House of Bishops

Not long after arriving in Bermuda, I received an invitation to attend the autumn meeting of The House of Bishops of The Anglican Church of Canada. As Bermuda was an extra-provincial diocese, I did not automatically belong to any House of Bishops and I accepted the invitation gratefully. I looked forward to the meeting eagerly, particularly since I already knew a number of the Canadian Bishops through my service with The Missions to Seamen.

I was received most warmly and told that I would be welcome at all meetings of the House in future. I became closely acquainted with all the Bishops over the five years I attended the meetings, and the fellowship within the group was stimulating, encouraging, sympathetic, friendly and generous. We spoke informally of the good things that were happening in our dioceses, and of our families. We relaxed with pleasure in each other's company. We also talked of the demands of being a bishop: the difficult decisions which only we could make; the misunderstandings which could occur because we must maintain confidentiality; the disciplining of errant clergy; and the feeling sometimes that the whole world was against one!

The Primate, Archbishop Michael Peers, presided over the meetings with gentleness, firmness and good humour. We discussed at length the major topics of the day, particularly our responses to the issues of homosexuality. We had excellent thought-provoking lectures from leading theologians and pastors. Much emphasis was laid on the constant nurturing of our spiritual lives. Among the 40 or so Bishops there was a wide range of opinion and a rich variety of churchmanship, but there was also an impressive unity of purpose and a determination to be a focus of unity, as far as was possible.

I made lifelong friends among the Bishops, and I learned much from them about being a Bishop. They welcomed me, taught me and gave themselves to me. My contribution to them was my knowledge of the Anglican Communion all over the world, my knowledge and experience of the maritime scene, and an irreverent sense of humour. It was a hard-working, responsible and happy House of Bishops.

**Visit of Canadian Bishops to Bermuda**
An integral part of the meetings of the full House of Bishops in Canada was the separate meetings of the individual Provincial Houses of Bishops. Ecclesiastically, Canada is divided into four Provinces, each with its own Archbishop. The Primate links up all the Provinces, and administers the Central Office in Toronto; he has no diocese of his own. The four Provinces are British Columbia and the Yukon, Rupert's Land, Ontario, and Canada. The Province of Canada is made up of the eastern seaboard, and includes the dioceses of Montreal, Quebec, Nova Scotia and Prince Edward Island, Fredericton, Western Newfoundland, Central Newfoundland, and Eastern Newfoundland and Labrador. Before becoming a diocese in its own right in 1925, Bermuda was linked with the dioceses of Nova Scotia and Newfoundland, and it seemed appropriate for me to be linked with the Province of Canada.

It was one of my keenest hopes that the Diocese of Bermuda would become more outward-looking and develop closer links with those parts of the Church with which we had natural affinities, such as The Church of The

Province of the West Indies, The Episcopal Church of the U.S.A. and The Anglican Church of Canada. We already had a strong link with The Church of England through the metropolitical jurisdiction of the Archbishop of Canterbury. As I got to know the Bishops in Canada through regular meetings, the idea formed in my mind of inviting the House of Bishops of The Province of Canada to hold a meeting in Bermuda. To my delight the Bermuda Church Society welcomed the suggestion, and offered to pay the accommodation costs of our guests. The visit was arranged for April 1993.

It was a memorable visit. The Bishops and their wives stayed at the comfortable Rosedon Hotel for the seven days of their visit, and we held our business meetings there. They were entertained to Dinner by the Governor at Government House, by the Premier at Camden (the official venue for such functions), and at Bishop's Lodge. Ted White, chairman of the Bermuda Church Society, hosted a lunch at the Royal Hamilton Amateur Dinghy Club, and the Minister for Tourism, Jim Woolridge, came to the hotel to address them. The Bishops preached in the parish churches on the Sunday morning, visited Burt Island (the Church's own island), and just before leaving were guests at the Annual Peppercorn ceremony at St. George's. There was much goodwill on all sides, and our links with Canada were duly celebrated.

## Appointing a New Archdeacon

A tricky situation which it was clear I could not avoid during my time in Bermuda was the appointment of a new Archdeacon. The role of an archdeacon is important in any diocese, but it takes on an added significance in Bermuda, where the Bishop combines the roles of Bishop of the diocese and Dean of the Cathedral. The Archdeacon is the Bishop's deputy and right hand man. He handles the applications for the Work Permits of the expatriate clergy. He is a parish priest and a counsellor to the clergy and the Bishop.

Tom Dyson was the Archdeacon when I arrived. He was in his 70's and it was clear that retirement might not be far off. He was a fine man, a good scholar, and an excellent parish priest of strong faith and deep devotion. English born and Oxford educated, he had been in Bermuda since 1957 and had been granted Bermudian status. He had a comprehensive knowledge of the Church in Bermuda and also of the history of the worldwide Church. By 1993 representatives of his parish Vestry were indicating to me that he should be gently encouraged to retire, and as his health began to deteriorate, I invited him, in April 1994, to discuss the matter with me. We had a most amicable talk, and we agreed a timetable for his future. He would retire as Archdeacon in September 1994 and as Rector of St. Mary's, Warwick, in January 1995. At the end of our meeting I made notes of what we had agreed, and gave him a copy.

He announced his retirement as Archdeacon at his Archdeacon's Visitation

Service in the Cathedral on June 12th 1994, and I appointed his successor on the following day. The new Archdeacon was to be Ewen Ratteray, a black Bermudian priest, Rector of St. John's, Pembroke, since 1980, and a priest of 28 years seniority. He was 52 years old and had served in parishes in the North of England for 14 years before returning to Bermuda.

As soon as I announced his appointment, I was confronted by several of the most senior priests, who felt that I should have consulted them before making the appointment. They also felt that the new Archdeacon was junior to them in terms of years of service, and that there was a case for appointing the most senior. Since three of the four who called on me considered themselves to be candidates for the appointment, I pointed out that the Constitution of the Diocese stated unequivocally that 'the Archdeacon shall be appointed by the Bishop,' and that it would have been difficult to consult with interested parties. I had had four years to think about how to make the appointment, and I could not see how a realistic consultation process could take place.

A major furore ensued, with letters appearing in the correspondence columns of *The Royal Gazette* (the daily newspaper), and a leading article in the same journal headed 'Perfectly entitled.' The editorial contained the following passage:-

> The Canons have asked what criteria the Bishop used in arriving at his decision. We can only think that he simply looked at finding what he considered, and the choice was his, the best person for the job...
>
> 'We can only think that Bishop Down did not consult the Canons because he was aware that all three wanted the job. It is, of course often difficult and unwise to discuss the choice for a job with people who are candidates for it. The conversation would go like this:
>
> 'Who do you think should be Archdeacon?'
> 'Me!'
> 'Me!'
> 'Me!'

A particularly unpleasant campaign of character assassination followed and rumbled on, but when I installed Ewen as Archdeacon the Cathedral was packed; and his new ministry made a most encouraging start. I had agonised over how to make the appointment, and I had known that it would provoke dissension among some who felt that they should have been appointed. But I do not regret for one moment making the appointment, painful though the aftermath was. Ewen rapidly grew into the job, and I had full confidence in him.

**Frustrations**
Bermuda's population, size, geographical isolation, history and prosperity make it a fascinating place in which to live. The total population is around

60,000, of whom some 25% at any one time are expatriates; 60% of the people are black, 40% white. With a total land area approximately the size of London's Heathrow airport, and situated 750 miles from the nearest landfall, it is very prosperous and has a high standard of living. All this makes for a community in which many people know each other well, and everybody thinks they know a lot about everybody else! It also produces an inward-looking and at times claustrophobic atmosphere.

Before formally inviting me to accept appointment to Bermuda, the Archbishop of Canterbury, Robert Runcie, outlined some of the difficulties involved. He spoke of the island's history, its wealth, its beauty, its racial background, the assassination of the Governor and his ADC in 1973, the repeated failures of the Synod to elect their Bishop, and the personalities and tensions holding back the progress of the life of the Church. He painted a challenging picture, but I was ready to accept the challenge.

★    ★    ★

As I read through the papers relating to the issue of my Work Permit I noted a requirement to begin training my successor, who should be a Bermudian, at once. I saw that as an expatriate I was considered to be a bird of passage. It was a new experience for me: in the United Kingdom I had the right of permanent residence, and when we had been posted to Australia with The Missions to Seamen we had been encouraged straightaway to settle permanently. The granting of a Work Permit for one year only came as a shock, and for a while I was tempted to regret my willingness to relinquish a fascinating and satisfying long-term appointment in favour of such uncertainty. However the conviction that God had called me to Bermuda stabilised my thinking, and I realised that the situation was one I would have to live with. I understood too that the rights of Bermudians had to be properly safeguarded.

The first renewal of my Work Permit proceeded smoothly but was not a formality. I was incensed when the Government formally requested the clergy to signify their approval of its renewal, and after a renewal for four years had been granted I wrote to the Archbishop of Canterbury setting out my unease at the process. During the next four years the Diocesan Registrar, Michael Woods, worked tirelessly to establish the renewal process on a more acceptable basis.

I took note of what happened as other expatriate clergy Work Permits became due for renewal. The process was slow, and sometimes dragged on beyond the expiry date of the existing permit. The priest and his family would become increasingly desperate to receive the decision, knowing well how much time it would take to obtain another appointment elsewhere. They knew that their applications, which were submitted by the Archdeacon on behalf of the parish and the diocese, were liable to be challenged by any

Bermudian with a grudge or by any Bermudian priest who wished to apply for the post himself. They also knew that the continuing uncertainty actively hindered the life of the parish and engendered resentment.

The second renewal of my Work Permit was a protracted and distressing process. The Minister for Immigration insisted that the Diocesan Synod should officially request renewal. This was unacceptable to me, since nowhere else in the Anglican Communion is a Bishop required to do this. Various high level submissions were made and rejected. Finally the Archbishop of Canterbury and the Foreign Secretary in London intervened. It was pointed out that the Diocesan Synod had had no part in my appointment, nor did it employ me; it had failed on two separate occasions to elect its Bishop. It was the Archbishop who had appointed me under the terms of the Constitution, and he wished me to continue in office. My Work Permit was then renewed for a further five years, until after my 65th birthday.

But the damage had been done. It was crystal clear to me that no expatriate Bishop could function effectively within such restrictive confines, and that the time had come when the Bishop must be a Bermudian whose tenure of office would not depend on a Work Permit. I therefore asked our diocesan legal officers to work actively towards the amendment of the Constitution of the Diocese so as further to facilitate the election of a Bermudian Bishop. With this achieved, I could consider an appointment elsewhere with a clear conscience.

★　　★　　★

A continuing frustration was the racial tension which was never far below the surface in many aspects of daily life. To the overseas visitor these tensions were rarely visible, Bermudians being by nature very friendly and courteous people. But below the surface a legacy of simmering racial distrust and resentment remained. I heard it said more than once that a black person could not be a racist; racism was a white person's disease.

Living as an expatriate in Bermuda for nearly six years made me understand that it was very important in such a small community to protect the employment rights of Bermudian citizens; that international expertise, experience, knowledge and business were vital to Bermuda's on-going life; that there needs to be a proper balance between protecting the rights of Bermudians and treating expatriates with due sensitivity; and that I was a bird of passage, who could not expect to stay on the island indefinitely.

My greatest frustration was the handling of Work Permits.

**Friends and Recreation**
In carrying out my ministry as Bishop, I came into contact with people from all walks of life, and I made a host of friends.

With Sally still in England, I had spent my first few days in Bermuda as the guest of Sir David and Lady Tibbitts. David was a retired Naval captain and former Deputy Master of Trinity House, and he and Mary made me most welcome. David was a true friend. He was wise, clear thinking, frank and generous, a man of great integrity and a wonderful sense of humour. He had introduced me to many people, helped me unpack and settle into Bishop's Lodge, and taken me sailing in his boat. We enjoyed each other's company, and I have happy memories of evenings on the patio of their lovely home and being utterly at ease with them both.

Paul Dean, whom I appointed as my Lay Chaplain, was another who went out of his way to welcome me and help me settle into Bishop's Lodge. A bachelor in his 30's, he had a managerial position with the English Sports Shop in Hamilton. He was a dedicated Anglo Catholic churchman with immense energy and a good knowledge of Bermudian society. Nothing was too much trouble for him and he had a glorious sense of humour. He could also express himself colourfully and forcefully. I recall a game of golf he and I were enjoying with a very gentlemanly English church friend of mine when things were not going well with Paul's game. After depositing golf balls into the sea on several successive holes, he was determined to drive his ball on to the fairway at the last water hole. Alas! Three more went into the water, and as the last dropped in with a resounding splash Paul's self-control deserted him. Even after 27 years in the shipping world, I had never heard such a flow of colourful and original invective! My friend's face was a picture!

Paul introduced me to Colin Fleming, another young Anglo Catholic bachelor, who had just successfully completed his final Chartered Accountant examinations when I arrived. I appointed Colin as my second Lay Chaplain, a job he filled with skill and enthusiasm until he accepted a position in Canada. In 2000 I went to Toronto to conduct his marriage service and I keep in regular contact with him and his wife Licia now that they are working in London.

When Colin moved to Canada, I appointed Walter Carlington, a black member of the Cathedral congregation, to replace him as Lay Chaplain. Walter was a delight to work with: thoughtful, sensible, hard-working, cheerful and sensitive, he was an ideal Bishop's chaplain.

I enjoyed many happy hours on Burt Island, the Church's 8½ acre island used mainly for young people's activities. There was a large hut with kitchen, washing and toilet facilities, mains electricity and a good water supply. There were excellent camping sites, a barbecue area, and a lovely open-air chapel in a hollow in the rocks. I often spent an afternoon helping with the grass cutting and maintenance; it was good working alongside the volunteers.

During most of my time in Bermuda I played golf on Saturday mornings. I became a member at the Riddell's Bay Golf Club and enjoyed a regular

*Bermuda, with Churchwardens, The Revd. Brian Melbourne and*
*Lay Chaplains Colin Fleming and Paul Dean, 1990.*

fourball match with Michael Woods, the Diocesan Registrar, Alistair Ritchie, an insurance executive, and Tony Goodfellow, a businessman and former Cambridge cricket Blue. Our matches were keenly contested in a wonderfully friendly atmosphere, and we enjoyed each other's company on all 19 holes! These games afforded a welcome release from the pressures of my daily life, and the course itself was magnificent. My golf improved: I played well enough to enjoy it and badly enough not to worry about it! I was very moved to discover that 15 people had got together to pay my first year's subscription, which was not inconsiderable; and later, on leaving Bermuda, when Honorary Life Membership of the Club was conferred on me.

Michael Woods was a staunch friend. A very able lawyer and Registrar of the Diocese, he and his wife Claire regularly invited me to meals on Sunday evenings in the 18 months before Sally arrived. We went sailing together and I came to have enormous respect for Michael's ability in the complex ecclesiastical legal business we dealt with. In retirement in Oxford we kept in regular touch, both on and off the golf course. Sadly, he died suddenly in July, 2004, after a distressing illness.

Richard Thornton and his wife Susie were also great friends. Richard had been Honorary Treasurer of The Marine Society in London, and was a strong supporter of The Missions to Seamen. When they came to Bermuda for

Richard to initiate a project for the Bank of Bermuda, we renewed and deepened our friendship. We sailed together and Sally and I were frequent guests at their lovely home. They worshipped at the Cathedral and gave strong support to the Restoration Appeal.

Bermuda is richly blessed with larger-than-life characters. The late Harry Cox was a prime example: warm-hearted, exuberant, shrewd, dynamic, and with a wonderful command of the English language, Harry loved talking. When I conducted his son's wedding service in the historic Old Devonshire parish church, the couple had invited him 'to say a few words' at an appropriate place in the service. Harry was delighted to oblige, and he began his address of $14^1/2$ minutes with a mention of 'iridescent rainbows'. He was still in full spate when the sight of me preparing to rise from my seat to stop him brought him to a swift conclusion!

We made many friends in Bermuda, and it is difficult and invidious to name some and not others. We appreciated them all. In my daily work I enjoyed excellent relations with the Governors and Deputy Governors, the Premier and the Government ministers. I would love to write about them all if there were space! I even had a good personal relationship with the Minister for Immigration; he had a difficult job to do, and even though I disagreed with him, I liked him as a person. I was most courteously received when I visited people seeking financial support for the restoration of the Cathedral, and I was very moved by the generosity of the gifts I received when I celebrated my 60th birthday. We were guests at meals in the homes of many people, and our own Christmas party at Bishop's Lodge was always a fabulous occasion; it was attended by the Governor and the Premier and their wives, and upwards of 100 guests from many walks of life. Baptisms and weddings were major occasions, and provided a great opportunity for Christian teaching and good fellowship. Funerals afforded pastoral opportunities and I got to know many people through them.

### Family

When I took up my appointment in Bermuda in March 1990, Sally and our younger son Tim, then aged 14, stayed on in the house in Bushey Heath we had lived in since 1974. It had been bought several years previously by The Missions to Seamen from the friends of my family who had very generously loaned it to us, rent free, for 10 years, and the Society graciously allowed us to continue to occupy it at a token rental for 17 months until Tim completed his GCSE (General Certificate of Secondary Education) examinations; it was a wonderful gesture.

As we planned to move from Bushey Heath in July 1991, we knew that we would need accommodation of our own for the times when we would be in England, and also as a base for Tim and our younger daughter Julia. Julia was about to embark on a three-year degree course in Occupational Therapy studies and training at St. Loyes College in Exeter, so we looked for a property to buy there. Sally found a lovely terrace house which had been built around 1900, and which we duly bought. We became very attached to its warm and cosy atmosphere and Julia and Tim loved it.

When Tim completed his GCSE course and Sally came to live in Bermuda, he went to live in school term time with his older brother Andrew and his wife Frances in Oxford. He attended Magdalen College School, where he enjoyed himself and did well. He came out to Bermuda for two holidays a year, and Sally spent much of the long summer holiday in Exeter with him and Julia. With good A Level results behind him, he went on to Warwick University to read Mathematics. University life suited him and he became deeply involved in the student radio station and made a number of lasting friendships.

Julia graduated from Manchester University in 1990 with a Bachelor of Science degree in Mathematics and Philosophy. She was a deeply committed Christian and felt called to serve as an Occupational Therapist. She took a gap year immediately after graduating and had three months' work experience in the Occupational Therapy Unit at Harrow Hospital. Then, after a short orientation course with the Church Mission Society, she spent the first six months of 1991 as a volunteer at the Christian Medical Centre at Vellore in South India. Her service there confirmed her conviction that this service was her calling: she loved the work, even though she suffered from protracted bouts of 'Delhi Belly.' She commenced her three-year degree course in Occupational Therapy studies in October 1991, and revisited Vellore to write a dissertation about the hospital's work as part of her course. On graduating in 1994, she was appointed to the O.T. department of the Salisbury District Hospitals Trust and started work there early in the autumn. She became an enthusiastic member of the congregation at St. Paul's church in Salisbury, where I had been Assistant Curate more than 30 years previously.

Helen, our elder daughter, and her husband Geoff settled first in Stanmore, where Helen taught English at a nearby comprehensive school and Geoff continued his research work with the General Electric Company, and then in Shepherd's Bush in West London, where Helen taught in a West London comprehensive school and Geoff lectured at Imperial College. Geoff had long been drawn towards ordination, and after being accepted for training by the Advisory Board of Ministry of the Church of England, he and Helen moved to Durham in 1993 for him to begin a three-year ordination training course at St. John's College. He decided to study simultaneously for a Bachelor of Arts degree in Theology. In September 1993 we rejoiced at the birth of their first daughter, Anna.

Andrew, our elder son, and his wife Frances moved into Oxford in the autumn of 1991 just after the birth of their first child Edward. Andrew was working in the Information Technology Department of the Anchor Housing Trust, and the whole family came out to Bermuda for Christmas just eight weeks after Edward's birth and moving house. They were ready for a break! Two years later there were more celebrations when their daughter Rebekah was born.

## Return to the United Kingdom

By the time Ewen Ratteray had been installed as the first Bermudian-born Archdeacon of Bermuda, and the protracted and unpleasant process of the renewal of my Work Permit had been settled, I had come to the conclusion that the constraints experienced by an expatriate Bishop made the election of a Bermudian as Bishop a top priority. After all the necessary steps had been taken to facilitate the election of a Bermudian, I would be free to consider an appointment elsewhere if and when one was offered. It still came as a pleasant shock when I received two invitations on the same morning to serve as Assistant Bishop in dioceses in England.

The dioceses were Bradford and Leicester, neither of which had a suffragan bishop, and I made a trip to England to visit the Bishops, both of whom I knew. After careful consideration I accepted appointment to Leicester as Assistant Bishop and Priest-in-Charge of St. Mary's, Humberstone, a parish on the outskirts of the city of Leicester. Geographically Leicester is a small diocese, but it has a population of around 1 million, some 350 churches and at that time 170 stipendiary clergy. The diocesan Bishop, Tom Butler, had many national commitments, and I realised that I would be very busy.

Humberstone was an ideal parish in which to be based. It was situated four miles from the city centre, and there was a frequent bus service into the city; this was a major consideration for Sally, who does not drive. There was just the one church, so with clerical assistance I would be free to carry out episcopal duties all over the diocese as required.

The time had come therefore to announce my resignation as Bishop of Bermuda with effect from November 30th 1995. I had been in Bermuda for five years and nine months, and I was very touched by the huge number of people who came to say how sad they were that we were leaving. But the time had come for the election of a Bermudian Bishop.

# CHAPTER SIXTEEN

# Leicester 1995-2001

## Back in England

I WAS LICENSED as Priest-in-Charge of St. Mary's, Humberstone, in the parish church on December 12th 1995, and as Assistant Bishop of Leicester on January 14th 1996 in the Cathedral. Both services were conducted by the Bishop of Leicester, Tom Butler, and they marked the beginning of a rich, exhilarating, busy and satisfying ministry in the parish and throughout the diocese.

The diocese of Leicester, which became a see in its own right in 1927, has never had a suffragan Bishop, and has relied on bishops returning from overseas appointments or moving from other responsibilities to provide several years of service as Assistant Bishops. With 350 churches, 150 stipendiary clergy and a population of one million, there is more work than he can cope with for a diocesan bishop with national responsibilities and no episcopal help. When Godfrey Ashby, the previous Assistant Bishop, indicated his intention of returning to South Africa to retire, Tom Butler knew that I was contemplating a possible return to the United Kingdom, and he wrote to me inviting me to consider moving to Leicester.

I had known Tom when I was General Secretary of The Missions to Seamen and he was Bishop of Willesden. The diocese of London is sub-divided into areas, each with its own Bishop, and we worshipped at Stanmore in the episcopal area of Willesden. Tom was a regular visitor to St. John's, Stanmore, and his visits were greatly appreciated. He was a dynamic man: forthright, likeable, clear-thinking and determined. He did not shrink from speaking on controversial and topical issues, nor did he hesitate to apologise if he made an error of judgement. His regular broadcasts on BBC Radio Four's 'Thought for the Day' were direct and challenging. When he contacted me about the possibility of an appointment in the diocese of Leicester, I arranged to visit him during a forthcoming visit to the United Kingdom. He then invited me to accept the position of Priest-in-Charge of Humberstone and Assistant Bishop of Leicester. I made a brief visit to the parish, and agreed to return a few weeks later for an official visit. Everything worked out smoothly, and I was duly appointed. We were to live in Humberstone Vicarage.

## Reflections on Bermuda

It was not until we had settled in the Vicarage that I had time to draw breath and review and assess our time in Bermuda. I had mixed feelings. On the one hand many good things had been accomplished, and positive contributions made to the ongoing life of the island; we had greatly enjoyed many aspects of Bermudian life, and made true and lasting friendships. On the other hand I had experienced regular and intense frustration over the constraints affecting the ministry of an expatriate Bishop, and I had been disturbed both by the hostility aroused in some quarters by my appointment of the Archdeacon and also by the continuing smouldering racial tensions. When Archdeacon Ewen Ratteray was elected to succeed me as Bishop I was thrilled. The lay people voted overwhelmingly for him, and he became the first elected Bermudian Bishop.

As I reflected, I was deeply grateful for the welcome and fellowship I had experienced in the House of Bishops in Canada. I learned a lot about being a Bishop there. We talked about the joys, satisfactions, frustrations and hurts which are an integral part of a Bishop's life and his 'care of all the churches.' In the House I had listened with heartfelt sympathy to a Bishop whose whole life was being overshadowed by protracted unpleasant litigation arising from a courageous and proper decision he had made; to Bishops who were agonising over decisions they were going to have to make which would affect people's lives and which they knew would be resisted; and to Bishops who could not, and would not, reveal confidential information which would manifestly justify actions for which they were being criticised. I had also rejoiced with them at the many wonderful signs of God's presence and activity in the life of the Church. It made me realise that my experiences were not unique. It was clear that integrity, love, hope and faithfulness are all-important, and that in the context of ministry, success and failure are words which are neither easily defined nor even necessarily relevant. It was invaluable experience.

## Humberstone

The old village of Humberstone had been gradually absorbed into the eastern suburbs of the city of Leicester. The parish was predominantly residential: there were a few large houses, many roads of well-established semi-detached residences, some large new housing estates, several areas of local authority-built houses and some streets of old terraced houses. There were approximately 12,000 residents. There were several good shopping areas, excellent Infants and Junior Schools, a major police station, a private hospital, a number of public houses, a Royal British Legion Club and a fine parish church. The main Leicester to Peterborough road and the outer city ring road ran through the parish.

St. Mary's Church stands in the centre of the old village in the middle of a large churchyard. It is sheltered on three sides by tall trees, and a long tarmac path leads to the south door through an avenue of ancient and imposing yew trees. It has a long history, the list of incumbents stretching back more than 800 years.

There was a long interregnum before we arrived, and the previous vicar, Stephen Haddelsey, had been taken seriously ill, and had subsequently died, soon after his own arrival following another lengthy interregnum. The churchwardens and parishioners had done a wonderful job in maintaining the worship and work of the church, but they were looking forward to welcoming a new parish priest. They were not expecting to be offered a Bishop, however, and were intrigued by the prospect! Because I would have wide responsibilities throughout the diocese, Bishop Tom Butler invited a non-stipendiary priest, Alistair Helm, to meet me to discuss the possibility of our working together. We took to each other immediately, and agreed both to work together and to be licensed at the same time. It was the beginning of a happy and fruitful partnership and of a deep and lasting friendship.

## Getting on with the job

The licensing of Alistair and myself by Bishop Tom Butler was a joyful and lively occasion. St. Mary's was packed, and the singing was enthusiastic. Clergy from neighbouring parishes, City Councillors, the Head Teachers of the Humberstone Infants and Junior Schools and representatives of many local organisations were present. It was a surprise and delight to welcome two priests from Bermuda days: Billy Hayward, Bermuda's Diocesan Curate, and Brian Melbourne, formerly Curate in Pembroke parish and now an incumbent in Canterbury diocese. The reception which followed the service gave us an opportunity to meet many of our parishioners, and Alistair and his wife Kate and Sally and I were made to feel very welcome.

The Churchwardens, Les Mitchelmore and Janette Sanders, were real stalwarts. They had driven to Heathrow to meet me on the day I flew in from Canada to visit the parish, and they impressed me with their outgoing attitude, strong faith and readiness to consider plans for the future. Janette was quiet, thoughtful, loyal and utterly reliable. She had been widowed fairly recently and was coping bravely with her loss. A serious person, she had a lovely sense of humour: her whole face lit up when she laughed. Les came to the Vicarage every day for several weeks when we moved in; he helped in all manner of ways, and nothing was too much trouble for him. As my diocesan ministry grew, I appointed him as my Lay Chaplain: he had a comprehensive knowledge of Leicester and Leicestershire, a keen interest in Church affairs, and an enthusiasm for this new task which eased my burdens considerably.

Roy Kirk, the Honorary Secretary of the Parochial Church Council, was the Librarian at the Leicester University Education Library, and he was another priceless asset. As might be expected of someone with his professional background, he was a superb secretary; careful, methodical, clear-thinking, thorough and plain-speaking. He loved the Church. He read well and spoke well in public, and offered wise advice in an unobtrusive and pleasant way. He had an attractive sense of humour, and was a true friend. He was the embodiment of what a good Anglican lay person should be.

Joan Garner, the Honorary Treasurer, watched over the parish finances with an eagle eye. She kept the accounts meticulously, but found presenting them at meetings something of an ordeal. We came to a happy solution to this problem: she briefed me fully, and I presented the accounts, after which she answered any detailed questions. She was a valued member of the church choir and of other church organisations.

With our licensing taking place less than two weeks before Christmas, Alistair and I had no option but to 'hit the deck running.' There were the Christmas services to prepare, and little time for prolonged consideration of possible variations from the existing pattern. We did the best we could, and the members of the congregation were very appreciative.

Alistair was a remarkable man. A Superintendent in the Leicestershire Police Force, in his early forties, he had been ordained to the non-stipendiary ministry four years previously, and had served as Assistant Curate at St. James the Greater in Leicester. He had been thoroughly trained, and he was an invaluable colleague. He was blessed with exceptional energy, and he loved preparing orders of service for special occasions. Despite his long hours on police duty, he always prepared his sermons thoroughly, often in the early hours of the morning: they were straightforward, down to earth, thought-provoking, and spiced with a rich element of humour. He was utterly reliable, and a man of unimpeachable integrity. He was highly efficient in his daily work and was promoted to the rank of Chief Superintendent not long after our arrival.

We were assisted by a retired non-stipendiary priest, Maurice Poyner, and by a retired Lay Reader, Joan Garner. Yes, we had two Joan Garners in the one congregation! Sally also joined the Ministry team in her capacity as a Lay Reader, and we all met once a month to review progress and plan the life and activities of the parish. We reinstated the 8 a.m. celebration of Holy Communion on Sundays, and were thrilled to see attendance at the Sunday evening service steadily increasing.

An emergency situation arose within a month of our arrival when a large lump of stone fell through the roof of the church from the tower, fortunately when nobody was in the building. Immediate action was essential. Authorisation to carry out the necessary work straightaway was obtained from the Archdeacon, and a temporary repair was effected. We learned that full repair and restoration would cost £20,000, and that there was no real alternative to doing it. The problem had been caused by wind-blown elder seeds taking root in the mortar of the tower some eighty feet above the ground. An elder bush had then started to grow out from the side of the tower, and its roots had grown inwards, thus loosening the blocks of stone and pushing them outwards until one fell. A section of the tower had to be dismantled, the tree roots dug out, and the tower rebuilt. The Parochial Church Council authorised the repair, and paid for it from a long-established and jealously-guarded Restoration Fund. Later in the year, and after a thorough publicity campaign, Alistair and I sat in our cassocks at a table in the lych gate to receive contributions from parishioners to help pay for the repairs. On the day itself we received more than £4,000 – and got very cold in the process! The response from so many people was heart-warming.

A top priority was to tidy up the churchyard. Over the past few years it had become overgrown to the point when some people wondered whether the church had been closed because the grass and brambles had grown so high. It was a huge churchyard, and it was obvious that clearing it would be a mammoth task, but it needed to be tackled. In the Spring of 1996 we organised a team of volunteers for a weekend's work. No fewer than 71 people came to help, and we got the grass cut to an acceptable height. It was very moving to see several ladies in their late seventies and eighties on their knees clipping the grass around the gravestones and helping in a variety of ways. For the next three years Alistair and I, with several volunteers, spent Saturday afternoons keeping the grass cut: it was hard but satisfying work. Then, after protracted correspondence, the Home Office issued an order closing the churchyard to new burials and requiring Leicester City Council to maintain it.

By the middle of 1996 the members of the Ministry Team could detect an encouraging spirit permeating the life of the parish. The congregation was responding to active leadership, and the Sunday services, which were thoroughly prepared and lively, were well attended. Geoffrey Carter, our admirable Organist and Choirmaster, was building up the choir and extending its repertoire. The churchyard was looking tidy, though not beautiful. The midweek celebration of Holy Communion was conducted by our retired non-stipendiary priest, Maurice Poyner. Maurice, a former Post Office telephones engineer, was ordained at the end of his professional career; young at heart, and with an engaging capacity to relate easily to people of all ages, he brought gentleness and humility to all he did, and he was much loved. Our retired Reader, Joan Garner, opened the church every day and said Morning Prayer there. She was a former Civil Servant, unmarried, and had a deep faith. She was an excellent preacher, and I was delighted when she volunteered to act as secretary to the Ministry Team. Both she and Maurice made a great contribution to the life of the parish.

Alistair and I did many things together. On Friday evenings we usually spent an hour or so in the Royal British Legion Club. Situated in the heart of the village, the club hummed with life at the weekend. We usually sat near the door, and chatted amicably to those around us and to people coming in or leaving. We kept quiet during the Bingo sessions, and chatted in the intervals; we never played Bingo, but nobody seemed to mind. We became an accepted part of the furniture, and as time passed more and more people came to talk to us. We learned a lot about our parishioners, and we dealt with many problems on the spot. When it came to the Remembrance Day service in church, the first rehearsal was distinctly sloppy, and I told them all in military language that it was not good enough. Thereafter our Parade services were a model of discipline and good organisation, and I do not think that my reputation suffered because of the reprimand! Several years later, when a serious disagreement over the club's future threatened to split the membership, the Committee asked me to chair a special meeting; disaster was averted.

Alistair brought a breath of fresh air to the life of the parish. We both saw the humorous side of events, and one particular incident is etched indelibly in my memory. Alistair had been visiting the home of a young man whose wedding date was approaching, and had been told by the person answering the door that the young man had gone away. 'Where has he gone?' Alistair asked. 'Can you give me his address?' Upstairs a window was thrown open, and a voice called out: 'What the f—-ing hell do you want to know where he's gone to for?' Forgetting for a moment that he was wearing his clerical collar and not his Police uniform, Alistair called back: 'Because I've got to read his f—-ing banns of marriage, that's why!' To this day I smile at every reminder of that story.

At the beginning of November 1996, almost a year after our arrival in the parish, we introduced an All Saints and All Souls service to remember God's servants who had died. I had organised World AIDS Day services in Bermuda, and had noted how moving and meaningful were the quiet moments in those services when individual members of the congregation brought forward candles, lit them, and placed them in specially constructed frames, in memory of departed loved ones. I sent invitations to the service to the families of all whose funeral services the parish clergy had conducted during the past five years, and also announced it in church. The church was packed for the service, which was deeply moving. It provided an opportunity for quiet reflection, remembrance and sharing of a sense of loss. It directed our thoughts towards Heaven through the readings and prayers. The music was carefully chosen, and the atmosphere was peaceful but not sentimental. Every year thereafter we held a similar service, and each time the church was full. We were meeting people at a point of need.

As we came to the end of our first year at St. Mary's, we could look back on solid achievements. The church had been repaired, the worship was lively, the congregation was in good heart, the churchyard was tidy, and the church was being talked about in the parish. There was an encouraging increase in the number of weddings booked for the following year, and the number of baptisms was also increasing.

## Ministry in the Diocese

When I was appointed as Priest-in-Charge of Humberstone and Assistant Bishop of Leicester, I welcomed a lessening of my responsibilities. I was 61 and for twenty years had been in overall charge first of a major missionary society and then of a challenging overseas diocese. On returning from Bermuda I had been diagnosed as suffering from high blood pressure and was receiving medication on a long-term basis. It was good to be a member of the senior staff team of the diocese without bearing the ultimate burden of leadership, and as I grew into my new position the local knowledge I was acquiring as a parish priest as well as a bishop became increasingly useful at staff meetings.

I was soon immersed in the busy life of the diocese. My first official function was to re-launch the Team Ministry in a group of churches in the centre of Leicester: the ministry team included chaplains of various colleges and institutions, and during the service I caught a glimpse of the rich mixture of racial and cultural elements in the city. In Leicester relations between Christians and members of other faiths are excellent, and I learned more of this three years later when I served as Lord Mayor's chaplain.

Confirmations became a regular feature of my ministry. I conducted an average of thirty services of Confirmation each year, and I loved them. It was encouraging and inspiring to see people of widely different ages and backgrounds coming forward to witness publicly to their commitment to Jesus Christ and to confirm the promises made on their behalf at Baptism. Talking informally to them before or after the service often brought forth moving accounts of their Christian experience or of how they had arrived at the point of Confirmation. In the sermon at these services I usually shared with them some incidents from my own Christian pilgrimage, and months later I was often reminded of the stories I had told by those who had been present. One of the challenges arising from conducting so many Confirmation services was the need to keep the sermons fresh; it is almost impossible not to repeat them, and I was thankful that I had such a long and varied experience on which to draw.

Many of these services stand out in my memory. On one occasion seven children from the top class of the Church of England Junior School in the village of Church Langton, where Barbara Knight, the parish priest, had a wonderful ministry among the children and staff, were confirmed during school hours. The whole school was present in church for the service, and many parents came too. Those who were being confirmed had been thoroughly prepared and were clear about what they were doing. It was a joy to conduct the service. On another occasion I confirmed 92 people from a number of parishes in the Cathedral. The actual laying on of hands took 27 minutes, but nobody seemed worried: my concern was to make it a deeply personal moment for each one. There were big services with large numbers of candidates in some churches, and smaller more intimate ones in some of the village churches; each was unique and individual.

A service in a house in my parish of Humberstone brought home to me what Confirmation can mean to the person being confirmed. Irene was a widow in her seventies, and had no living relatives. She lived in a small but comfortable house in a busy road. She was confined to a wheelchair, having had both legs amputated above the knee because of diabetes and being unable to cope with artificial limbs because of the nature of her illness. She had not been out of her house for more than five years, and lived alone. Nursing staff and Home Helps visited her daily and cared for her. It might have been expected that she would be angry and bitter about all she had suffered, but she was not. She had a radiant Christian faith, which she was ready to talk about whenever it was appropriate. She managed to get herself out of bed and into her chair on her own every morning, and she began her day with a reading from the Bible and a time of prayer. Many times every day she would quietly say 'Thank You, Jesus.' I visited her regularly, and celebrated Holy Communion with her. One day she confessed to me that, although she regularly received Holy Communion, because she was housebound, she had not actually been confirmed. She asked me if I would confirm her. We arranged a date, and I confirmed her in her wheelchair in the lounge of her home. It was profoundly moving. We talked a lot, and thereafter we prayed for each other every day at 7:30 a.m. The monthly celebration of Holy Communion in her home was something I looked forward to.

The licensing of clergy to new appointments and their inductions into new livings was another regular feature of my ministry. It was always exciting to see a full church with people eager to meet and greet their new priest, and to feel the sense of anticipation at a fresh beginning. Here again the sermon was an important part of the service, and I took great care to have in mind an up-to-date assessment of the life of the parish, general background information, and an accurate picture of the incoming priest, particularly if he/she was coming from another diocese. I wanted them to feel at ease with us from the outset, and even if I had not actually met them beforehand I received a thorough briefing from the Archdeacon concerned.

Special occasions in the life of the diocese, the city, the county, a parish or an organisation were often celebrated with a church service, and there were regular requests for one of the Bishops to preach, lead prayers or conduct the service. Diocesan occasions at which I preached included the Commissioning of a Rural Dean, the Diocesan Readers Service, the Diocesan Choirs Festival, the Commissioning of Lay Pastoral Assistants, the Bishop's Lay Congress, the Installation of Honorary Canons, the Ordination of Priests and the Church House Staff Eucharist. In parishes I preached at Patronal Festivals, Music and Flower Festivals, anniversaries, Re-dedications of Church Bells, the Dedication of a Chapel and at Lent Courses. The range of organisations at whose services I preached was vast, and included the Girl Guides' Thinking Day Service, the Royal Naval Association Annual Service, the 35th Anniversary of the Independence of Trinidad and Tobago Service, the Police Christmas Carol Service, the George Cross Island (Malta) Association Service, the St. George's Day Boy Scouts Service and the Prayer Book Society Service. There were particular one-off services at which I preached, such as the 25th anniversary of a priest's ordination and a service of Thanksgiving for the Lord Mayor's Year of Office. There were ecumenical occasions, such as Prisoner Week, the 750th Anniversary of the presence of the Dominican Order in Leicester and the Week of Prayer for Christian Unity. There were also official occasions, such as Civic Services, County Services, the Dedication of the Dunblane Memorial in the National Forest, The Battle of the Atlantic Service in Liverpool Cathedral, the Trinity House Annual Service in London and the Armada Sermon in Leicester. I have deliberately written about these engagements, for each of which I prepared carefully, with a minimum of detail, in order to give an idea of the number and range of them. To say that I was kept at full stretch would be an understatement.

I became well versed in consecrating new burial grounds at parish churches. These services were held in the open air, seldom in perfect weather conditions or on smooth level ground, and I was always relieved and quietly triumphant when the solemn procession around the boundaries passed without mishap!

Another satisfying feature of my espiscopal ministry was regular interviews with clergy and ordinands. These lasted usually for at least an hour and often touched on matters at the very heart of our lives; they brought to the surface hopes, dreams, uncertainties, fears and questions of belief. Praying with them and blessing them at the end of the meeting was particularly meaningful.

Combining diocesan and parochial duties demanded careful planning of my time and strong support from the members of the parish ministry team. At the beginning I had the invaluable assistance of Maurice Poyner, the retired non-stipendiary priest who had lived in the parish for many years and had an encyclopaedic knowledge of it. It was a heavy blow when he was taken ill in church one Sunday evening in 1998 and died shortly afterwards. Alistair was a tower of strength, but he had a phenomenally busy daily workload and could not reasonably be called on at short notice. So when Maurice died, I was in urgent need of the back-up of another priest. Susan Paterson proved to be the answer. She was a non-stipendiary priest who lived in Humberstone and was coming to the end of her first curacy. She readily accepted an invitation to join us and proved her worth immediately. I also had assistance from Helen Bence, who was the Principal and proprietor of an excellent nursery school. She revolutionised the ministry to the young people of the parish: she established a mothers and toddlers group called 'Holy Chaos', which got off to a flying start and has never looked back. So at Humberstone our ministry team consisted of a part-time parish priest who was also a Bishop with extensive diocesan duties, a very senior Police officer who was also a non-stipendiary priest, two school teacher non-stipendiary ministers, an active Reader who was also my wife, and a retired Reader. Finding a mutually convenient date and time for a staff meeting often challenged the administrative skills of us all!

In the Spring of 1998 Bishop Tom Butler advised me that he had accepted appointment as Bishop of Southwark and would be leaving Leicester in the middle of the year. His decision had important implications for me: since Leicester does not have a suffragan bishop, I would be in charge of the diocese during the episcopal interregnum. I attended the Lambeth Conference of Bishops in July/August 1998 as Bishop Commissary of Leicester ('the one to whom charge is committed' – Chambers English Dictionary) and not as Assistant Bishop. I became Bishop Commissary as the Lambeth Conference began.

# CHAPTER SEVENTEEN

# Leicester 1995-2001:
# The Lambeth Conference of Bishops
# July/August 1998

EVERY TEN YEARS all the serving Bishops of the Anglican Communion come together at a residential Conference at the invitation of the Archbishop of Canterbury. So far all the Conferences have taken place in England, though there are currently moves to hold future gatherings outside the United Kingdom. Each Conference is a momentous event. The first was held at Lambeth Palace in 1867, and the most recent at the University of Kent in Canterbury in 1998. The Conferences are traditionally referred to as the Lambeth Conference of a particular year. The Bishops meet 'to worship and pray, to talk and to study the Bible together,' as Archbishop George Carey expressed it in his Introduction to the Official Report of the Lambeth Conference 1998.

From the outset it has been made clear that the purpose of the Conferences is not legislative. In 1867 Archbishop Longley wrote that 'such a meeting would not be competent to make declarations or lay down definitions on points of doctrine. But united worship and common counsels would greatly tend to maintain practically the unity of faith; they would bind us in straiter bonds of peace and brotherly charity.' In practice the decisions and resolutions of the Conferences have been very influential at defining moments in the life of the Anglican Communion. At most of the Conferences there has been at least one major issue demanding clear, considered and constructive guidance: in 1867 there was widespread concern over the unorthodox and allegedly heretical views of Bishop Colenso in South Africa; in 1988 the thorny question was the possible consecration of women bishops; and in 1998 it was homosexuality.

When I was consecrated as a Bishop in 1990 it was just 17 months after the previous Conference, and the next one seemed a long way ahead. I looked forward to attending the 1998 conference, if indeed there was one. As General Secretary of The Missions to Seamen, I had become very aware of the importance and impact of the Conferences, and when my appointment as Bishop of Bermuda was announced, the prospect of participating myself was very exciting. The invitation arrived three years before the 1998 Conference, and I was delighted that the spouse of each Bishop (by now there were a number of women bishops) was invited. There was to be a separate Spouses' Programme in addition to the Bishops' meetings. When the Conference opened on July 18th 1998, the experience far exceeded my hopes and dreams.

The University of Kent was an ideal venue for a three-week Conference with 2000 participants. Set in lovely country overlooking the city of Canterbury, the residential accommodation was good and the conference facilities excellent. A huge Sports Hall, suitably furnished and discreetly camouflaged, was an admirable venue for plenary sessions and the daily Eucharist, and several large marquees in the spacious grounds housed the Spouses' Conference, the buffet lunches, the displays of ecclesiastical merchandise, and the Lambeth Conference shop, where high-quality commemorative items could be purchased. We prepared our own breakfasts in our accommodation, and evening meals were served in some of the College Halls.

No praise could be too high for the brilliant logistical planning. Coaches to convey all the participants to services in Canterbury Cathedral and for a whole-day visit to London were always there at the right time. The complex and diverse programmes ran to time; instructions, written and verbal, were clearly and concisely expressed; up-to-date technological aids worked efficiently; the residential accommodation and the Conference rooms were maintained in immaculate condition; telephones, Fax machines and E-mail facilities were freely available; and excellent temporary toilets were provided in the grounds near the main conference hall and near the spouses' marquee. It was a masterpiece of careful, thoughtful and imaginative planning and execution, and afterwards I wrote to David Long, the Conference Manager, both to congratulate and thank him. There were no domestic distractions.

The Conference itself was also well thought out and superbly planned. Each day began with a Eucharist at 7:15 a.m., the service following the pattern of the worship of a different Province or Church of the Anglican Communion. A book entitled *Lambeth Prayer; Daily Worship for the Conference 1998* was given to each participant at the beginning of the Conference; it set out each day's service in full, and gave the text in both English and the native language of the Province concerned. Another book, *Lambeth Praise*, provided the words and music we sang; it was, and still is, a wonderful resource, and included hymns and songs from all over the world.

Breakfast was followed by Bible Studies in groups of twelve for one and a half hours. We kept the same groups throughout, and these times were a highlight of the Conference for me. In the group I was in there were Bishops from Brazil, Canada, Congo, Cyprus and the Gulf, New Zealand, North India, the Sudan, the United Kingdom, the U.S.A., and a Roman Catholic official observer. All the groups studied St. Paul's Second Letter to the Corinthians. As the days passed and we learned more about each other, we became more relaxed and shared our deepest feelings and experiences. The fellowship deepened: it was uplifting and strengthening.

There were also some marvellous lighter moments. Our Canadian Bishop was speaking one day about how Christians are sometimes over-protective of their own interests. He related an incident from the time when he had been the Rector of a busy parish. In the Parish Hall kitchen no fewer than seven different women's organisations each had its own crockery and equipment; each had its own padlocked cupboard: there was no sharing of resources. He pondered long and hard over this, not liking the atmosphere of suspicion. Eventually he came to a decision. One Saturday evening he went into the kitchen with a hacksaw. He cut off the padlocks, then gift-wrapped each one separately. On Sunday morning he had the gift-wrapped parcels carried into church on a cushion. During the service he invited a representative of each of the seven groups to come forward. He gave each of them a parcel and asked them to unwrap them. When the paper was removed the sawn-off padlocks were revealed. There was a deathly silence. Then somebody laughed, and then another; soon the whole congregation joined in. He confessed to having had some bad moments anticipating what might happen, but a salutary lesson had been learned. Many of our sessions brought forth similar pearls.

The remainder of the day was given over to plenary sessions and section meetings. There was seldom more than one plenary meeting in a day, and the topics covered included two presentations on 'The Bible, the Church and the World' by Dr. David Ford, Regius Professor of Divinity at Cambridge University; 'Making Moral Decisions' by Bishop Rowan Williams of Monmouth; three on 'International Debt' by the President of the World Bank, the Archbishop of Cape Town and the Bishop of Worcester; and 'A Youthful Spirit' by the Bishops of Waikato and Horsham.

The broad spectrum of the Church's calling and concerns was covered in the work of the Sections, which met most days. There were four Sections, which divided into a number of sub-sections. Each Section considered one major theme, and its sub-sections dealt with particular aspects of it. Towards the end of the conference formal resolutions to be placed before a plenary session were prepared. The four Sections were these. First, 'Called to Full Humanity': this Section reflected on subjects including Human Rights and Human Dignity, The Environment, Human Sexuality, Modern Technology, Euthanasia, and International Debt and Economic Justice. Second, 'Called to Live and Proclaim the Good News': the eight sub-sections considered issues including The World God Loves, God's Call to Mission, Being a Missionary Bishop in a Missionary Church, and How to support each other in Mission. Third, 'Called to be a Faithful Church in a Plural World': the sub-sections drafted resolutions on The Authority of the Bible, The Unity of the Anglican Communion, The Future Shape of Lambeth Conferences, Marriage and

Family Life, and Religious Freedom. Fourth, 'Called to be One': the sub-sections reviewed the current complex ecumenical scene, with its signs of hope and its disappointing setbacks; considered progress in official ecumenical conversations; and looked at issues arising from the emergence of New Churches and Independent Christian Groups. I was a member of Section Four, and enjoyed the often spirited discussions of our sub-section. A frustration of our full Section meetings was that a small number of Bishops tended to dominate proceedings. We were a large group, often with more than a hundred Bishops present, and despite the considerable efforts of the Section leaders, the sheer size of the meeting hindered lively spontaneous discussion.

## The Homosexuality Debate

As the conference drew towards its close we were all aware of the attention being focussed on the forthcoming debate on the homosexuality issue. The media were reporting differing views among members of the sub-section discussing the subject, and there was a widespread feeling among the Bishops that this was a vitally important issue requiring thorough and careful handling. There were deeply-held opposing convictions and opinions among us, and a number of Bishops who had met in Kuala Lumpur before the Conference had publicly expressed uncompromising views based on their understanding of Scriptural teaching about homosexuality.

The sub-section of Bishops who had worked together for nearly three weeks to produce a report and resolution had spent many hours, often late into the night, agonising over the complexities of the issue. They concluded that:-

> We must confess that we are not of one mind about homosexuality...It appears that a majority of Bishops is not prepared to bless same sex unions or to ordain active homosexuals. We have prayed, studied and discussed these issues, and we are unable to reach a common mind on the scriptural, theological, historical and scientific questions that are raised. There is much that we do not yet under-stand...The challenge to our Church is to maintain its unity while we seek, under the guidance of The Holy Spirit, to discern the way of Christ for the world today with respect to human sexuality. To do so will require sacrifice, trust and charity towards one another, remembering that ultimately the identity of each person is defined in Christ.

They were well aware of the size and complexity of the subject, and the resolution they put forward, which was a model of integrity, compassionate thinking and succinct formulation, recognised this.

The stage was set for drama.

There was considerable media interest in the proceedings, and there was strict security at the entrance to the Hall to ensure privacy. The chairman for the debate was Archbishop Robin Eames, Primate of Ireland, a man noted for his outstanding ability to draw together people of widely divergent views. As proceedings got under way it was soon clear that the balanced resolution so carefully worded by the sub-section fell far short of the wishes of the uncompromisingly anti-gay Bishops. Amendments were proposed and accepted which included phrases such as homosexual practice being incompatible with Scripture, and being unable to advise the legitimising or blessing of same sex unions. Other Bishops, concerned for the impact the resolution would make on gay and lesbian people, proposed an amendment 'committing ourselves to listen to the experience of homosexual persons'. Eventually the resolution read as follows:-

This Conference:

(a) commends to the Church the subsection report on human sexuality;

(b) in view of the teaching of Scripture, upholds faithfulness in marriage between a man and a woman in lifelong union, and believes that abstinence is right for those who are not called to marriage;

(c) recognises that there are among us persons who experience themselves as having a homosexual orientation. Many of these are members of the Church and are seeking the pastoral care, moral direction of the Church, and God's transforming power for the living of their lives and the ordering of relationships. We commit ourselves to listen to the experience of homosexual persons and we wish to assure them that they are loved by God and that all baptised, believing and faithful persons, regardless of sexual orientation, are full members of the Body of Christ;

(d) while rejecting homosexual practice as incompatible with Scripture, calls on all our people to minister pastorally and sensitively to all irrespective of sexual orientation and to condemn irrational fear of homosexuals, violence within marriage and any trivialisation and commercialisation of sex;

(e) cannot advise the legitimising or blessing of same sex unions nor ordaining those involved in same gender unions;

(f) requests the Primates and the ACC to establish a means of monitoring the work done on the subject of human sexuality in the Communion and to share statements and resources among us;...

Clause (g) noted the significance of the Kuala Lumpur Statement and other resolutions of the Conference.

In its final form the resolution was overwhelmingly approved, and I was one of those who voted in favour of it. But many Bishops were left feeling bruised and unhappy; the last word on the subject most certainly had not been spoken.

## Highlights of the Conference

During one of the most concentratedly satisfying three week periods of my life a number of memorable events and moments stand out.

The majesty and brilliance of the Opening Service, in the magnificent surroundings of Canterbury Cathedral, and with all Bishops fully robed and many of the wives resplendent in clothes reflecting their national backgrounds, set the tone for the whole Conference.

The cheerful friendships and fellowship Sally and I enjoyed with the two South African Bishops and their wives in the excellent student accommodation where we stayed, and where we took turns in preparing breakfast for all six of us, ensured a happy start to each day.

The whole-day visit to London, with lunch in an enormous marquee at Lambeth Palace and an address by Prime Minister Tony Blair, a Garden Party at Buckingham Palace hosted by The Queen, and a boat journey down the Thames on our way back to Canterbury, gave us a wonderful day out.

The meticulously prepared daily Eucharists celebrated by different Provinces were outstanding. We were privileged to see the richness, variety and diversity of our Anglican worship. The Vigil of Meditation, Prayer and Washing of Feet conducted by Father Jean Vanier of the L'Arche Community was deeply moving. Relaxed evenings at the campus pub with good friends from the Anglican Church of Canada sent me to bed in a pleasant state of mind. The lively and imaginative 'Crowning Glory' musical drama, written and produced by the Spouses' Conference, restored calm after the tensions of the Homosexuality debate of the previous day. The closing service at the University of Kent provided a wonderful climax to an unforgettable experience.

# CHAPTER EIGHTEEN

# Leicester 1995-2001:
# Bishop Commissary of Leicester,
# and Afterwards

WHEN BISHOP Tom Butler advised me in the Spring of 1998 that he would be moving from Leicester to become Bishop of Southwark in the middle of the year, a legal document transferring episcopal authority in the Diocese of Leicester to me was drawn up. It was entitled 'Instrument of Delegation,' and read as follows:-

---

### DIOCESE OF LEICESTER

#### Church of England (Miscellaneous Provisions) Measure 1983

#### INSTRUMENT OF DELEGATION

**WHEREAS WE THOMAS** by Divine Permission **BISHOP OF LEICESTER** will vacate our said Bishopric upon our translation to the See of Southwark **AND WHEREAS** there is no person in Episcopal Orders in the Diocese who is for the time being authorised to discharge our functions as Diocesan Bishop **WE DO** hereby delegate in accordance with Section 8 of the Church of England (Miscellaneous Provisions) Measure 1983, as amended by Section 12 of the Church of England (Miscellaneous Provisions) Measure 1995 and after consultation with our Bishops Council and Standing Committee, all of our functions as Diocesan Bishop to **The Right Reverend WILLIAM JOHN DENBIGH DOWN** such delegation to take effect and remain in force from the confirmation of our election to the See of Southwark, until the election of our successor has been confirmed.

**GIVEN** under our hand this _11th_ day of June One thousand nine hundred and ninety-eight.

+Thomas Leicester

---

Without doubt the episcopal interregnum was going to be the most concentratedly busy period of my whole ministry. In addition to carrying out all the regular episcopal duties myself, I was still responsible for the parish of Humberstone, and I had already committed myself to act as Lord Mayor's Chaplain for the Civic Year! I was thankful for the experience of administration at the highest level which I had acquired during the past twenty years, because it was obvious that I would need to be extremely well-disciplined and to delegate to others as many duties as I reasonably could. I would aim to do first only the jobs that I alone could do, at the same time keeping in the closest touch with what my colleagues were doing.

The beginning of my service as Bishop Commissary coincided almost exactly with the start of the Lambeth Conference in July 1998. We returned from the Conference reinvigorated and with a fresh vision. Five days later, and a week after the widely publicised Conference debate on homosexuality, I received a telephone call from *The Times* newspaper. I was told that in the next day's edition of the paper a report would appear of an interview with a priest in Leicester diocese, Simon Long, in which he had spoken of his relationship with his partner Kevin. The reporter asked for my views, and I agreed to speak to him later in the day when I had had time to make some enquiries and to marshal my thoughts. I rang Simon, in order to confirm the story, and also the Archdeacon and our Diocesan Communications Officer, Sue Kyriakou. We agreed that we would issue a statement after the publication of the article.

Next morning a report headed 'Rector comes out in gay vote protest' appeared on page 1 of *The Times*. It began with these words:-

> An Anglican priest has responded to the Archbishop of Canterbury's plea for the Church to 'listen to the experience of homosexuals' by announcing that he has had a 'gay wedding' with the man who shares his rectory...Simon Long, 58, is risking his job by 'outing' himself in protest against the overwhelming vote condemning homosexuality by the Lambeth Conference of Bishops a week ago.

He had met Kevin at a homosexual club in Leicester in 1990, and in 1993 they agreed to have a blessing ceremony, 'the nearest homosexuals can come to marriage.'

> The Anglican Church does not officially approve these so, like many gay Christians, they turned to the Metropolitan Community Church for a 'service of union'. In Birmingham, surrounded by friends, they stood in matching white dinner jackets to exchange rings and wills, a gesture of protest against the absence of inheritance rights for homosexual couples under British law. Mr Long has not officially 'come out' to his parishioners.

I realised that a potentially explosive situation could go badly wrong if it was mishandled, and that much patience, care and sensitivity would be required in order to discern the right course of action. I accordingly issued a Press Statement on the day *The Times* article appeared. It read as follows:-

> The article referring to The Revd. Simon Long in today's edition of '*The Times*' has come to the attention of the Bishop Commissary of Leicester. The Bishop will review all aspects of the matters raised with all concerned. This will necessarily involve time, sensitivity and care, and no further public statement will be issued at this time.

I had a long conversation with Simon, for whom I had great respect. I had been aware of his sexual orientation, because almost two years previously he had himself brought it to the attention of the diocesan Bishop, Tom Butler, and at Tom's request I had visited Simon and Kevin at the Rectory and had had a frank, positive and friendly discussion with them. At that time Simon was thinking seriously of issuing a statement to his churchwardens setting out his situation. He had a real dilemma: he loved and valued the Church, his parish and his people; he did not want to leave them; but he felt that by not issuing his statement he would be living a lie. He eventually decided against 'coming out' at that time, but it was plainly a situation which would not go away. The debate at the Lambeth Conference had decided him.

I had further lengthy conversations with the Archdeacon of Leicester, Mike Edson, the Diocesan Communications Officer, Sue Kyriakou, our diocesan legal officers and Bishop Frank Sargeant, Head of Staff at Lambeth Palace. All were very helpful, and I was grateful for their advice and support.

Six days after the appearance of the newspaper article, I had a long meeting with the churchwardens of the six churches in Simon's parish. There was sadness that the situation had arisen at all. There was sympathy for Simon himself. There was hurt at the way they had found out. There was some anger at Simon's perceived abuse of his position. There was also a strong feeling, confirmed at the end of the meeting by a confidential canvass of their views, that he could no longer continue in office.

I discussed the situation again with Simon. We were frank with each other, and we respected each other's positions. We also got on well together. For my part I knew that I must proceed with sensitivity along the lines set out in the Lambeth Conference resolution, for which I had voted. I also had a number of very good friends who were gay. I had reached the conclusion that some people are born with homosexual orientation, and I understood the anguish and despair some of them had experienced as they strove to come to terms with their sexuality. I had a lot of sympathy for Simon. I did not want to proceed quickly, because I believed that when feelings calmed down we would be able to work towards resolving the situation. I called another meeting of the churchwardens a month or so after the first one; it was friendly and positive, but it was also clear that there was no significant change in their view that Simon should not continue in office. I then called a meeting of the

District Church Councils, representing the churches of the parish, and a similar picture emerged there.

I advised Simon of the feelings of his people and of the strength of their view that he could not go on in such circumstances. We concluded that he should resign as Rector of his parish, and he intimated that he was considering working in a secular capacity. I talked to the officers of the Church of England Pensions Board, and they were very helpful in sorting out Simon's pension entitlements quickly. Nine months after the appearance of the newspaper article, Simon and Kevin opened a restaurant and bookshop in Scotland, which is doing well. We parted on good terms, and I was delighted that his parishioners gave him a warm and generous send-off.

Throughout the whole process Simon was frank, courteous, dignified and sensitive. I respected his integrity, and the courage with which he had faced his difficulties, and I was well aware that the Church has a lot of serious thinking to do over the issue of homosexuality.

★   ★   ★

The episcopal interregnum lasted almost a year, and I was at full stretch throughout. I was clear that there could be no major policy changes while I was in charge: existing practices would continue; I would concentrate on my pastoral duties; and I would prepare the way for the incoming bishop.

There were, however, some logistical arrangements to make straightaway. The Bishop's office was in a new building adjacent to Bishop's Lodge, four miles from Humberstone Vicarage. All the office equipment and records were there, overseen by the Bishop's Personal Assistant, Penny Russell. So for the duration of the interregnum I moved into the Bishop's office; I spent several hours a day there, and conducted most personal interviews there. It was necessary also to maintain my office at Humberstone, where a parishioner, Jan Zientek, was my part-time Secretary.

Penny Russell was a tower of strength. She loved her work, and was very good at it. She had an encyclopaedic knowledge of the diocese, and her judgment was sound. She was thoughtful and courteous, and had a pleasant manner with people. We worked together very happily: we respected each other, we discussed problems carefully and in depth, and I could rely on her to do what she said she would do. She had a marvellous sense of humour, and many a busy day was enlivened by her pithy comments. She dealt very competently with the many letters we received every day, and we successfully avoided any diary mix-ups. This was a major achievement, as I had to break the practice of my whole working life by transferring my desk diary daily to and from Bishop's Lodge. Normally the diary never left my office, and I made appointments only from there. Throughout my ministry I missed only a handful of appointments through my own mistakes.

During the interregnum I had to delegate responsibility for most of the day-to-day work of Humberstone parish to my non-stipendiary clergy colleagues and Readers and to a temporary assistant, The Revd. Peter Hebden. Between them they worked wonders, and I was able to participate in the Sunday morning services in the parish church some twenty times in the year. On weekdays I conducted Confirmation and Licensing of Clergy services, interviewed clergy and lay people, attended meetings of the House of Bishops and of Regional Bishops, visited parishes, attended a whole range of official functions, chaired committee meetings and kept up with correspondence. A feature of my ministry as Lord Mayor's chaplain was composing and leading the opening prayers at meetings of the City Council. I did not want the prayer to be a mere formality, so I asked the Town Clerk to give me a brief summary of the agenda beforehand. I was then able to weave this information into a prayer relevant (I hoped!) to the meeting.

Halfway through the interregnum it was announced that the new Bishop of Leicester would be The Right Reverend Tim Stevens, Suffragan Bishop of Dunwich in the Diocese of St. Edmundsbury and Ipswich. We contacted each other immediately, and we enjoyed a happy and fruitful start to our ministry together which continued undisturbed after his arrival.

During the year I was fortunate to have three short breaks overseas. Sally and I spent ten days in Bermuda after Christmas and enjoyed meeting many friends again. I went to Bangladesh for ten days to represent the Oxford Mission, with whom I had been associated for more than twenty years, at a 'Partners in Mission' consultation. I also flew to Canada for six days to conduct the wedding of my former Lay Chaplain in Bermuda, Colin Fleming. These breaks were a godsend to me: they provided a complete change of scene.

## After the Interregnum

### The New Bishop of Leicester

With the arrival of our new diocesan bishop, Tim Stevens, I reverted to my role of Assistant Bishop and parish priest. I realised that during my three and a half years in the diocese, and particularly during the year in charge, I had learned a great deal about the diocese and our people. I felt that this knowledge might be useful to Tim as he settled in, so although I was approaching retiring age, I offered to stay on for two years. He welcomed and accepted the offer.

Tim was enthroned as Bishop of Leicester in a dignified, moving service, rich in symbolism, in the Cathedral. Early in the service it was my privilege to anoint his hands. In that deeply significant moment I felt that I was extending my hands in welcome, handing over to him my temporary charge of the

*Leicester Cathedral, with June and Maurice Mawdsley, 2000.*

diocese, and asking God's blessing on him as servant of the servants of The Lord.

He was a good person to work with. He never hesitated to seek advice or information. He consulted widely, and was concerned that every aspect of a decision should be considered carefully and prayerfully before committing himself to it. He was not afraid to stand up and be counted when a situation required this. He placed great importance on our Senior Staff meetings, which comprised the Bishops, the Provost, the Archdeacons, the Director of Ministry and Training and the Diocesan Secretary; every meeting began with a celebration of Holy Communion in the Bishop's chapel at 8 a.m. and continued until 5 p.m. We had lunch together in Bishop's Lodge, and it was always a delightfully happy and relaxing break. He was keen that our meetings should not be restricted to dealing with the day-to-day business of the diocese, important though this was; he introduced regular training sessions for us and an annual residential meeting.

I enjoyed our work together. I did my best to keep him fully informed about what I was doing, and he shared many concerns with me. There was a lovely atmosphere of trust between us. I greatly appreciated his entrusting to me the role of Sponsoring Bishop for the ordinands proceeding to their selection conferences; this involved monitoring their individual progress through training, meeting regularly with the Diocesan Director of Ordinands to discuss the overall training picture, and officially endorsing each candidate.

I felt that the senior staff was a happy group moving forward with a sense of purpose and under wise leadership. We all had our part to play, and we valued the appreciation shown to our work.

A few months after Tim's arrival the regular four-yearly residential clergy conference was held. It was a splendid conference at which he made a great and favourable impact.

## The Cathedral

A major project with which I was associated throughout my ministry in Leicester was the acquisition of a suitable building for a Cathedral Centre, and the building, in partnership with Leicester City Council, of the long-planned Visitor Centre at the West End of the Cathedral and adjoining the medieval Guildhall. Leicester did not become a separate diocese until 1927, so there was no Cathedral at that time. The inner-city parish church of St. Martin's was designated as the Cathedral, but it lacked many of the ancillary amenities which form an integral part of a modern Cathedral. There was no Chapter House, there were no Cathedral staff offices, no adjacent Hall, no kitchen, no public car parking, and just three toilets. The Provost's secretary worked from a room in the Provost's residence, and the Residentiary Canons from their homes, only one of which was near the Cathedral.

There was a strong feeling among the members of the Cathedral congregation, staff and clergy that there was an urgent need for a Cathedral Centre which would offer appropriate facilities for hospitality, counselling, committee meetings, office work and functions. With strong support from The Hon. Mrs. Ann Brooks, wife of the Lord Lieutenant of Leicestershire, Geoffrey Simpson, Chairman of the Cathedral's Fabric Committee, and the Cathedral clergy, I became Chairman of a small committee formed with the approval of the Bishop to press forward with the acquisition and financing of the purchase of a suitable building. The Provost, The Venerable Derek Hole, took charge of the negotiations with the City Council to implement the plans for the Visitor Centre.

Comprehensive estimates of the finance required to carry out and complete both projects were obtained, and it became clear that we should need to launch an Appeal for £2 million. A Feasibility Study commissioned by the Cathedral concluded that this was an achievable target, and professional fundraising consultants were employed at the start of the Appeal. Local staff were later engaged to carry through the project. Brian Wakefield, an early-retired Area Manager of a major Bank, took charge, with Don Salt, a member of the Cathedral Choir, as his assistant and Margaret Sharman as their secretary.

A lovely old building adjacent to the Cathedral came on to the market, and the Cathedral Chapter purchased it. It was exciting and very satisfying to see it being transformed into a Cathedral Centre of great character, and it was a proud moment for us all when Her Royal Highness The Princess Royal, who gave us strong support throughout the Appeal, opened it. Slowly but surely the money came in, and there was a further great occasion shortly after I retired when His Royal Highness The Duke of Edinburgh opened the Cathedral Visitor Centre during a Royal visit to Leicester. The amenities of the Cathedral had been augmented and enhanced by these substantial additions, and it was good to know that they had been paid for!

With the Appeal already under way, we were delighted to welcome the new Provost of Leicester, The Very Revd. Vivienne Faull, to the Appeal Committee. Viv had succeeded Derek Hole, who had retired, and was the first woman to be appointed as Dean or Provost of an English Cathedral. She brought experience of ministry in Gloucester and Coventry Cathedrals to her task in Leicester, and it was a joy to work with her.

## The Diocese

Alongside my involvement with the Cathedral Appeal, I continued to carry out my regular diocesan engagements, which included Confirmations, Licensing of clergy to new appointments, preaching at special occasions, clergy appraisal interviews, social functions on behalf of Bishop Tim, dedication services, and being ready to deal with emergency situations as and when they arose. These last could seldom be predicted, and I spent many hours pondering over, dealing carefully with and recording some of the unjust and damaging accusations levelled by private persons and even official bodies against individual clergy and their families who had done little or nothing wrong. There were also engagements outside the diocese from time to time, such as the annual three-day Bishops' Conference in Liverpool, the twice yearly Regional Bishops' Meeting, and invitations to preach.

## St. Mary's Humberstone

It was good, too, to be able to devote more time to St. Mary's, Humberstone, after my year of mainly episcopal duties.

An old church needs plenty of tender loving care, and we all worked hard to achieve and sustain a high standard of maintenance at St. Mary's. A Children's Corner was established and later equipped with new furnishings. Toys and musical instruments were purchased for the very young children who came to Holy Chaos, our excellent group for mothers and toddlers established by Helen Bence, a nursery school Principal and ordinand, who became a non-stipendiary member of our ministry team when she was ordained. The choir and clergy vestries were painted, carpeted and refurnished. The church was redecorated inside, and a contract was signed to renew the electrical wiring and lighting. A trumpet stop was added to the

*Leicester, with Churchwardens Les Mitchelmore (left) and
Stan Cunningham (right) at St. Mary's, Humberstone.*

organ in memory of a much-loved parishioner. A beautifully crafted wooden
surround for the lectern was installed. Many hand-worked kneelers were
made and presented by parishioners. A Book of Remembrance in a lovely
wooden display case, and inscribed by Lawson Mapp, Cathedral Warden in
Bermuda, was presented. The massive church doors were taken down,
cleaned, oiled and replaced. The Church Hall was decorated inside and
outside, its wiring and lighting renewed, new chairs and tables purchased, and
a contract signed to extend the building and add storage space. The long
tarmac path from the Lych Gate to the church was re-laid, and rose beds were

planted near the church for a memorial to past parishioners. When I retired the buildings and surrounds were in good order.

But a church is about people rather than buildings, and knowing my parishioners and being known by them gave me great satisfaction. In parish ministry there is constantly a rich variety of daily experience: there is the joy and happiness of baptisms, confirmations and marriages; the satisfaction of leading and being an integral part of a regular worshipping community; the calling to care for the sick, the elderly, the vulnerable, and those who are going astray; and the ministry to the dying and the bereaved.

It was good to see an increase in the number of baptisms and marriages at St. Mary's, and the members of the ministry team took great care in our preparation for these. I personally saw each wedding couple at least once before either arranging further meetings with them, if I was going to conduct the service, or introducing them to the member of the team who was to marry them. I also saw the parents of each child to be baptized at least once, and followed this up with a home visit. As time passed my knowledge of the parish and our parishioners grew; constantly meeting them kept me in touch with what they were thinking, and this in turn helped in the preparation of sermons.

One of the major drawbacks of being both a bishop and a parish priest was that there was simply not enough time to meet all the demands on my time and energies. As usual it became a matter of establishing priorities, and it was not easy to be even-handed. I had to be firm with myself in delegating particular tasks. I allocated as much time as possible to visiting the housebound, the elderly, the bereaved and the sick. I knew from my own time in bed for a year as a teenager with tuberculosis how much they appreciated an unhurried visit, when they could receive Holy Communion and then talk without reserve to a sympathetic and discreet listener. Irene Johnson, the diabetic lady whose legs had been amputated, was one such person, and Joy Bennett was another.

Joy lived in a small bungalow, and was virtually housebound; walking unaided was very difficult for her. She had a number of serious physical ailments, and in 1994 was diagnosed as having a tumour on the brain; she was told she had no more than six months to live. She was then in her mid-seventies. She had experienced much suffering in her life: brought up by her grandparents, and with a strong Christian faith, she nursed at Great Ormond Street Hospital for Sick Children in London before her marriage. Her only child, a son, died shortly after his birth, and her husband also died young. She married again, and had twelve years of great happiness until her second husband died. She then moved into her bungalow, and as she grew older her health deteriorated. She might have been expected to feel sorry for herself, but she did not. Her tumour did not affect her thought processes, and she was nearly always bright and cheerful. When I arrived each month to celebrate Holy Communion with her a small table would already be set with a clean white cloth and tiny candles. She participated in the service with enthusiasm and reverence, and I always came away uplifted by her company, and fortified by a generous glass of whisky! Against all the predictions, her tumour did not kill her, nor did she lose all her sight, as had been forecast. She resolutely refused to undergo further chemotherapy treatment, declining it in robust terms. Now in her mid-eighties she lives on, tended by loving carers and friends. She was Joy by name and Joy by nature.*

Saturday afternoons at St. Mary's were the time for keeping the church neat and tidy and doing all the odd jobs. Alistair and I cut grass, weeded rose beds, stained floor boards, hoovered the carpets and swept the floors. It was a refreshing change from the pressures of our daily work. We were joined by Susan Adams, a young woman whose parents had recently died and who missed them greatly. She was an enthusiastic cleaner, and took over the care of the church's linen and some Sacristan's duties. She had considerable secretarial skills, and I am deeply grateful to her for typing this book so willingly and competently.

To write about the host of wonderful characters who made up the family of St. Mary's would fill a book and still run the risk of omitting some, but I will mention one more. Maurice Mawdsley suffered a serious heart attack at home, and only prompt action by his daughter Rose, a nurse, saved him. I went to see him in hospital as soon as I heard the news about him. Maurice was a man of decided opinions, never afraid to call a spade a shovel, and when I arrived at his bedside in the Coronary Care Unit he was telling the doctor that his pain was caused by indigestion. The doctor disagreed, and a lively debate between the two of them ensued, with Maurice reluctant to concede an inch! He was an interesting person. I visited him regularly after his heart attack, and later after two knee replacement operations, and I learned a lot about him. He had served in the Armed Forces in the Second World War, been an apprentice butcher, and then run a busy Post Office for many years. He had served as Churchwarden at St. Mary's and was a long-serving member of the Parochial Church Council. Some of his opinions were extremely provocative, and he occasionally drove his devoted family to distraction. But he was the salt of the earth, a man who could be relied on.

A parish priest needs to be prepared to react swiftly and at any time in emergency situations and domestic crises, and we had our share of these during the years at St. Mary's. There were the tragic deaths of five young people in a holiday motor accident; the arrest in Venezuela of two young parishioners on drug-carrying charges; the break-up of marriages;

---

*Joy died peacefully early in February 2004.

employment crises; the problems which came my way when I was Chairman of Governors at our local Infants and Junior schools; the care and counselling of the bereaved; the abandonment of a bride on her wedding day, and a host of unpredictable situations. My daily time alone with God each morning was vital.

### Approaching Retirement

With Bishop Tim well established, Sally and I gave serious consideration to retirement, and one of the first questions to deal with was where we would live. We owned our house in Exeter, and it had been let since Julia completed her degree course and we returned from Bermuda. Much though we loved Exeter and our home, we did not feel that Exeter was the ideal place for us to retire to. Our children were living in Oxford, Cornwall, Bosnia and Warwickshire, with Andrew and his family in Oxford the most likely to be permanently settled. We decided to look for a house in the South Midlands within reasonable reach of Oxford.

In September 1999, during a fortnight's holiday, we drove around Oxfordshire and the neighbouring counties looking at likely locations. Witney was one of the places we visited, and we were immediately attracted by it. We made a round of the estate agents, and toured the town looking at the exteriors of properties for sale. One property seemed to meet our requirements, and we arranged to return the next day to look at it. It was a compact four-bedroomed house built in 1985 in a quiet residential estate six or seven minutes walk from the town centre and with a small garden. It needed some attention, but we liked it and thought that it would be suitable. We discussed it with the estate agent, and then put in a bid, which was accepted three hours later. We spent an uneasy night wondering whether we had done the right thing!

The purchase took three months to complete, during which time we sold our house in Exeter to the tenants who had been living there for four years. We were very fortunate that everything proceeded so smoothly, and since there would be a period of eighteen months before I was due to retire, we decided to let the house for a year. The income from the letting covered the cost of putting the house in good order, and the tenant looked after it very well. Before we moved in ourselves in July 2001, we extended the kitchen to include a utility room.

As I prepared to retire I looked back over forty-two years in the ordained ministry of the Church. Two thirds of that time had been spent serving with The Missions to Seamen, and I had travelled all over the world. I had been a Bishop for more than eleven years, and had experienced the joys and the challenges of the calling. We had made lasting friendships wherever we had been, and enjoyed the heart-warming welcome Christians everywhere extend to each other. I could look back over solid achievements and humbling failures. As the years had passed I had come to know God more deeply and to depend more and more on my daily time with Him. I brought to Him my hopes and dreams and achievements as well as my sins and failures, and I received forgiveness and the strength to pick myself up and carry on. I read the Bible every day, and meditated upon it, and I saw every day as a fresh opportunity for service.

I was looking forward to retiring from full-time ministry, although I knew I would miss many aspects of it. I wanted to write this book, and I was physically and mentally tired. I wanted a good break for a few months. I looked forward to helping in the parish of Witney and the Diocese of Oxford, and to playing golf. When the time came to leave Humberstone and the Diocese of Leicester, we were given a wonderful send-off and many generous gifts. My ordaining the new priests of the diocese in Leicester Cathedral marked the first day of my retirement. I appreciated Bishop Tim's generosity in inviting me to do this: it was a climax to my full-time ministry and a happy baptism into retirement.

# CHAPTER NINETEEN

# Retirement in Witney 2001-

THE OFFICIAL DATE of my retirement from the full-time ministry of The Church of England was Saturday June 30th 2001. The following day, Sunday July 1st, I ordained the new priests in Leicester Cathedral: it was a wonderful privilege, a climax to forty-two years in the ordained ministry, and a happy reminder that a Christian's ministry continues through retirement to the end of his or her life. My first sensible thought on Monday July 2nd was that I had no more official engagements and there was nothing I was required to do! A new way of life stretched ahead for Sally and me. In the quiet of my study early that morning I committed myself afresh to God: in new and unfamiliar circumstances and surroundings I would continue to seek to discern and follow God's call for the future.

**Early Days**
While there were no official duties on that first Monday, there was plenty to do. We planned to move to our new home in Witney a week later, and the last-minute preparations had to be made. The house we were moving into was much smaller than the Vicarage, and there were items of furniture and other possessions to dispose of, so we arranged for a large skip to carry away unwanted goods and clutter; we had no difficulty in filling it! The moment when we finally left the Vicarage was poignant: it had been a pleasant home; we had loved its spaciousness, and been happy there; and it was the end of a chapter of our lives which had spanned all our married life.

Getting ourselves sorted out in the house in Witney took time. An extension to the kitchen, which we had planned and authorised in good time, was not quite finished when we moved in, so we had workmen in the house as we sought to unpack. Cupboards and bookshelves had to be constructed in the bedroom I was going to use as my study, which delayed my being able to arrange it as I wanted. Despite our efforts in Humberstone, we discovered that we still had too much furniture and too many books, so further pruning was necessary. Eventually order emerged from chaos, and we began to settle into life in Witney.

Much of the summer still lay ahead of us, and we took advantage of the long days to explore the countryside around us. We revelled in the freedom of being able to go out for the day if we wanted to, and to stop for a meal as the fancy took us. We travelled on minor roads through breathtakingly beautiful and unspoiled villages and landscapes in Oxfordshire and the Cotswolds, and it was lovely to return to our very own home at the end of the day.

After forty-two years of active, absorbing, challenging and satisfying ministry I felt that I both wanted and needed a complete break from Church duties and activities for a while. I wanted to be able to go to church and just be a member of the congregation. We worshipped initially at the parish church of St. Mary's in Witney, and enjoyed the pleasure of being able to sit together during the services. The parish of Witney has four churches – St. Mary's and Holy Trinity in the town, and Curbridge and Hailey on the outskirts – and is served by a Team Ministry. When we arrived, there were three full-time clergy (the Rector and two Team Vicars) and a non-stipendiary Associate Priest. But it was known that one of the Team Vicars who was about to move on would not be replaced. Sally was keen to continue as a Lay Reader and also as a member of a church choir, and when she visited Holy Trinity to experience the worship there, she liked what she found. She was soon welcomed into the choir, and her ministry as a Lay Reader was also welcomed. She was licensed as a Lay Minister in the Cathedral in the autumn.

After six months of settling into retirement, I felt ready to undertake a gentle programme of Church duties and activities. The Rector of Witney, Cameron Butland, invited me to preach and celebrate Holy Communion on a regular basis, and I happily accepted. I went to see our area Bishop, Colin Fletcher, Bishop of Dorchester, to offer my services in any capacity he might consider appropriate, and I intimated to both of them that as I was planning to write this book, my available time would be limited. Both were very understanding, and I settled down in earnest to write.

Before embarking on *Down to the Sea* I arranged for ultimate publication of a collection of the Graces I had written and delivered at public functions. I had kept copies of them all, as each was written for a particular occasion and with different people in mind, and Jeremy Gotch, a good friend and former Master of The Worshipful Company of Carmen, had been pressing me for several years to publish them in aid of a charitable cause. I duly put together the collection, and wrote a connecting commentary: the collection is currently being illustrated and will be sold to raise funds for The Mission to Seafarers and The Worshipful Company of Carmen.

An early feature of retirement was the opportunity to play some golf. Two good friends from Bermuda, Michael Woods and John Ellison, had both retired to the Oxford area, and they introduced me to some of the local courses. John is a member of the Chipping Norton club, and proposed me for membership there. It is an excellent course, with a fine modern clubhouse on high ground overlooking glorious countryside. John and I play once a week, and our modest efforts give us a lot of pleasure: on the nineteenth hole our conversations range over a wide variety of subjects, and we enjoy each other's company.

Retirement was proving decidedly pleasant!

## Involvement with the Church and the Local Community

Sally's entry into the Church life of Witney was a model of good sense and initiative. She took a good look at the two Anglican Churches in the town, and concluded that she would be happy at Holy Trinity. She was made most welcome there, and is fully involved in a number of activities. She knew that I would become involved in the wider life of the diocese, and would often be conducting services away from Witney, and she continued her practice, adopted when I was a port chaplain, of worshipping regularly in our parish church. As a Licensed Lay Minister she is invited to conduct services in other parishes from time to time. She also sings with the Eynsham Choral Society throughout the year.

With the passing of time I have become steadily more involved in the life of the Diocese of Oxford and the parish of Witney. I have been a member of a small group led by the Archdeacon of Berkshire which has been preparing a guidebook for Church fundraising. I have also served on The Cutting Edge Ministries committee, which, under the leadership of the Bishop of Dorchester, is charged with initiating and supporting new and visionary ministries with which to engage our constantly changing society. I have conducted services in a number of local churches during interregna, and preached for friends and former colleagues in Buckinghamshire, Berkshire, Hertfordshire and Gloucestershire. During 2003 I conducted fourteen Confirmation Services, mostly in the Reading episcopal area during the episcopal interregnum, and I also preached at the annual Licensing Service of the Lay Ministers in the Cathedral.

In Witney itself I continue to worship regularly at St. Mary's and take part in activities there and at Holy Trinity. I have spoken to the Witney Rotary and Probus clubs, and I usually meet people I know on my daily walks. I treasure the fact that I have very few evening engagements: after a working life in which I was out most evenings it is a great joy just to read and watch television.

Beyond the Diocese of Oxford, I have enjoyed my Presidency of The Oxford Mission. The Oxford Mission '...consists of three religious communities, the Brotherhood of St. Paul, the Sisterhood of the Epiphany and the Christa Sevika Sangha. (It) has houses in India and Bangladesh. Their work is pastoral, medical and educational, and is carried on in the dioceses of Kolkata and Dhaka' (Church of England Yearbook 2004). Since retirement I have made two visits to Bangladesh and one to Kolkata on behalf of the Mission, and it has been exciting to see how the changed political scene in both India and Bangladesh has resulted in the birth of The Brotherhood of St.

Paul, a totally Bangladeshi community succeeding The Brotherhood of the Epiphany, and the Christa Sevika Sangha (The Handmaids of Christ) as the long-term successor of The Sisterhood of the Epiphany. The ministry of The Oxford Mission is held in high esteem and affection in The Church of North India and The Church of Bangladesh, and it is encouraging to see how the dioceses are assuming responsibility for the work. Economically, Bangladesh is one of the poorest countries in the world, and I have been enormously impressed by the imaginative and energetic outreach of the Church of Bangladesh, of which the Oxford Mission is an integral part.

The Church of Bangladesh is tiny numerically, having some 15,000 members in a country with a population of more than 130 million, most of whom are Muslims. It is a United Church, bringing together Christians of various reformed denominations. Small in numbers, it is large on practical outreach. Because evangelism by word of mouth is almost impossible for legal reasons, the Gospel is proclaimed by practical action. The Church runs a number of Self Help projects, and I spent a full day with one based at the Oxford Mission in Barisal. With capital provided by Churches overseas and missionary societies, the Self Help groups assist people in the greatest need for whom some initial finance is essential in order to initiate work which will make them self-sufficient. The Self Help project team helps them to identify their skills, provides them with practical basic training, and makes loans to start the business. With the Project's local Director, Florence Sarkar, I visited a home where a tailoring business had been started by a mother to whom a loan had been made to purchase a sewing machine, another who was rearing chicks for the market, and a third where one cow had been purchased followed later by several others. In all I saw at least a dozen small thriving home-based businesses. The day of my visit coincided with the time for repaying part of the loans, and all who had received cash made payments. There is almost 100% repayment of loans. Because of this practical help, questions are asked as to why the Church offers this assistance, and honest answers can be given. The Gospel is preached by love in action as well as by word of mouth.

There will be a continuing need for the Oxford Mission committee in England to remit funds to support work there; however, the funds in the United Kingdom are dwindling, and far-reaching decisions about the future will soon have to be made.

I am also a member of the Council of USPG, the United Society for the Propagation of The Gospel, for whose work I have great respect. My interest was aroused when I was General Secretary of The Missions to Seamen and came into regular contact with successive General Secretaries of the Society. I keep in close touch with The Mission to Seafarers, as it is now styled, to whom I owe an immense debt of gratitude for twenty-seven wonderful years of ministry. It will always have a very special place in my affections.

## Family

Our family continues to give Sally and me enormous pleasure. Our older son Andrew and his wife Frances live in a lovely house in Botley, ten miles away, with their children Edward aged twelve, Rebekah aged ten and Samuel aged 6 months. Samuel brought great joy to the family, even if he was unexpected and interrupted Frances's teaching career! Andrew continues to work with the Anchor Housing Trust. Helen, our older daughter, was ordained deacon in Canterbury Cathedral in June 2003, and is serving as Assistant Curate of Eythorne and Elvington with Waldershare etc (six churches in all). She and her husband Geoff and their daughters Anna aged ten and Catherine aged seven moved from Cornwall to the Vicarage at Whitfield near Dover just before she was ordained, and are very happily settled. Geoff is currently working for a Doctor of Philosophy degree. Julia, our younger daughter, has been working in Bosnia for nearly seven years. She is National Director for Hope and Homes for Children, a charity established in 1994 to care for child victims in war-torn and underprivileged countries. She enjoys her work, and has learned to speak Bosnian fluently, which is a tremendous asset. Our younger son Tim spent a year at home with us after graduating from Warwick University before taking up appointments first in the Accounts Department of Warwick University and a year later with a progressive Information Technology company in Leamington Spa.

## The Future

One morning soon after I retired I was reading Psalm 92. I lingered over verses 12 and 13:-

> Those who are planted in the house of the Lord:
> shall flourish in the courts of our God.
> They shall still bear fruit in old age...

Those words were a pointer to the future.

I have always been very conscious of my faults and failings, and been frustrated by my inability to overcome some of them, but I do know that I was in earnest when I committed myself to love and serve the Lord Jesus Christ when I was twenty. I knew that if I was going to preach the Good News of Jesus I had to live by His teaching. As I read the words of that psalm, I felt that I truly am 'planted in the house of The Lord,' and I pray that God will use me for His purposes as long as I live.

As I look back over my life I can trace God's guiding hand throughout. He was there in my childhood, in the Church training I received. He was there when I was desperately ill with a burst appendix at the age of ten. He was there in the year I spent in bed with tuberculosis. He pointed me towards the ordained ministry of the Church. He led me to Sally, who has given me love, encouragement and strength; her sound commonsense and Christian commitment have been an anchor for me. She is a wonderful wife and mother, and has made many sacrifices for us all. God has been with us throughout our life together and in our ministries.

May we bear fruit in old age.

# Three Important Sermons

1. At my Enthronement as Bishop of Bermuda, 25 March 1990
2. Before a General Election in Bermuda, 12 September 1993
3. My last sermon at St. Mary's, Humberstone, Leicester, before retirement, 17 June 2001

# Sermon on the Occasion of my
## Enthronement as Bishop of Bermuda
### 25 March 1990

Jesus said, 'I am among you as one who serves.' (St. Luke 22 Verse 27)

A Bishop's Enthronement Sermon is a very important occasion for him. He stands at the threshold of a new stage in his life. He has high hopes for the life of the diocese he will serve. He looks forward to working in close partnership with his clergy and lay people. He looks forward to working with Christians of all denominations. He looks forward to becoming an integral part of the community in which he will live and serve. And he finds the prospect both exciting and also somewhat daunting.

But he starts this new stage of his life with priceless assets. First, like every servant of Jesus Christ, he knows that he is not called to undertake these new responsibilities on his own or in his own strength. Our Lord Jesus Christ lives in him, is present in him, guides him, forgives him, encourages him, enlightens him, and strengthens him. He is never alone. Second, he is surrounded by fellow Christians, whose love reaches out to support and encourage him. And third, he has a rich inheritance: all around him there is visible evidence of the work of the Church in the past and in the present. He is aware that he too, in a wonderful way, is part of God's eternal purpose.

As I stand here before you all, there are many things for which I give thanks to God:

- thanks for being called to serve in this lovely place, where so much of the beauty of God's creation is apparent;
- thanks for being made to feel welcome by so many people here, who have brought gifts of food and flowers to Bishop's Lodge, invited me into their homes, waved to me from their cars, or greeted me in the streets, or wherever I have been;
- thanks for the rich inheritance into which I am entering; and
- thanks for a task to undertake.

I see this task of mine as one in which all of us share. It is the calling of each and every one of us to work constantly to improve the quality of life of the individual and of the whole community. The Church has a vital role to play in this.

The Church derives its role from its head, our Lord Jesus Christ. Jesus was not the average person's idea of a great leader. He didn't flaunt his power. He didn't spend all His time with the rich and powerful. He never scorned the humble person. On the contrary, He went about proclaiming love as the supreme force for good in the world. He chose fishermen, tax collectors and very ordinary people to be His closest friends, and to literally change the course of history. He had compassion for people, healing their illnesses, and comforting their hurts. He voluntarily took upon Himself the sins and wickedness of us all, and gave His life to redeem us. Events vindicated Him. The powers that be of this world could – and did – kill Him, but on the third day He was gloriously raised to life. He was alive! He is alive. His lives now. And His way of doing things, the way of love, is the right way. He came to serve, not to be served.

The role of the Church is to serve, just as Jesus served. Its role in the community has many aspects and is all-embracing. Let's think about this together for a few moments.

★    ★    ★

The Church's calling is to proclaim good news for everybody. The good news is that this is God's world: He made it and He sustains it. In God's world God cares about all He has created, including each of us. The good news is that God loved the world so much that He gave His only son, so that everyone who has faith in Him may not die but have eternal life. The good news is that love will always ultimately triumph over evil. The Church's message is exciting, uplifting, inspiring, positive, world changing. Its message is filled with power when Christians show by the quality of their lives, and the quality of their service, that they live daily with Jesus. We need to lead holy lives as far as we can.

★    ★    ★

The Church's calling is to promote reconciliation:

– reconciliation between people and God and God and people;
– reconciliation between its own members who are at variance with each other;
– reconciliation between the many branches of the one Church;
– reconciliation between hostile sections of the community; and
– reconciliation between nations in conflict.

But the Church's work of reconciliation is only truly effective when the Church takes to heart the need to get its own act together. Today it gives me great joy that there are so many representatives of other Christian traditions here. Thank you for coming. I hope and pray that our partnership in the Gospel will be happy and fruitful.

★    ★    ★

The Church's calling is to be involved at every level in the total life of the community. Here in Bermuda, I believe that there are wonderful opportunities for the Church to grasp.

Bermuda is an island community. The sea surrounds us for many miles in all directions. A very significant part of our trading is based on sea transport. The Church has a calling to minister to seafarers, who come here as strangers in an unfamiliar place. It has a calling to minister to those who service ships from the shore. And it has a calling to minister to those who make decisions affecting the lives and work of seafarers. (There is a similar need to serve the airline personnel who stop over here.) The sea also provides a living, food, sport and relaxation for many Bermudians. The Church has a calling to provide a relevant and appropriate ministry to them.

Bermuda is a centre of international business and commerce. In recent years large international companies with worldwide trading activities have established themselves here. They bring revenue to the island, and they bring an international dimension to a relatively small community. The Church has a calling to minister to those involved in making decisions which have far-reaching implications both here and beyond our shores. We have much to offer them.

Bermuda is a tourist's delight. A great part of the island's income derives from tourism. We should not forget, though, that tourists are people like ourselves. On holiday they hope to leave behind the cares and concerns of their daily lives. Some of them can't do this. The Church must be alert and sensitive to the needs of those far from home who just can't cope. And for the vast majority of happy tourists, the Church has a calling to seek to enhance their enjoyment of a break from routine. Welcoming congregations, smiling guides in the churches, and genuine love for people should be, and often are here, the hallmarks of the Church's witness.

And Bermuda has a vigorous Church life. In the short time I have been here, I have seen how Christians are witnessing to their faith in many areas of the community's life. My hope and prayer is that the Churches here will draw closer together through practical collaboration and joint acts of worship, until we attain that unity which is our Lord Jesus Christ's will for His Church. Last Sunday it gave me great joy that so many Christians from many denominations joined together as soloists, and as members of the choir, the orchestra and the audience, to produce a stunning performance of Verdi's *Requiem*. It was an example of ecumenical collaboration. I pray too that we may reach out to contribute in a variety of ways to the life of the Church beyond our shores.

★    ★    ★

Our Lord Jesus Christ came to serve. He called the Church He came to build to serve. And the Bishop is called to serve the servants of the Lord. When I was consecrated Bishop in St. Albans' Abbey in England two months ago today, the Archbishop of Canterbury said this:-

'A Bishop is called to lead in serving and caring for the people of God and to work with them in the oversight of the Church. As a chief pastor he shares with his fellow Bishops a special responsibility to maintain and further the unity of the Church, to uphold its discipline, and to guard its faith. He is to promote its mission throughout the world. It is his duty to watch over and pray for all those committed to his charge, and to teach and govern them after the example of the Apostles, speaking in the name of God and interpreting the Gospel of Christ. He is to ordain and to send new ministers, guiding those who serve with him and enabling them to fulfil their ministry. He is to baptise and confirm, to preside at the Holy Communion, and to lead the offering of prayer and praise. He is to be merciful, but with firmness, and to minister discipline, but with mercy. He is to have a special care for the outcast and needy; and to those who turn to God he is to declare the forgiveness of sins.'

★   ★   ★

I will end by saying this. I have come to serve:

– to serve God,
– to serve His Church,
– to serve you all, and to serve Bermuda.

I shall surely make mistakes – we all do. But I trust that in His providence God will use us all to His glory. I believe the life of the Church in Bermuda has a glorious future as well as a great past and present.

Jesus said, 'I am among you as one who serves.'

Amen

### Sermon preached in the Cathedral in Bermuda
### prior to a General Election
### 12 September 1993

In St. Paul's Epistle to the Romans, chapter 13 and verse 1, we read this: 'Everyone must submit himself to the governing authorities, for there is no authority except that which God has established. The authorities that exist have been established by God.'

The theme of the prayer and readings for today is 'People in positions of authority.'

The prayer for today asks God to govern the hearts and minds of those in authority.

The first reading, from the Book of Daniel, was the dramatic story of the downfall of the arrogant and foolish King Belshazzar of Babylon.

The second, from the Acts of the Apostles, was the story of St. Paul being very properly protected by Festus, a newly appointed just and conscientious Roman Governor.

The theme, 'People in positions of authority', is very appropriate for us here, as we prepare for an election.

\*    \*    \*

When we think about elections all sorts of pictures flash through our minds. We think about candidates canvassing for votes; politicians of different persuasions slanging each other unmercifully; members of government stoutly defending their record; opposition members fiercely attacking them; wild, extravagant promises being made; party political debates on TV and radio; media commentators confidently telling us who is going to win, and by how much; public election rallies; and wholesale rubbishing of opponents. All this is part of an election scene. By the time the day of the election comes round, most of us want to get it over and get on with living!

Beware of treating elections lightly!

Think about what is at stake. Ask yourself what politics is really about. Think about the role politics plays in your life. Think about the role it ought to play. Ask yourself what sort of person you want to represent you in Parliament. Ask yourself where God comes into politics. Work out for yourself where you stand.

Let's think together about some of the issues for a few moments.

\*    \*    \*

First, let's be clear what we mean by the word 'politics'.

Politics is the process of governing people and nations. It is the civilian side of government as opposed to the military side. It is about making laws which

271

affect people's lives, and about making far-reaching decisions about what is in their best interests. It is about our elected representatives coming to a majority view about what is best for us. It is about the exchange of views, the to-and-fro of debate, and the heated arguments which are all part of the process.

At its best politics is lively, stimulating, robust, and healthy. It brings out depth of thought, skill in presenting arguments persuasively, a high level of debate, a rich variety of views, and strongly held convictions. At its worst it is pigheaded, uninformed, rude, ignorant, arrogant, and self-centred; it is more concerned with clinging on to power and privilege than with serving people.

Politics is about the whole process of government.

★    ★    ★

Next: some people say that the political arena is no place for a Christian, that it is impossible for Christians to be involved in party political activity, and still retain their integrity, and that God is excluded from political life.

That has to be wrong.

Politics is about making decisions here on earth which affect God's world. The welfare of God's people is what politicians are concerned with every day. The proper and responsible use of our freedom of choice and action is vital. It is quite clear, therefore, that as God's servants committed Christians should be involved right at the heart of the process.

Christian politicians have a responsibility to apply their Christian principles to decision-making. They have a duty to state plainly that this is God's world in which we are living, and that God cares profoundly about it. And they are called to show the dignity, the courtesy, the firmness, and the graciousness which Jesus showed.

Christians have a vital role to play in politics.

★    ★    ★

Next: we need to be clear that the calling to hold office in government is honourable, important, and worthy.

The Bible is quite uncompromising about this.

The Old Testament teaches that it is God who calls people to positions of leadership, responsibility, and authority. Remember how Saul, and then David, were called to be kings of Israel. They were God's choice.

In the New Testament Jesus spoke specifically about this to the Roman Governor, Pontius Pilate. Pilate had asked Him: 'Do you refuse to speak to me? Surely you know that I have authority to release you, and authority to crucify you.' (John 19 verses 10 and 11) Jesus replied: 'You would have no power at all over me, if it had not been granted to you from above.'

St. Paul expanded on this in the 13th chapter of his letter to the Church in Rome. 'There is no authority,' he wrote, 'but by act of God... The existing authorities are instituted by Him... They are God's agents working for your good... The authorities are in God's service, and to these duties they devote their energies.'

St. Paul had no cause to love the authorities of his day. He knew at first hand the humiliations and indignities of house arrest. He had experienced the squalor of jails. He had suffered a lot at the hands of some people in authority. But he was clear in his own mind that it is God who calls people to take office.

St. Peter wrote in similar vein. He refers to the Christian's obligation to 'submit to every human institution for the sake of the Lord, whether to the sovereign as supreme or to the governor as his deputy, for the punishment of criminals and the commendation of those who do right.' (1 Peter 2 verses 13 and 14)

The calling to hold office in government comes from God.

★　★　★

Next: in a country where governments are elected democratically, we should consider carefully what sort of person or persons we are electing to represent us and govern us.

To the Christian the criteria are clear.

We should vote for people who have high standards; people whose integrity in business, in their personal affairs, and in their family life is plain for all to see; people who are concerned for the welfare of the individual as well as for the community; people who have a vision of what our country and the world could be like, and the energy and enthusiasm to turn dreams into reality; people who respect the dignity and value of every human being; people who are prepared to read, study, and discuss so as to be informed: people of courage and determination, who won't give up or give in; and people prepared to give themselves freely for others.

We want people of sound principles to represent us.

★　★　★

Let me summarise what I have said so far.

- Politics is the process of governing people and nations,
- Christians should not shrink from taking their place in the political arena,
- Holding office in government is a calling which comes from God Himself; and
- The people we elect to represent us should be persons of high calibre.

★　★　★

Now I want to talk about our attitudes towards people in authority.

The Bible is perfectly clear about this, too.

Jesus told us to respect earthly authority. 'Give to Caesar what is due to

Caesar,' He said, in answer to a question, 'and give to God what is due to God.' (Matthew 22 verse 21) In other words, get your priorities right! Pay earthly rulers what is their right to demand. Give God the love and respect and service which is due to Him.

St. Paul spelled it out, too. 'Every person must submit to the supreme authorities,' he wrote. 'Anyone who rebels against authority is resisting a divine institution, and those who so resist have themselves to thank for the punishment they will receive.' (Romans 13 verses 1 and 2) We obey the authorities because of our Christian commitment, not because we are afraid of them.

And St. Peter wrote: 'Give due honour to everyone: love to the brotherhood, reverence to God, honour to the sovereign.' (1 Peter 2 verse 17)

★   ★   ★

My last point is a word of caution.

We need to remind ourselves frequently that every leader, every person in a position of authority, is very human. They are as subject to temptation and mistakes as we are. Sometimes the temptations can seem irresistible. The course of history is liberally sprinkled with instances of leading people falling from grace in moments of weakness. Kings, Queens, Presidents, Congressmen, Members of Parliament, leaders of nations, Bishops and other clergy, teachers, bankers, social workers – none are immune from temptation. Any of us can fall.

As Christians we have a duty to pray, and pray regularly, for our leaders. 'I urge,' wrote St. Paul, 'that requests, payers, intercession and thanksgiving be made for everyone – for kings and all those in authority, that we may live peaceful and quiet lives in all godliness and holiness.' (1 Timothy 2 verses 1 and 2)

Don't rubbish our politicians – pray for them!

Let us pray:

The prayer for today:
Almighty Father,
whose will it is to restore all things in your beloved Son, the King of all:
govern the hearts and minds of those in authority
and bring the families of the nations,
divided and torn apart by the ravages of sin,
to be subject to His just and gentle rule;
who is alive and reigns with you and the
Holy Spirit,
One God, now and for ever.

Amen

### My last sermon at St. Mary's, Humberstone, Leicester, before retirement
### 17 June 2001

As I was preparing this sermon I thought back to May 24th 1959, Trinity Sunday, when I was ordained Deacon in Salisbury Cathedral.

I was approaching my 25th birthday. I had just completed two years ordination training at Ridley Hall in Cambridge. That had followed on from three years at St. John's College, Cambridge, where I studied French and Latin. I was still recovering from tuberculosis, which I had picked up before my 18th birthday, and which had kept me in bed for more than a year.

Conflicting thoughts and feelings assailed me.

On the one hand I was strongly convinced that God had called me to ordination. I had worked through a number of intellectual obstacles, and I had come to a firm belief and trust in God. I was excited by the prospect of living out my faith in the real world.

On the other hand I had a strong sense and awareness of my inadequacy for the task. I was aware of shortcomings in my own character. I felt unworthy of my calling. I was very aware of the responsibility which ordination would bring. And I just didn't know how I would get on.

Coupled with all these feelings was the inescapable fact that I didn't actually want to be ordained. I had for years wanted to make my career in the Royal Navy, and I was very sad when that became impossible because of my illness.

I struggled with all this right up to the day of my ordination.

In the days, weeks, months and then years which followed my ordination I discovered gifts I didn't know I had. I found a deep joy and satisfaction in what I was doing. And I came to the conclusion that I was a round peg in a round hole. I made mistakes. I still felt unworthy – but I knew I was doing what was right for me.

★    ★    ★

Through these 42 years I have learned a great deal, and I want to talk about just three great truths which I have discovered and proved for myself.

The first is that God can be trusted.

When I was ordained I had had no experience of earning my living; I didn't know how I would cope with the life of a priest; and I didn't have any money!

On the day I was ordained my Bank balance was 4 shillings and 11 pence, I had £5 in my wallet, and five and a half weeks to wait before I would be paid. I was enormously relived and grateful when the Parish Treasurer anticipated my need without my having to ask for help.

In the early years of our married life we were very poor, but never in debt.

When things looked really tough something always arrived to keep us solvent. We always managed to pay our bills.

I discovered, too, that you are called, often, to take steps of faith in the ordained ministry:-

- you see something that needs to be done,
- you work out what it will cost,
- you wonder how you are going to raise the necessary finance,
- you discuss your plans with fellow Christians, to see what they think,
- you worry whether you can actually complete the task if you embarked on it,
- you make tentative enquiries about finance, and you often end up with conflicting advice and considerable worries!
- you pray for guidance, and often you don't seem to get a clear lead; you don't get overwhelming negative responses, but you wish the positive ones were stronger,
- you consult those who must back you if you decide to go ahead, but in your own mind you know that you are responsible, and
- so you decide to take the step of faith, and you wait anxiously for confirmation or rejection of what you are doing.

I have learned that when you take a step of faith, after doing all you can to check whether or not what you are doing is right, God always does His part.

I have learned that God can be trusted in every aspect of life. He can be trusted:-

- in personal matters,
- in financial matters,
- in major decisions, and
- in small decisions.

What He needs from us is a willingness to genuinely seek His will, to take time to find out what is His will, and to do things His way. He will soon show you if you are going wrong. And He will never abandon you.

★    ★    ★

The second great truth I have discovered, and proved for myself, is that we should not be afraid to take steps of faith.

As little children we follow what our parents tell us to do, trusting that they know what is best for us. As we get older, increasingly we make our own decisions. Sooner or later we are confronted with the need to make a decision about how we are going to lead our lives, what standards we will have, and whether or not we will follow Jesus.

The most major step of faith we take is when we willingly and deliberately commit ourselves to love and serve and follow Jesus Christ. I was 20 when I made that decision. I knew that I meant it, but I had no idea where it was going to take me.

That decision had immediate implications.

I knew:-

- that my way of life had to change; what God wanted had to take precedence over what I wanted,
- that I had to consider with God how I would earn my living, and
- that I had to find out more about the Living God who wanted me to love and serve Him.

Further decisions followed:-

- I had to witness publicly to my changed way of life – and I had to begin by telling my parents,
- I had to struggle with the call to be ordained,
- I had to get used to the idea of serving God where He wanted me to be, and
- I made the decision to be ordained.

We were married a year after I was ordained, and since then we have made our decisions together.

After 3¹/₂ years in the ministry it was time to consider moving on, and after a lot of heart-searching I joined The Missions to Seamen as a chaplain.

We went where God led:-

- first to South Shields, to learn the job,
- then to Hull, and
- next to Fremantle, in Western Australia.

We went to Australia as a family, without any previous visit there. It was a giant step of faith, leaving all our relatives behind.

12 years after joining The Missions to Seamen I became its Chief Pastor, or General Secretary. I served in that capacity for more than 14 years.

Throughout 26¹/₂ years in The Missions to Seamen I was faced with one major step of faith after another. There was:-

- the decision to go to Australia, and
- the decisions to build new seafarers' centres in Singapore; Jakarta; Tomakomai (in Japan); Pusan; Port Walcott and Dampier (in N.W. Australia); Dubai; Napier (in New Zealand); Fos (near Marseille); Richards Bay (in South Africa); Lagos (in Nigeria); and other places.

Then came the invitation to become Bishop of Bermuda. It was another great step of faith.

All steps of faith cause you heart-searching and a degree of concern. You weigh up the various possibilities. You are aware of what could go wrong. You feel the weight of responsibility. And you take the step of faith – to discover once again that God is there with you; He doesn't abandon you; and He leads you along the right path, if you will let Him.

★   ★   ★

And the third great truth I have discovered and proved for myself is that we should not be anxious about tomorrow – 'sufficient unto the day is the evil thereof.'

In many ways this has been the hardest of all lessons to learn.

Over the years I have worried about things. I have imagined the worst case scenarios. I have been anxious about the outcome of my actions. I have been anxious about unpleasant threats. I have worried about whether I could raise the necessary money for new projects.

But through experience I have learned much more how to take each day as it comes, and to leave the worrying to God. After all, He has the complete picture. He knows us better than we know ourselves. And He is faithful to His promises.

So 'do not be anxious about tomorrow. Tomorrow will take care of itself. Sufficient unto the day is the evil thereof.' (Matthew 6 verse 24)

★   ★   ★

Sally has been a wonderful partner throughout these 42 years. We have enjoyed wonderful times, and we have weathered storms together. Now the time has come to move into a slower mode, and I rejoice in the words of Sir Francis Drake's great prayer, which has always inspired me:-

'O Lord God, when you give to your servants to endeavour any great matter, grant us also to know that it is not the beginning, but the continuing of the same to the end, until it is thoroughly finished, which yields the true glory; through Him who for the finishing of Your work laid down His life, our Redeemer Jesus Christ.'

Amen

# Index